HENDERSON STATE COLLEGE:
The Methodist Years, 1890–1929

CHARLES CHRISTOPHER HENDERSON
(1850–1923)
Namesake of the College

HENDERSON STATE COLLEGE:

The Methodist Years, 1890-1929

---

by

JOHN GLADDEN HALL

HENDERSON STATE COLLEGE ALUMNI ASSOCIATION
Arkadelphia, Arkansas

Library of Congress Catalog Card Number: 74-26368

Manufactured in the United States of America by
Kingsport Press, Inc., Kingsport, Tennessee

TO

HENDERSON STATE COLLEGE
Past—Present—Future

Foreword

INVESTIGATION of the role of the small college in the overall prospectus of American higher education has suffered much neglect. Especially is this true in the state of Arkansas. No comprehensive narrative has been published on Henderson State College. Only a twenty-five-page sketch prepared by the late Professor William Ritchie for the college's semi-centennial celebration in 1940 has been made available to the general reader. With this thought in mind this work found its origin. The study began in the graduate school of the University of Mississippi under the direction of Research Professor Allen Cabaniss and was submitted to that university in 1972 in partial fulfillment of the requirements for the degree of Doctor of Philosophy in history. For this volume much of the original manuscript has been extensively re-worked; some things have been deleted, others expanded.

In accordance with the statement by Historian Gerald M. Capers, Jr., that a research work need not be dull, I have attempted to present the history of the Methodist years of Henderson State College for both the layman and the historian. Conscious that each of us to some degree invariably interprets the facts as he sees them, I have strived toward an objective stance. I have not been hampered by any obligation to the United Methodist Church or to the Henderson State College administration. I am not a graduate of the school; therefore, I have no fond memories to elaborate. My purpose is to describe the concentration of ideas that have determined the profile of the institution during its historical development. The principal sources for the study have been the minutes of the trustees, of the Arkansas Methodist conferences, and of the Henderson-Brown Club; official school publications; and three newspapers: the *Arkansas Methodist*, the Arkadelphia *Southern Standard*, and the Henderson *Oracle*.

Henderson State College possesses a colorful past, and this book is intended as a chronicle of that past. An institution of higher learning is of necessity more than bricks and mortar and mathematical figures in record books; consequently, personalities of founders, administrators, and professors have been considered. No attempt has been made to discuss the college's numerous distinguished alumni; only when they were instrumental in forwarding the narrative were individual students included. Because the college began in the minds of the Arkadelphia townspeople, especially the congregation of the First Methodist Episcopal Church, South, some discussion of the town and its personages has been included to portray the environment in which the school began and grew. Additional information is also found in the notes and appendices at the end of the book.

I am indebted to Research Professor Allen Cabaniss, Professor Joseph Kiger, and Assistant Professor David Sansing, all of the University of Mississippi, for their criticisms and suggestions, both general and detailed; to the staff of the Arkansas History Commission for help in research; and to Margaret Ross of the *Arkansas Gazette* for her valuable assistance in providing research materials. I should like to thank Peggy Lynch Underwood who typed and proofread the manuscript. Finally, I should like to express my appreciation to my wife, Julia Ann, upon whom I have called for assistance and advice more than on anyone else.

JOHN GLADDEN HALL

Arkadelphia, Arkansas
March 24, 1974

Table of Contents

HENDERSON STATE COLLEGE:
The Methodist Years, 1890–1929

ARKADELPHIA METHODIST COLLEGE
1902 Lithograph

Hudson-Kimberly Pub. Co.

CHAPTER I

Introduction

ENDERSON State College is heir to property, traditions, and spirit of a liberal arts school which opened in September, 1890, in Arkadelphia, Arkansas, under the auspices of the Methodist Episcopal Church, South. The college has a unique past, for it is the only Arkansas institution of higher learning which has been controlled by both church and state, and it is the only state supported one to bear the name of an individual. Considering its years as a Methodist institution (1890–1929), it is the oldest state college in Arkansas, with the exception of the University of Arkansas.[1]

Located in one of the state's oldest communities, the college was founded through the efforts of the local Methodist congregation and the townspeople, somewhat reluctantly accepted by Arkansas Methodism, and later transferred to the state. The college has operated continuously under five names in succession. From 1890 to 1904 it was called Arkadelphia Methodist College; in the latter year the name was changed to Henderson College; in 1911 the trustees voted to insert Brown in the title. The institution continued to be known as Henderson-Brown College until 1929 when the Methodist Church withdrew its support and retroceded the property to the city of Arkadelphia. Thus after thirty-nine sessions her doors as a Methodist institution were closed, but on an optimistic note, for the college was continued without interruption as a state school. In 1929 the town deeded the property to the state which assumed control of the facility and operated it under the name Henderson State Teachers College. In 1967 by legislative act the name was amended to Henderson State College.

Seven presidents served the Methodist school which was besieged by chronic financial plights, personality conflicts between administrators and patrons, a disastrous fire, and finally the emotional issue of consolidation with a Methodist rival. Triumphantly overcoming these challenges, the institution advanced to a mature college fulfilling a vital service in providing quality education. With the end of the Methodist era, the school could look confidently toward its future role as a state institution.

Here, within the first thirty-nine sessions (1890–1929), is the story of the Methodist years of Henderson State College.

CHAPTER II

The Setting

ON the morning of June 3, 1929, Charles Wooten Pipkin, professor of government and soon-to-be dean of the graduate school at Louisiana State University, stood before the assembly convened for the commencement exercise ending the thirty-ninth annual session of Henderson-Brown College. The surroundings and many faces were familiar to him, for only eleven years earlier in 1918 he was graduated from the small Methodist institution with the Bachelor of Arts degree. During those intervening years he had brought honor and prestige to his alma mater. A Rhodes Scholar, a Doctor of Philosophy from Oxford University, and a recently-appointed Carnegie Fellow in International Law to the University of Paris, Pipkin had returned to receive the college's highest honor, the Doctor of Laws degree.[1]

Friends of the school attending that commencement needed no Pipkin to remind them of the academic achievements of many Hendersonians; but neither distinguished graduates nor liberal contributions from loyal patrons could prevent the Methodist Church from merging the institution with rival Hendrix College. Although those present felt pride in the accomplishments of this eminent graduate, the awarding of the degree was a solemn occasion; it was the last ever conferred by the Methodist institution and its authorization was the final act of the Henderson-Brown College board of trustees.[2]

A contemplative person departing that commencement ceremony, the last of the Methodist era, might well have paused at the

5

gateway of the iron fence separating the campus domain from the
town of Arkadelphia then observing more than a century of éxist-
ence. Looking eastward a short distance to the end of Henderson
Street, he would have viewed two familiar landmarks. Facing
each other at the corner of Henderson and Tenth streets were
the Greek revival mansion of Walter Eugene Barkman, grandson
of the "Father of Clark County," symbolic of Arkadelphia during
her antebellum years; and the largest residence in town, the pseudo-
classical dwelling built for Charles Christopher Henderson, namesake of the college, symbolic of the postbellum period. Characteristic of the Old and New South, no two structures are more
representative of the history of Arkadelphia and Henderson State
College. These houses would have called to mind the loyalty and
financial support that their owners and numerous other Arkadelphians had long given to the school, for the spirit of determination
to found and maintain the institution had taken its roots from the
backgrounds and traditions of these persons who had struggled
to develop their town into one with a cultural and intellectual atmosphere. Their sacrifices had often been required, and each time
they had responded to the call. It was their pioneer spirit which
had led them to give freely of their money, love, and concern,
especially in the final struggle waged to save the college for the
town and its name Henderson.

Arkadelphia is an old town whose history is closely connected
with the development of Arkansas. Situated in the southwestern
part of the state, it is located on a bluff on the west bank of the
Ouachita River [3] some thirty-five miles south of the "hot springs."
Known as Blakelytown until about 1842, it is one of the oldest
settled points in Arkansas and probably the first in what is now
Clark County.[4] Clark, of which Arkadelphia is the county seat, is
one of five counties predating formation of Arkansas Territory
(1819). Carved from lands of the Louisiana Purchase (1803), it
was created December 15, 1818, by the last territorial legislature

of Missouri and named for William Clark of expeditionary fame.[5]

History holds no record of anything pertaining to Arkansas antedating the year 1541, and Hernando de Soto holds the distinction of being the first European to traverse the Ouachita Valley, where he reportedly encamped on Saline Bayou some two miles from the site of Arkadelphia.[6] The first people known to have inhabited the place were the Caddo Indians who offered no resistance to Manifest Destiny.[7] Perhaps the first Anglo-American settler was Patrick Cassidy, who as early as 1800 resided on a twelve hundred-acre tract purchased from Frenchman Louis Cavet.[8] Following acquisition of the Ouachita River Valley by the United States, President Thomas Jefferson authorized its exploration in 1804.[9] Permanent white settlement began shortly afterwards with the arrival of a few families of French and English descent. It is believed that the first building at the site of the town was a blacksmith shop built near the river by Adam Blakely who had arrived around 1809.[10] Although legal title could not be secured to lands in the region until 1820, people continued to locate there.[11]

The settlement made few strides, however, until the coming of the two men credited with its permanence. Among the early settlers arriving in 1811 were John Hemphill and Jacob Barkman,[12] pioneers in manufacturing and river commerce in Arkansas. Soon after their arrival, Hemphill secured from the Indians the salt wells supposedly visited by De Soto, and there in 1812 he opened a salt refinery, possibly becoming the first industrialist in Arkansas.[13] It is probable that the availability of salt was responsible for attracting the first white settlers. In 1814 Hemphill traveled to New Orleans to purchase a number of large kettles used in boiling down sugar cane juice. At the salt works these kettles, holding as much as two hundred gallons each, were put into service boiling salt from the water through evaporation, making it possible for the budding entrepreneur to accommodate the demands of his rapidly growing business. One of these kettles rests today on the Henderson State College campus.[14]

Before his unexpected death in 1818, Hemphill had the foresight to draw up a will. Aside from his being a successful industrialist, little is known about him except a clue from his will. Expressing concern for the future of the settlement and interest in learning, he directed that "It is my will and Desire that all my children may have a good English Education." [15] This early immigrant's concern for education did not go unheeded, and by the decade preceding the Civil War, Arkadelphia was becoming an educational center, a position the town has held for over a century.

Jacob Barkman, "Father of Clark County," was attracted to the alluvial bottom lands at the confluence of the Ouachita and Caddo rivers. He settled at that location some four miles north of Arkadelphia and with considerable speed began building an agricultural "empire" which at the time of his death (1852) encompassed some twenty-two thousand acres, stretching all the way from the Caddo River to the town on the Ouachita.[16] The college campus is situated on lands that were once a part of that empire.

The future of Arkadelphia and a portion of Barkman's estate were both jeopardized when Stephen F. Austin, speculating in New Madrid land claims, envisioned a town at the juncture of the Caddo and Ouachita rivers.[17] Austin's plan depended on the opening of this part of the public domain to persons holding such land certificates. But until a survey of the lands had been made, no titles to claims could be secured. The future Texas hero, learning that no order for such surveys had been issued, realized that nothing could be done with the New Madrid claims at that time. Consequently, he abandoned his plan for developing a town at the location. Nevertheless, Austin remained convinced that his choice was among "the best that could have been made in the country. . . ." [18]

A history of river commerce between southwestern Arkansas

and New Orleans should properly credit Jacob Barkman with being its founder. The necessity of transporting his cotton and other products resulted in his opening regular commercial shipping services in 1812 between the upper Ouachita River and the "Crescent City." [19] Using pirogues manned by six slaves, the round-trip took six months, but it launched his career in river transportation.[20] Barkman, whose arrival antedated that of the first steamboat on western waters, also inaugurated steamboating on the upper Ouachita. In the 1830's his small sidewheeler, *The Dime*, was making regular round trips to New Orleans in a matter of days. These shipping interests accounted for a large part of his fortune.[21]

Barkman's affluence made possible the construction of a dwelling which would do justice to his growing wealth and prestige. In 1815 he erected a handsome two-story brick mansion on the bank of the Caddo River.[22] The grounds were beautified and as the years passed, the magnificence of the estate made vivid impressions on some who otherwise were critical of Arkansas.[23]

The large house was destined to play an important part in the political, social, and economic life of Clark County. The first term of court was held there on June 14, 1819, less than one month before Arkansas acquired territorial status.[24] One of the most persistent complaints of any frontier area was mail service, or rather the lack of it. Next to the court, however, the oldest continuous public service in Clark County is the post office, which, like the court, was inaugurated at the Barkman house when a monthly delivery was begun between there and Little Rock in 1819. By the end of the decade this service had been expanded to a weekly one.[25] The mansion located on the Military Road, the main land route from St. Louis, via Little Rock, to the Southwest, became a familiar stopping place for men of note on their travels and was designated as a stop when stagecoach service was initiated over that route in 1831.[26] All that remains of the great house is the massive stone doorstep which rests at the east end of the stately portico fronting the entrance of "Homeplace," since 1969 the official residence for the president of Henderson State College.

The stream of immigrants into the area had been meager until the period following the War of 1812. Arkadelphia could boast only a handful of white residents, and with the advent of territorial status, the entire county had only 1,040 residents, including seventy slaves.[27] But during the next decade the population increased as settlers laid out farms on the rich lands bordering the Ouachita River and its tributaries.[28] A special census in 1827 revealed that the county population had risen to 1,452; of these, 474 resided in Caddo Township which embraces Arkadelphia.[29] Though such numbers would not rank the town or county high populationwise, they are indicative that the region was one of attraction in the expanding Mississippi Valley frontier.

Accounts of travelers and adventurers in Arkansas Territory show remarkable consistency in reproving the entire region. In 1819 British-born Thomas Nuttall of the Philadelphia Academy of Natural Sciences observed that as far as he was concerned all inhabitants beyond Arkansas Post were "chiefly renegade Americans who have fled from honest society."[30] Several years later George W. Featherstonhaugh, a geologist from England on a journey through the South, visited for three days at the Barkman house. He predicted a dismal future for the territory and "declared that Arkansas would not follow in the footsteps of former frontier states, since they had solid immigration."[31]

But contrary to such impressions, many of the pioneer immigrants to Arkansas were men of intellect and refinement; several persons of this background chose to settle in Clark County. One was Michael Bozeman, a promoter of education. Arriving in 1835, the young Alabamian located some six miles west of Arkadelphia and began an extensive farming operation which soon rivaled that of Jacob Barkman.[32] For the historian, a carefully kept day-by-day journal reveals the meticulous care this learned man gave to every detail of the management of his growing enterprise.[33] His Greek revival house is thought to be the oldest existing residence in the county. Interested in education for his neighborhood, Bozeman opened Oakland Academy in 1847, the first county school. Though relocated twice, the academy maintained its identity until consolidated with the Gurdon Public Schools in 1946.[34]

The most noted of the Clark County pioneers was Meriwether Lewis Randolph of Virginia, grandson of Thomas Jefferson. Randolph, who had studied law at the University of Virginia, was commissioned in 1835 by President Andrew Jackson as the last territorial secretary of Arkansas.[35] While serving in this capacity, he became a partner in and an agent for the firm of Randolph, Nichols, Hearch, and Lyons which was buying lands in the territory for speculation.[36] With commissions received for this service, Randolph bought choice lands in Clark County. In November, 1836, he brought his wife Elizabeth [37] and their infant son to his first purchase—nearly seven thousand acres—to reside in a small log house located approximately fifteen miles southwest of Arkadelphia. Randolph's faith in the county was evidenced when he purchased additional lands, bringing his total holdings to almost eleven thousand acres.[38] His plans to build "a Monticello in Arkansas" were never realized. In September, 1837, shortly before his twenty-eighth birthday, he died and was buried near the house.[39] Thus a Randolph of Virginia lies interred in Clark County. After Randolph's death his wife returned to her native Tennessee. The landed estate she left behind was lost to taxes and tax-title disputes.[40]

Although the Barkman house had served as the first courthouse, the thriving town on the Ouachita River did not become the county seat until 1842. As the town advanced to its new role as the seat of justice, the residents changed the name of the community from Blakelytown to the more sophisticated *Arkadelphia*, by which the town was referred to in the county court proceedings

on January 11, 1842. Following the court's removal from Barkman's home in 1825 until its permanent location in Arkadelphia,[41]
it seems that every prominent man within a ten-mile radius could
claim that a term of court had been held in his parlor and that his
barn had been the jail.

Although Arkadelphia was first incorporated in November,
1846, for some reason the plat of the town was not filed and the
act was invalidated. Consequently, the town did not come into
corporate existence until January 6, 1857.[42] Records concerning
the origin of the name are lacking, but several stories persist. One
account is that the name is a compound word formed of *arc*, a part
of a circle, as a rainbow, and the latter part of the name of that
city of the Quakers and brotherly love, Philadelphia, thus making
the name *Arcadelphia*, as it was first spelled, to signify an arc or
rainbow of brotherly love, as indicating an imaginary halo of
fraternal friendship arched above the little town. Later, for the
sake of euphony, *k* was substituted for *c*, and the autograph of the
name became *Arkadelphia*. Another version is that it is a combi-
nation of *Arkansas* and *Philadelphia*, devised by the Barkman-
Maddox family because they believed the name Philadelphia to be
dignified. The former theory is probably erroneous, since Arkadelphia does not mean "arc of brotherly love." The Greek word
philos means "love of" and *adelphos* pertains to brothers. The
wrong syllables were taken to justify "arc of love." An etymologist
would find "brotherly circle" more correct.[43]

The town's commercial development from Blakely's blacksmith
shop of 1809 to the brick business houses of the present day has
been continuous and constant. The earliest trading establishments
were built along the river where Blakely and Barkman had operated
trading posts. It was there that John S. T. Callaway, who had arrived in 1817, opened the first general store.[44] In 1839 the town
was laid out according to the present plan, with one block being
reserved for public buildings. The village's growth like the nation's

was to the west, and the first brick courthouse, located three blocks from the river wharf, became the nucleus around which the town developed. Completed in 1844, the two-story Georgian structure served the county until construction of the present building in 1898.[45] Now standing like a lonely sentinel, a white painted brick house at 410 Main Street is the sole survivor of the antebellum business establishments. The historic structure, built in 1846, is believed to be the oldest structure in the town.[46]

Early visitors to the hamlet who sought elegant lodging would have met with total disappointment, but accommodations did exist. In 1824 William Blakely was granted a license to operate a tavern to provide food and lodging, but the establishment generally credited with being the first hotel was not opened until 1843. Jonathan O. Callaway, a great-grandson of Daniel Boone, and his wife, Amy, a daughter of pioneer John Hemphill, operated a two-story log inn at the corner of Fourth and Main streets, which for more than a decade was the scene of numerous social events. In the mid-1850's it was demolished and replaced by the Spence Hotel, a two-story edifice fronted by massive columns, which served travelers until its destruction by fire in 1872.[47]

Conspicuously absent from the business district until the middle of the nineteenth century was a saloon. Although liquor was made locally from corn, it was not sold commercially until 1851 when Jewell Stafford opened a taproom with a supply of "spirits" imported from New Orleans.[48] No doubt this delay can be attributed to a temperance crusade then sweeping the United States. Approximately twenty-five years later, in 1875, taverns were required to locate at least three miles from the city limits by an act of the state legislature which prohibited the sale of intoxicating liquors within that proximity of "any Academy, College, or University in the state."[49]

Facing the courthouse at 320 Clay Street stands the law office of Municipal Court Attorney B. W. Sanders. Constructed in 1855 by Attorney James L. Witherspoon,[50] this small brick building has continually housed a law firm. Witherspoon came from Alabama in 1849 and shortly thereafter formed a partnership with Harris Flanagin, an Eastern lawyer, who had preceded him to Arkadelphia in 1842.[51] From this first law office, these men brought acclaim to the town. Witherspoon was one of the founders of the state school for the blind, which opened in Arkadelphia in February, 1859,[52] and Flanagin served the state as governor during its most crucial period: the Civil War.[53]

Flanagin's election to the state's highest office was indicative of Arkadelphia's prominence in government, for from territorial days Clark County citizens had distinguished themselves in the political arena. The first territorial legislature had elected Jacob Barkman to sit in its upper chamber, and the fourth had chosen him to be its president.[54] Ill-fated John Wilson, president of the Real Estate Bank, served as president of the first constitutional convention; and when Arkansas entered the Union in 1836, he was elected Speaker of the House of the first state legislature.[55]

Medical services were made available before 1830 with the arrival of a Dr. Busnine who was a member of the Royal College of Surgeons in London, the faculty of medicine in Paris, and late surgeon to the East India Company. A distinguished physician, he set a high standard for the profession in early Arkansas.[56] But the first resident dentist, W. W. Hamilton, did not open his office until May 1, 1869.[57]

Local interest in events of national scope was sustained largely through newspapers from New Orleans. For regional news Arkadelphians relied on the Little Rock *Arkansas Gazette*.[58] The town's first newspaper, the *Sentinel*, began weekly publication in 1850 under the editorship of J. L. Pignes.[59] The oldest paper in circulation is the weekly *Southern Standard*, founded in 1868 by Adam Clark and J. W. Gaulding.[60] The city's daily, the *Siftings Herald*, dates from 1881.[61]

The newspapers kept their readers informed on a variety of topics and promoted civic affairs, but it was the church that exerted the most influence. Although pioneers had brought the Baptist, Methodist, and Presbyterian faiths to this backwater settlement, no congregation was formally organized until the decade of the fifties. Earlier, services had been conducted by itinerant ministers in homes and in the courthouse. During the summer seasons traveling men of God preached to interdenominational assemblies outdoors. The Baptists formed the first congregation on July 15, 1851, with the Reverend H. H. Coleman as pastor.[62] Their original building, a two-story frame completed in 1853, was constructed in conjunction with the Masonic Lodge,[63] which had received its charter in 1848;[64] the Baptists occupied the lower floor, the fraternal body the upper.

The fall of 1851 saw the organization of the Methodists with Circuit Rider the Reverend J. F. Biggs preaching in a small frame building at Sixth and Caddo.[65] Though it was in many ways a pretentious congregation, one of the state's noted ministers of Methodism was apparently outraged with the impropriety of some of its members when he prefaced a sermon with "Our church requires all her congregation to kneel when they pray and it is impossible for ladies to kneel in light dress when tobacco juice is an inch deep on the floor."[66] The First Presbyterian Church was founded in 1858. Their minister, the Reverend A. E. Beatties, preached in the town's first brick church building which was completed in 1859.[67] (The Hardman Lumber Company presently occupies the historic structure.) By 1859 all three houses of worship were ringing bells to remind their congregations of their duty to attend religious services.[68]

Leisure time of Arkadelphians was not completely devoted to public worship and other church related functions. The sport of kings, horse racing, had long had its own particular clientele. From as early as 1836 there was organized racing on the Barkman plantation which drew horsemen from Arkansas, Tennessee, and Kentucky, and involved large wagers. William N. Wyatt notes in his travel diary that in the fall of that year, races on the Barkman estate drew a crowd of "some two or three hundred persons," one-fourth of whom were well dressed young women.[69] The circus, another mode of exciting and suspenseful entertainment, was also popular among residents of all ages. The town's first visit from a circus was in 1842; the popularity of these spectacles is evidenced by the report that a circus even played the town during the Civil War years.[70] By the mid-forties, the Debating Society, Agriculture Society,[71] and Athena Reading Club, which ultimately became the public library,[72] were offering diversions to various groups. Also, barbecues and ladies' bazaars were held for special occasions.[73]

Manufacturing interests in Arkadelphia partially refute the theory that the antebellum South scorned factories and strove to keep the section dependent on one or two staple crops. No town in Arkansas was more prominent in industrial endeavors during that era. In addition to the existing industries of a grist mill, cotton gin, sawmill, and the aforementioned salt works, a tannery was opened in 1830 by Nazareth Mooney. In 1842 James Harrison Obaugh, a nephew of President William Henry Harrison, built a brick factory, which would be maintained for three generations and would eventually manufacture the bricks used in construction of the first building of the college.[74] The $30,000 cotton spinning factory opened by Jacob Barkman in 1848 was among the first textile mills constructed in the state.[75]

The most spectacular factory was the arsenal operated for the Confederate States of America. Begun by Major-General Thomas C. Hindman in the summer of 1862, the plant was designated to serve the entire Trans-Mississippi Confederate States Army.[76] In addition to repairing and fitting cannons, the ordnance works produced percussion caps, rifles, gun carriages, and caissons. The chemical laboratory made medicines, such as calomel, castor oil, and iron tonic. During the war years, shoes, harnesses, and wagons were also manufactured. The Confederate government also re-opened the defunct salt works and in 1863 erected a textile mill.[77]

Although Arkadelphia was an industrial center, its society was agrarian and cotton was its raison d'être. As early as 1840 Clark County produced approximately 300,000 pounds of the staple.[78] The increase in cotton production was paralleled by a sharp rise in the slave population. In the decade preceding the Civil War, nine men in the county owned more than twenty slaves each,[79] and on the eve of the conflict, of the total county population of 9,735, slaves numbered 2,214.[80] Within a half-century since its founding, the town on the Ouachita with a population of 817, including 217 slaves, had developed by 1860 into the state's seventh largest community.[81]

Arkansas officially cast her fortune with the Confederacy, and Arkadelphia, home of a wartime governor and the "great depot for the Trans-Mississippi Confederate States Army," was catapulted into a hub of activity under the new flag. But despite its key to commerce, transportation, and industry, only a meager attempt was made to defend the place and in March, 1864, the town was occupied by Union soldiers.[82]

Impressions recorded by two Union soldiers after they saw Arkadelphia reveal that they must have felt much like crusading knights of the eleventh century when they viewed the wondrous sights of Constantinople. An Iowa farm boy noted:

> After crossing the Caddo river . . . [the] country [was] much richer and plantations well improved. . . . The city . . . on the west bank of the river . . . has been a fine and flourishing city. Costly mansions and buildings stand deserted and desolate. . . .[83]

This private's view was shared by a lieutenant-colonel who reported "Everything in and around this place indicated its former prosperity."[84]

A gracious way of life was no myth in Arkadelphia, and the residences, like those of many urban centers in the antebellum lower South, though based on cotton, were built of wood. More than a dozen of these houses stand today, a few in a state of excellent repair, as witness to that past prosperity. "The finest in the state architecturally," they are adaptations of the classical revival fever that swept the cotton states. The most palatial is the ten-room, two-story house built by James E. Barkman, a son of Jacob Barkman.[85] It was occupied by the builder's son Walter E. Barkman, a founder, trustee, and patron of the college, until his death. In 1968 the stately house became the property of the college, and it now serves as Panhellenic House for the six campus sororities.[86]

The surrender of Robert E. Lee ended the war for Confederate independence. But "the marks of the war, although visible, were not so legibly written on this portion of the country." [87] Emerging from the conflict without physical damage, the town continued to grow and prosper. At the beginning of the new decade the population had increased to nearly 1,000 and "never in the history of Arkadelphia before the War or since" had the trade equalled that of the 1870 season.[88] In the early seventies the *Southern Standard* stated that Arkadelphia could boast of "five dry-goods and four grocery stores, one of the best hotels in the state (the Spence), one restaurant, one tin and two blacksmith shops, one livery stable, one steam grist mill, one brickyard, one cotton gin, two excellent female schools, one male academy, three churches . . . and several lawyers and physicians." [89]

A unique business operating in the town was the city-owned meat market which had opened in 1866 and, by city ordinance, excluded all competition by other butchers.[90] Beginning in 1869 a bell placed on the premises was rung to announce the slaughter of a beef. From the time of the market's closure in 1873 until 1930, this bell was used as the town's fire alarm.[91] The site of the old market is today occupied by the city fire department.

The year 1873 was a significant one in transportation and commerce, as it witnessed the demise of river traffic and the advent of the railroad. The importance of the Ouachita River in the settlement and development of Arkadelphia cannot be overemphasized, for it provided direct passage to the Mississippi River and for over sixty years afforded this area in the heartland of North America with a vital avenue to New Orleans and ultimately the ports of the world. During the flourishing years of river travel numerous steamboats crowded the wharf at the foot of Caddo Street; the largest was the *Will S. Hays*. The coming of the Cairo and Fulton Railroad in 1873 resulted in immediate decline of this medium of transportation.[92] The first passenger train arrived amid pomp and splendor on June 27 of that year, bringing a delegation of railroad and state officials, including Governor Elisha Baxter. The toast for the occasion was proposed by Civil War Governor Flanagin and "real champagne was in the glasses." [93]

The era of the seventies also observed the organization of a Protestant Episcopal Church, the development of a baseball "league," and the formation of a brass band.[94] The town's first theatre, Grayson Hall opened in 1873, provided entertainment by road shows and afforded accommodations for the productions of the local Dramatic Club which organized in 1875.[95] Seeing need for better trade practices, businessmen organized the Chamber of Commerce in 1872. In addition to the Masons, other fraternal orders including the Odd Fellows and Knights of Pythias were active by the end of the decade.[96]

In 1879 another Iowa visitor's impression of Arkadelphia as being "the garden spot of the South" [97] was somewhat reminiscent of the Union private's account. This traveler, arriving by train from St. Louis, described the town and vicinity:

I passed many good towns . . . until I reached Arkadelphia, . . . [the] best [town] suited for a colony of Iowa, or Northern men . . . [and] one of the nicest sites for a town I have ever seen . . . with a good business outlook, society, and schools not excelled in any town its size. The Country . . . is high and covered

with very fine timber. The valleys are considered the most productive land, especially for cotton. Sawmills are plentiful.

Lands are cheap; prices ranged from $2 to $10. The soil is good
. . . more corn is raised to the acre than in Guthrie, Iowa. Cotton,
however, is king . . . as this is the center of the cotton belt. This
is the place for a northern man to go and raise corn, wheat, cattle
and hogs, for he will have a better home market.

The prevailing cry that to go South is to be slain on account of
any political opinions you may have is a myth. There is no more
benevolent and hospitable people living than there are in Arkadelphia.

The people have no labor saving devices to farm with, like in
the North, but with Northern men the tools will follow.[98]

The Arkadelphia of this description must have been similar to
that seen by Charles Christopher Henderson, who arrived at approximately the same time. Although he was not from Iowa or the
North, it was at this location that he settled and began a diversified
career in lumbering, railroading, and banking. But if Henderson is
to be remembered, it is for his devotion to the cause of higher education and his patronage of the college bearing his name. Discussion
of Henderson is reserved until he becomes intricately involved
with the institution.

Arkadelphians had early expressed sincere interest in some manner of schooling; William Callaway in 1820 offered instruction in
the fundamental three R's to students on a subscription basis. During the following years other teachers taught varied subject matters in private tuition schools.[99] Their success is partially attested by
the fact that in 1840 of 2,309 county residents, only twenty-two
whites over twenty years of age could not read or write. By 1850
the county and town were providing thirteen one-teacher schools
for 196 pupils.[100]

In 1855 Samuel Stevenson built a two-story wood school house
crowned by a cupola [101] and employed a number of notable instructors; among them were Mary Connelly, a graduate of Washington

Female Seminary,[102] and Elizabeth Webb, a native of Cobh, Ireland, who had been presented at Queen Victoria's Court.[103] With the opening of the first public school in January, 1870, the private academies began to decline.[104]

The year 1859 was especially significant in scholastic achievements for the citizenry. It witnessed both the founding of the town's first institution of higher learning and the establishment of the state Institute for the Education of the Blind. Arkadelphia Female College, begun by the Methodist Episcopal Church, South,[105] was incorporated by the state to have "succession for ninety-nine years." The act empowered the school's board of trustees, to be elected by the Little Rock Conference, "to confer such literary and scientific degrees and honors as usually conferred by institutions of learning of a like character, and to grant such diplomas or certificates, as be necessary to attest said degrees and honors."[106] The Reverend James E. Cobb served as the institution's only president and financial officer. During the second year of his presidency, he was also assigned the pastorate of the Arkadelphia Methodist Church.[107] Unfortunately during the short military occupation of the town in April, 1864, the two-story frame building which housed the seminary was vandalized by Union troops. One account records that "Led on by the demon of mischief, some of our men . . . ransacked the building from end to end, tore up the maps and papers, destroyed the benches, and smashed the piano into ruins. The whole seminary was left in a perfect mess."[108] Such was the fate of the college: it did not survive the conflict. In 1869 Mary Connelly purchased the academy owned by Samuel Stevenson and instituted a preparatory and college-level curriculum for young ladies. Using the name of the defunct Methodist college, she operated her school as Arkadelphia Female College until 1874.[109]

The Institute for the Education of the Blind, Arkansas' oldest state institution, began operation in February, 1859,[110] on land overlooking the Ouachita River. In 1868 it was removed to Little Rock [111] and the property donated to the city of Arkadelphia upon condition that the citizens establish a free high school. Later the property was sold to the Red River Baptist Association which opened a Baptist academy in the facilities in 1875.[112] It was maintained by the Association until 1886. The Baptist State Convention meeting in Fayetteville in 1883 had resolved that a college under control of the Baptist Church was a necessity, and after several years of preliminary investigation the organization announced in April, 1886, that the Convention would accept the buildings formerly belonging to the Institute for the Blind at Arkadelphia [113] and operate an institution there. Appropriate for the river the new institution overlooked, the name Ouachita Baptist College was selected, and the school opened in September, 1886, with 160 students.[114] This action resulted in the determination of the local Methodists to establish a college in the town, and the final step toward the creation of that school was taken in 1890.

CHAPTER III

The Founding of the College

ARKADELPHIA Methodist College was founded March 24, 1890, through the joint instrumentality of the local congregation and citizenry. The minutes of the trustees' first two meetings refer to the institution as The Arkadelphia College of the Methodist Episcopal Church, South. The school, however, was incorporated June 10, 1890, as Arkadelphia Methodist College.[1] Higher education was no stranger to Arkadelphia, and when the Baptists opened Ouachita Baptist College in 1886, the local Methodists, recalling that their denomination had operated an antebellum conference school (Arkadelphia Female College), resolved to have a new institution. Thus the rivalry which presently persists between the two institutions began, as one loyal alumna stated, "before Henderson ever existed." [2]

Although interest in a college had been expressed as early as 1886, efforts to build one did not materialize until late 1889.[3] On November 6 of that year, a town meeting was held for furthering that purpose. A five-member committee was appointed to canvass the area to obtain subscriptions amounting to $20,000 for the venture.[4] Backers of the proposal, however, became convinced that the interest of the community and church could best be served by securing Hendrix College, an established Methodist institution then subject to relocation.

Arkansas may be censured for its role, or rather its lack of one, in higher education until the founding of the University of Arkansas in 1871. Although provisions had been made by acts of

23

Congress in 1818 and 1827 to reserve lands for a "seminary of learning," all hope for a state university vanished when the legislature of 1844 memorialized Congress for the right to use the lands for support of common schools.[5] The state's failure to provide a tax-supported college had left total responsibility of higher education to private endeavors and various Christian denominations. For several years following Arkansas' admission into the Union, there was hardly a session of the legislature that was not called upon to incorporate one or more academies. Some dignified by the name "college" were chartered, though in reality they were little more than high schools. All proved to be failures; however, for none survived the Civil War. And Arkansas, one of two Confederate States without a state university, did not open her first such institution until 1872, almost ten years after the passage of the Morrill Act.[6]

Although Methodist societies had existed in the American colonies within the Church of England, the Methodist Church was not officially organized as a separate ecclesiastical body in America until 1784. When Arkansas achieved statehood (1836) the General Conference of the church designated the new state Arkansas Conference and made it independent from that of Missouri. Later, for convenience of administration the area was apportioned into three conferences: Arkansas; Little Rock (known for a time as Ouachita), 1854; and White River, 1870.[7]

At its initial session in November, 1836, Arkansas Conference expressed concern for the education of its young people and resolved to found three schools: a manual labor one for boys and two "respectable female institutions." [8] This commitment was not fulfilled; but the next year Fayetteville Female Academy, the first chartered institution in Arkansas for the instruction of women which had opened in 1836, was placed under the patronage of the conference, although the school did not belong to the Methodist Church.[9] Both church and laity continued to agitate for educational facilities; and finally in 1844 the conference voted to establish "two seminaries of high order," one in the southern part of the state, the other in the northern.[10]

Two years later a charter was issued for Washington Male and Female Seminary at Washington in southwest Arkansas, and in 1849 Solesbury College was opened at Batesville. The Washington school remained under Methodist control only a few years,[11] but Solesbury became the "pride of the Arkansas Conference" and continued to function until the trying circumstances of civil war forced its closure at the end of the summer session in 1861.[12] The Methodists also operated two other prewar colleges: Arkadelphia Female College and Ouachita Conference Female College, chartered in 1857 [13] at Camden and relocated at Tulip in 1860.[14] Efforts were made to create a male college at that location; although some progress was achieved, secession suspended the movement.

Following failure of the Confederacy, the Little Rock Conference assumed jurisdiction over Camden Female College and Camden Male College; neither school, however, fared well.[15] The former must have failed to impress church leaders that it possessed sufficient potentiality to develop into a first-class institution, for at its 1869 meeting, the conference resolved to found a female college in the state capital.[16] Full strength of Arkansas Methodism became involved in that endeavor in 1873 when the White River and Arkansas conferences joined the enterprise to build a "college of high rank" for the women of the state.[17] This venture materialized in 1874 [18] with the installation of Arkansas Female College. However, the school failed to prosper as had been anticipated, and after twelve years it was sold to private owners.[19]

In reality, Quitman College, founded in 1870 by Arkansas Conference,[20] was the first Methodist institution to offer courses of collegiate standing. A charter obtained in January, 1873, empowered the trustees to establish departments of liberal arts and science, and to confer the customary degrees.[21] Attempts to designate Quitman College the male institution for Arkansas Methodism met much opposition; because of the school's somewhat remote location, the three conferences could not agree that such action would be wise.[22] The college continued, therefore, under the single patronage of its founder until its closure in 1898.[23]

Arkansas Methodists, anticipating the approaching centennial of American Methodism, established a centenary committee in each of the three conferences during the 1883 sessions.[24] In keeping with plans to celebrate the occasion and since for a number of years the church had been considering the question of establishing a quality male college in a central location,[25] the Centenary Committee initiated steps to acquire Central Collegiate Institute, a privately-owned college located at Altus in the northwest part of the state.[26]

A primary concern to those who met in June, 1884, to negotiate purchase of the institution was denominational unity on educational policy.[27] The delegates pledged themselves to support a plan recommended in 1882 to maintain only two colleges in the state, one male and one female.[28] In pursuance of this goal the Arkansas and Little Rock conferences, meeting in the fall of 1884, approved a proposal to buy the institute and operate it for males.[29] Two years later the White River Conference endorsed the transaction,[30] thus by 1886 all three conferences were supporting the institution. In 1889 the school was renamed Hendrix College in honor of Bishop Eugene R. Hendrix.[31]

With purchase of Hendrix College, church leaders committed themselves to the establishment of a senior college for women. Following abandonment of Arkansas Female College at Little Rock, Presiding Bishop Charles B. Galloway appointed a committee in 1887 to pursue establishment of such.[32] The result was a recommendation that the institution be located at Searcy, that other schools related to the church be correlated with it and Hendrix College, and that the conferring of degrees be restricted to these two colleges. In December, 1888, the conferences accepted the proposal along with the enticing subscription of $25,000 from the citizens of Searcy.[33] Named in honor of the bishop, Galloway Female College opened in September, 1889.[34] And the church, marked with wrecks of many weak institutions perishing from lack of adequate support, frankly recognized that its only hope of operating a reputable educational system depended upon adherence to this united policy.

From the beginning of Methodist control there had been a growing conviction among members of the board and church leaders that Hendrix College could obtain permanent success and fulfill its intended mission only in a larger, stronger, more central location than was afforded by the hamlet of Altus. In 1889 the conferences authorized its relocation and, resolving that "prolonged agitating of the question of the removal of Hendrix would be dangerous to the best interest of the college and unsatisfactory to the citizens of Altus," instructed the board of trustees "to settle the question definitely as soon as possible." [35]

The trustees met in Little Rock, January 1, 1890, to consider the question of relocating Hendrix College. After hearing reports from both sides, including the special plan of a citizens' committee from Altus, the board voted to relocate the institution and announced that it would entertain bids for prospective sites.[36] The removal aroused deep interest throughout the state and resulted in keen competitive bidding from Van Buren, Clarksville, Morrilton, Stuttgart, Searcy, Conway, and Arkadelphia.[37]

Arkadelphia's bid was most significant, for some members of the local congregation were contemplating plans to operate a college, thereby jeopardizing the Methodist Church's more realistic approach to higher education. When removal of Hendrix College was announced, rather than continuing plans for founding a new school, Arkadelphians accordingly made an all-out effort to obtain that institution. The local press discussed the movement over a period of weeks and argued "that the established good will of Hendrix College would be an asset which a new college would not have" and, therefore, that "Hendrix would be more desirable than the proposed new institution." [38] Attention was also called to economic prosperity which would accompany the college. It was argued that money given to secure Hendrix College would not be lost, "nor thrown away, nor simply money lent to the Lord as missionary money, but an investment that would pay a handsome and perpetual dividend." [39]

A large, enthusiastic group met on Monday night, March 17, 1890, in the Methodist Church to hear Dr. J. R. Harvey deliver a speech citing the advantages to Arkadelphia if Hendrix College were located there.[40] As a result, the citizens pledged a site and $30,000, and appointed a committee of prominent men to journey to Little Rock to lobby for the institution. Notable among the committeemen were W. E. Barkman, Dr. J. T. McLauchlan, Dr. J. R. Dale, Mayor L. J. Weber, and Ouachita Baptist College President J. W. Conger.[41]

The Hendrix College trustees reconvened in Little Rock on March 19 to determine the issue and for three days heard reports from the delegations of the seven vying communities. After a few ballots the voting centered on Conway, Searcy, and Arkadelphia, one town located in each of the three conferences. The competition was so intense that it took more than twelve hours to reach a decision. On the fifty-first ballot, March 22, 1890, Conway was selected.[42] Apparently the choice was based on Conway's more central location and Searcy's recent selection as the site for Galloway College. Although the trustees had committed themselves and the church to abide by the final settlement, they could not compel the rival cities to submit, and Arkadelphia's ultimate failure to secure Hendrix College resulted in immediate implementation of her original plan.

Arkadelphia's action was not exclusive; Van Buren was the only town which did not use the funds subscribed for securing Hendrix College to build an institution of its own. Morrilton, Searcy, Clarksville, and Arkadelphia each built a college; Stuttgart erected an academy.[43] The colleges at Morrilton and Searcy functioned for only a few years; the institution at Clarksville was later sold to the Presbyterians who operate it today as The College of the Ozarks. When the trustees approved removal of Hendrix College from Altus, they conveyed the college property to the town; Altus reconveyed it to I. L. Burrow, the founder and original owner, who continued to operate the institution as Hiram and Lydia (Burrow) College until closure in 1906.[44] The founding of these colleges by the various towns and the loyalty given them by local and regional congregations all but destroyed the united policy of 1886 and created a situation which led to the survival of the fittest.

Formation of the college in Arkadelphia began when the minister of the First Methodist Church, Dr. John McLauchlan, called a mass meeting for March 24, 1890, to seek continued support of the citizenry in efforts to build a co-educational college. R. W. Huie presided, but it was McLauchlan's ringing speech which stressed that Hendrix College was to be a school for males and Galloway for women and that the church needed a co-educational institution. Recounting that a site and $30,000 had already been pledged to aid in the securing of Hendrix College, McLauchlan had little difficulty in convincing the donors to channel their gifts to the proposed institution. Approval was given and optimism was expressed that the college would be "a credit not only to the city, but to the state as well." [45]

News of the decision to build was greeted with great enthusiasm as evidenced by the local press: "Our citizens are enterprising and know no such word as fail." [46] All were encouraged to contribute to the new co-educational school for "when built it will greatly enhance the growth and prosperity of this place." [47] The press also noted that "the people of Arkadelphia intended to build a college in their town before the removal of Hendrix College was ever thought of." [48]

Aware of the precariousness of their college's future without official acceptance and support from Methodism, the townspeople invited the board of education of the Little Rock Conference to attend the organizational meeting on April 16, 1890,[49] and made them the following proposition:

> The citizens of Arkadelphia tender to the Board of Education of the Little Rock Conference . . . a building worth $30,000 and sufficient land site, upon condition that they establish and maintain a conference co-educational college at that place, and the control of said college be vested in a board of trustees named by said Board of Education.[50]

Learning that $28,000 had been subscribed and witnessing the pledging of over $1,000 more, the board unanimously adopted the following resolution:

> Whereas: We recognize the importance of sustaining the two connectional schools [Hendrix and Galloway] of the three conferences in Arkansas and—
> Whereas: It is apparent that the establishment of a co-educational college in Southwest Arkansas is a matter of urgent necessity to the welfare of Methodism and Christian education in this section—and—
> Whereas: We believe such a school may be established without material injury to our connectional schools, Therefore be it—
> Resolved: That we accept the liberal proposition from the citizens of Arkadelphia to establish a co-educational college and pledge to the enterprise our warmest sympathy and most earnest support.[51]

These representatives agreed to present Arkadelphia's generous proposal to the Little Rock Conference at its December meeting, provided that "the curriculum should be equal to that of Ouachita Baptist College." [52]

Fifteen prominent men were then elected to serve as the board of trustees, with terms extending from one to three years. Of this number six were ministers, the Reverends J. T. McLauchlan, J. H. Gould, H. D. McKinnon, C. D. McSwain, A. O. Evans, and J. R. Moore; five were businessmen, R. W. Huie, W. R. White, E. H. McDaniel, R. H. Featherston, and H. A. Butler; two were physicians, J. R. Dale and C. H. Cargile; J. R. Harvey was a dentist; C. V. Murry an attorney.[53] McLauchlan held the Doctor of Medicine degree; Harvey and Murry were ordained Methodist ministers. Three of the trustees served dual roles: Evans and Moore were members of the Hendrix College board, and Butler was a trustee and a later president of the board of Galloway College.[54] Only one member was from north of the Arkansas River; eight were residents of Arkadelphia.

Immediately following their election on April 16, 1890, the board of trustees of Arkadelphia Methodist College held its first meeting. Nine members were present; also in attendance was the board of education of the Little Rock Conference.[55] The meeting opened with a prayer, a ritual followed at every session until the state assumed control. The trustees did not define their own powers or their relationship to the future college. Such a procedure did not suggest itself. The trustees apparently assumed that they were the absolute masters of the institution. It probably occurred to no one present that the trustee system of university government is an American invention. In Oxford and Cambridge the faculty is the governing body; on the Continent the university is an organ of the church or state.[56]

The first order of business was the election of officers. John T. McLauchlan, a minister, lawyer, and physician, was elected chairman, a position he held until his death in 1896.[57] Regarded as the "Father of the College,"[58] he had been born in Perth, Scotland, December 13, 1825. At the age of seven he emigrated with his family to America. He was graduated from the Louisville Medical College with the Doctor of Medicine degree and practiced in Kentucky before settling at DeWitt, Arkansas, in March, 1870. Following his arrival in the state he turned to law and followed that profession for three years until 1873 when he was licensed to preach by the Little Rock Conference. Arriving in Arkadelphia from a pastorate in Camden, he served a three-year appointment to First Methodist Church where he crowned his twenty-three-year ministry with the founding of Arkadelphia Methodist College.[59]

Completing official positions of the board were secretary and treasurer. Chosen secretary was Eli H. McDaniel who held the position until his death in September, 1905. Born in South Carolina, he settled in Arkadelphia in 1879 and became a prosperous businessman. He had been among the first to enter the campaign to locate a Methodist college in the town.[60] R. H. Featherston, another local resident who also from the conception of the school had been eminently connected with the movement, was elected treasurer.[61]

Perhaps the most prominent businessman in the group was Robert W. Huie who served as a trustee for twenty-seven years. Born August 1, 1845, in Scott County, Arkansas, his life's story could well have appeared in a Horatio Alger book. "From jeans to broadcloth, from day laborer to captain of industry, from penny saver to philanthropist," [62] he began his Arkadelphia career at the age of seventeen. Returning from Confederate service he became an employee in the mercantile business of R. H. Featherston and within eleven years was the owner. From time to time he entered into lumbering, railroading and banking partnerships with Dr. John R. Dale, Charles C. Henderson, and Walter W. Brown, three other men who were to play enduring roles in the history of the institution. He served as president of Arkadelphia Lumber Company, one of the largest in the world, and was a co-owner of the Ultima Thule, Arkadelphia, and Mississippi Railroad.[63] In 1889 he founded Citizens National Bank, the only national bank to operate in the town. A Mason, a faithful member of the Methodist Church, and a man interested in civic affairs, he contributed liberally to Ouachita Baptist College and gave the land and furnished the architect for the first federal building constructed in Arkadelphia. The death of this benefactor and patron ironically occurred in 1929, the year that the institution was transferred to the state.[64]

The most noted member of the board, however, was Dr. John R. Dale, a fellow in the American College of Surgeons. Born in Mississippi in 1848, he came to Arkadelphia in 1866 and served an apprenticeship in a drug store. He later entered Louisville Medical College and was graduated with the Doctor of Medicine degree from Jefferson Medical College of Philadelphia in 1872. In 1879 he was awarded a gold medal by the Howard Medical Society, of which he was then serving as secretary, for his work in the Memphis yellow fever epidemic.[65] A surgeon of national reputation, in 1894 he accepted the chair of operation surgery at Beaumont Hospital Medical College in St. Louis.[66] In the years following, he made weekly trips from Arkadelphia to that hospital to perform surgery and conduct classes. Dale held memberships in the American Medical Association, the Southern Surgical and Gynecological Society, and the Arkansas Medical Association. An influential man in the business world, he was a founder and for years vice-president of Citizens National Bank, a major stockholder in the Arkadelphia Lumber Company located at "Daleville," [67] and a director of the Ultima Thule Railroad.[68] The only trustee not a Methodist, Dale was a member and strong supporter of the Presbyterian Church and an active member of the Masonic Lodge. He donated the lands for the present public library building and a Presbyterian house of worship. He served faithfully on the board and was the college physician until 1902 when he moved to Texarkana where he established Dale Clinic and continued to practice medicine until his death in 1927.[69]

Following the election of officers, a motion prevailed that "we endeavor to open school at such time in September next as may hereafter be determined by the board." [70] To implement this motion, Claud V. Murry, attorney for the board,[71] moved the naming of committees to procure a charter and draft a constitution, to purchase a site, to engage an architect to submit plans for a suitable building and dormitory, and to employ a president. With appropriate committee appointments made, Chairman McLauchlan designated Featherston, Murry, McDaniel, Cargile, and himself the executive committee "with power to act in all matters between sessions of the board," which then recessed until June.[72]

The trustees held their second meeting June 4, 1890; the proceedings were a formality.[73] A charter and constitution were read and adopted. The latter provided that direction and control of the college would be administered by a fifteen-member board, to be elected or appointed by the Little Rock Conference to three-year terms, five to expire at the end of each conference year. While the constitution stated that all trustees were to be residents of the conference, it did not require that they, or any portion of them, be members of the Methodist or any other church. It stipulated that they would hold an annual board meeting on the Monday of commencement week. The constitution also provided that an executive committee, consisting of three trustees, the chairman and secretary serving as ex-officio members, would have supervisory control of the college's business affairs between board sessions.[74] This committee was destined to exert profound influence on the institution's operation.

The chairman then reported the purchase of a nine-acre campus site, costing $1,500, from Harriet Barkman.[75] Formerly a cotton field within the Barkman plantation, the campus, located on the northern edge of Arkadelphia, fronted the Barkman and Henderson mansions. It was separated from the Ouachita Baptist College campus by approximately three blocks and two deep ravines. This latter geographical feature was incorporated into the rivalry which soon developed between the institutions: their displays of hostility and competition became known as the "Battle of the Ravine." The building committee announced employment of architect Thomas Harding to superintend erection of a $30,000 "handsome structure to house the college." [76]

The trustees voted unanimously to accept the presidential selection committee's recommendation that George Childs Jones be employed as president for one year. They agreed that Jones would "bear all necessary expenses of the school and receive all the profits," while the board would furnish "all necessary school furniture and the heavy furniture for bedrooms." [77] In reality, the college was a joint undertaking between the citizens of Arkadelphia and the president of the institution! Next, the trustees empowered the president to select a faculty to provide instruction from primary through collegiate departments and scheduled the first term to begin the first Wednesday in September, 1890.[78]

The trustees associated themselves together under the name Arkadelphia Methodist College to secure legal existence for the institution under an Act of Incorporation provided by state law. They filed the "Articles of Association of Arkadelphia Methodist College" in the office of the Secretary of State on June 10, 1890. Therefore, the charter was granted to the trustees themselves and their successors as the body politic and corporate, and not to the Methodist Episcopal Church, South. The school was incorporated for the purpose of Christian education in literature, science, and art, for both sexes with no racial restrictions.[79]

CHAPTER IV

The Launching of the College

THE arrival of a dusty vehicle from the town of Amity with three girls and their trunks in early September, 1890, marked the coming of the first students to Arkadelphia Methodist College.[1] Their first view of the campus no doubt was one of disappointment; the "handsome structure to house the college" was only a promising pile of bricks. President Jones had, however, secured the temporary classrooms and boarding facilities to accommodate the 110 students who enrolled for the first session which began September 3, 1890.[2] The public school's fall term was delayed and that building was obtained for class recitations and the study hall; the George Walker Reed house, the large two-story antebellum mansion of Charles Christopher Henderson's uncle which stood at the location of the present First Baptist Church, was used for the women's dormitory and president's home. The male students were boarded with approved families in the town; no college housing was made available for men until 1903.[3]

The large enrollment was due to the energetic canvassing of President Jones. Arkadelphia was proud of the new school and furnished many of its students; more than one-half of those enrolled were from the bluff city. There were three out-of-state students, two from Texas and one from Mississippi. In addition to the 110 students in the collegiate department, thirty-two were attending the preparatory department.[4] The school was co-educational, and in the beginning session women outnumbered men, seventy to forty,[5] establishing a trend which would continue throughout the years of Methodist control.

That George Childs Jones, known for his scholarship, character, and administrative ability, was, as the minutes book of the trustees stated, a suitable person for the presidency,[6] he soon proved beyond question as he directed the college for its first fourteen years, its entire life span as Arkadelphia Methodist College. Born August 29, 1859, in Jackson, Tennessee,[7] Jones was only thirty years old when elected president. The son of a noted Methodist minister and educator, Amos W. Jones, who for fifty years held the presidency of Memphis (Methodist) Conference Female Institute, President Jones was descended from a long line of teachers.[8] Class valedictorian, in 1876 he received the Bachelor of Arts degree from Southwestern Baptist University (Union University),[9] which eventually awarded him the Doctor of Laws degree;[10] three years later Jones obtained the Master of Arts degree from Vanderbilt University. In 1881 he graduated from Comer's Commercial College, Boston, and following the educational vogue of the day continued his intellectual pursuits in Europe. After studying under renowned masters of science and philosophy at the Royal University, Berlin, he concluded his studies in Paris.[11] Following extensive travel, Jones returned to America and began duties as professor of mathematics and science at Memphis Conference Female Institute, a position he held until 1889 when appointed headmaster of Stuttgart Institute, a Methodist high school in Arkansas.[12] Less than one year later, he left this position to assume the presidency of Arkadelphia Methodist College. An ordained minister,[13] Jones served as an elder in the Little Rock Conference; but in 1901 he surrendered his parchments and stated that he had devoted himself exclusively to work in education and could better serve the church as a layman than as a minister.[14]

Proclaimed *par excellence* the president of Arkansas colleges,[15] the young Jones was equally commanding in appearance. Possessing an attractive physique and an engaging personality, he dressed conservatively in dark colors; and to give the appearance of an older man he wore a neatly trimmed, full beard, but in later life only a mustache. Nevertheless, he was not handicapped by his young age; rather, it seemed an asset; and he soon became a familiar figure on the campus and in the town.[16] "Of first-class executive ability, equal in literary attainments to any man his age, and inferior to none as an enthusiastic teacher, he seemed born to rule. Firmly without harshness, he directed and controlled the school without appearing to govern at all. There was found in him an absence of self-consciousness and no shadow of pretense."[17] A man of ideals and mottos, he lived by many; one well remembered by his daughter was "One's heritage means a great deal more than one's inheritance."[18] A member of the class of 1891 described President Jones as a "prince of a man" and remarked that the students "loved him dearly."[19]

The institution was divided into two departments: the collegiate and the preparatory, usually referred to as the academy. Fourteen schools comprised the collegiate department: ten academic—mathematics, natural and physical science, mental science, English, history, reading, Latin, Greek, French, and German; and four non-academic—music, elocution, art, and typewriting and shorthand.[20] In addition to serving as president, Jones was professor of physical science, mathematics, and Latin. He and nine others completed the first faculty; three who instructed in the ten academic schools and six who were associated with the four non-academic.[21]

Jones was assisted in the academic courses by J. Howard Sledd who instructed in languages and natural sciences and served as Chapel-keeper. The thirty-five-year-old professor held the Master of Arts degree from Randolph-Macon and was later awarded the Doctor of Letters degree from Franklin College in Texas.[22] Also, the Reverend Boone Keeton was professor of ancient and modern languages; he too held a Master of Arts degree.[23] The popular Arkadelphia teacher, Fannie A. Cook, niece of former United States Attorney General Augustus H. Garland, taught English and history.[24]

In the arts, Irene Inez Ice, who had been educated at Lebanon (Tennessee) University and Boston School of Oratory and who held the Bachelor of Science degree, conducted classes in elocution and calisthenics. Lizzie E. Cannon, who had attended the Chicago Art Institute and schools in Kentucky and Ohio, was the art teacher; H. W. Estes, a graduate of Zaerian Normal Penmanship College, offered courses in plain and ornamental penmanship; [25] and Lizzie Miles taught music.[26] Completing the instructional staff were Ruth Johnson, who taught shorthand and typing, and Mrs. George C. Jones, wife of the president, who offered the first course in homemaking, "fancy cooking." [27] Lizzie McKinnon, daughter of Trustee H. D. McKinnon, served as principal of the preparatory department; Dr. F. R. Fleming and Dr. J. R. Dale, a trustee, were the physicians.[28]

It was only the second day of school when impudent cupid attacked this august body. Winning as he usually does, he carried away Miss Miles, the music professor, to become the wife of a local citizen. Tessie Moore, a graduate of Memphis Conference Female Institute and Chicago Musical College, was then employed in her place.[29] It is interesting to note that even on this first faculty there was nepotism, including the president's and board's families. Notwithstanding, it was an admirable faculty to have been assembled in a short period of time.

In addition to multiple teaching assignments, the professors were expected to fulfill additional duties. They were required to make monthly reports of recitations and deportment to the president; to be present at prayers and the daily exercises opening and closing the school day; to be in the recitation room in advance of the class; and to report to the president any element of disorder. They were prohibited to receive calls except of a professional nature during school hours. Women instructors were allowed to receive visitors only from 7:00 to 10:00 p.m. on Fridays and Saturdays. All were restricted from engaging in additional employment, and they were expected to carry out faithfully all regulations of the college and to avoid that centuries-old faculty vice of criticizing each other, the college, and its program.[30] Jones regarded a harmonious faculty as essential to good work, a criteria desired by all presidents of the college, but attained by few.

Beginning operation in an era when accrediting and standardizing agencies for admission and graduation requirements existed only in the Northeast,[31] Arkadelphia Methodist College, like other Southern educational institutions, determined its own way. At the outset, almost any person of good moral character could get into the institution. Though the charter contained no racial restrictions, it was September, 1955, before the first full-time black student, Maurice R. Horton, was admitted.[32]

Students were classified according to qualifications at entrance as determined by examination. But once admitted, a student had to work. The curricula consisted of three degree programs: the English, the scientific, and the classical; these were pursued from ten "schools."[33] The English curriculum required completion of all courses included in the schools of mathematics, natural and physical science, mental science, English, history, and reading. The Bachelor of Philosophy degree was presented to young men completing this outline of study, the Mistress of English Literature degree to young ladies.[34] In 1893 requirements for the Bachelor of Philosophy and Mistress of English Literature degrees were reduced to include completion of all courses through only the junior year.[35] The scientific curriculum leading to the degree of Bachelor of Science required completion of the English program, the school of Latin, and either the school of German or the school of French. The most difficult curriculum was the classical which led to the degree of Bachelor of Arts and required completion of the scientific program and the school of Greek. The degree of Artium Magister (M.A.) was to be conferred on those who completed the English curriculum and all four language schools. The most popular courses of study were those in the four non-academic schools: music, elocution, art, and typewriting and shorthand. These special schools permitted students to elect particular courses not leading to degrees, but to Certificates of Graduation.[36]

The ten academic schools were divided into classes, freshman through senior; each class consisted of two prescribed courses. In contemporary terminology one would say that successful completion of one course was a prerequisite for the next. Academic electives were allowed only in the scientific and classical degree programs; a student could choose either French or German to satisfy the modern language requirement. Degree requirements were met through completion of courses, not by acquiring a specified number of credit hours. The schools of mathematics, English, history, natural and physical science, and reading offered sub-freshman courses for those who were deemed deficient; spelling was emphasized throughout the curricula.[37]

That a school of history requiring seven courses of all degree candidates would be included in a curriculum initiated in 1890 in an infant Arkansas college is a credit to the first president. Only nine years had passed since the 1881 appointment of Moses Coit Tyler at Cornell University as the first professor of American history in this country;[38] yet two courses in that subject were required of freshmen at Arkadelphia Methodist College. Histories of England and France were required of sophomores; juniors took Roman history and the history of Greece and Eastern Nations. A general history course was pursued by seniors.[39] (Although in 1970 course offerings in this discipline had been increased to thirty-seven, a student who had passed only one history course could receive a degree![40])

Greek, Latin, German, and French, a valid linguistic wealth, were offered. Courses in the ancient languages included works by Homer, Demosthenes, Sophocles, Caesar, Cicero, Virgil, Horace, Livy, and Terence. Jones, having recently returned from studies in both Germany and France, was especially concerned with work in these modern languages. Six courses were required in each of the two. The school of English was taught through grammatical and rhetorical approaches. In the senior year emphasis was given to written and oral application of the previous courses. The school of reading encompassed works from Aesop's *Fables* to selections by John Ruskin, with all five of the major literary genres being perused. A noteworthy requirement in the school of mathematics was a senior course in surveying and navigation. The school of natural and physical science offered twelve courses, ranging from geography to astronomy, to physics, to mineralogy. The school of mental science was open only to seniors and involved the students with problems of logic.[41]

Optional studies in music, elocution, and art included instrumental (piano, organ, guitar, and violin) and vocal music; painting; drawing; penmanship; and fancy cooking. An interesting feature of this liberal arts college was the inclusion of a school of business. Instruction was offered in bookkeeping, typewriting, and shorthand, but this school attracted only eight students the first year.[42] The most ironic feature of the college, church oriented as it was, was the absence of a school or even one course in Bible! Such was the case for thirteen years until the fall semester of 1903, when Charles C. Henderson funded a course of Bible study.[43] But all students were required to attend a thirty-minute devotional exercise at the beginning of each school day.[44]

The academic year was divided into two terms of five months (twenty weeks) each. There was no intermission between sessions, the semester break being a creation of a later day. In fact, the president encouraged students to remain on campus throughout the entire school year; he believed that absence from the academic environment, especially for visits home, was detrimental to the student's scholastic welfare.[45] School hours were from 8:30 a.m. to 12:00 noon, and from 1:30 to 4:30 p.m., five days per week;[46]

thus the students were spared a twentieth century discomfort: Saturday classes.

As previously mentioned, each class consisted of two courses taken within the academic year. Although examinations were given to determine whether a student would advance from one course to the next, the final evaluation for a class was not given until the completion of both prescribed courses constituting a class. Held at the close of the spring session, the annual tests were required in writing and were subject to presidential approval before a student could advance. In the spring semester, one month before the annual scheduled review period, all candidates for graduation were required to take a "strict" preliminary in the entire curriculum; this too was liable to the president's approval. Following medieval practice "patrons were cordially invited to be present at these exercises and examinations." [47]

The president was completely responsible for the welfare of the pupils. The sole authority, he decided all questions relating to the studies, examinations, habits, social privileges, visits, and recreation of the students. Entrance into the institution was a contract among the student, his parents or guardians, and the president. While the college recognized and respected home authority, parents could not authorize their children to deviate, in any degree whatever, from the rules.[48] Among them were: to explain to the president the cause of every absence before returning to recitations; to attend Sunday school and church every Sunday morning; to attend no ball, party, or any public gathering during school or study hours (7:00 to 9:00 p.m., except Saturday and Sunday); to be in place of residence daily by 7:00 p.m., except Sunday when attendance at evening worship was permitted; to use no tobacco or obscene language on the campus; not to leave the city without special permission; and not to give or receive attention from the opposite sex, either by visits or correspondence. To aid enforcement of the last all communications had to be directed to the president or his wife.[49]

Students not willing to conform to regulations were advised not to apply for admission, and were warned that discipline would be firm.[50] And firm it was! Those accused of violating the rules were suspended during the investigation period and the guilty were subjected to both private and public reproof. Public censure was administered by the president before the student body. Likewise, students who failed to show proper incentive to study were liable to public chastisement. In order to achieve more perfect discipline, a merits system was adopted. Ten demerits subjected a pupil to private reproof; twelve, public; and twenty, dismissal.[51]

Boarding students were required to furnish their own napkin, napkin ring, and linens. Books, stationery, sheet music, art and ornamental materials could be bought at the college for publisher's prices; all transactions were in cash, and it was recommended that parents deposit funds for purchase of the mentioned items with the president.[52]

The cost for the ten-month opening session was $160, to include tuition, board, fuel, lights, and laundry. Freshmen and sophomore day students paid $40; advanced students, $50.[53] Students residing in private homes obtained room and board for from $10 to $12.50 a month.[54] Optional studies, i.e., music, art, commercial, carried additional fees from $2 to $50. Special rates were offered to families with two or more college age children and to ministers' families, regardless of denomination. Parents enrolling two or more boarding pupils in the academic schools were charged tuition for only one. Children of ministers were admitted tuition free, and if five from the same family were boarding students, one was given total expenses.[55] All fees were payable monthly from local patrons; one-half in advance from boarding pupils. A ten percent deduction was granted on advance payment for the collegiate year. Final settlements were due the first Monday in June. Remindful of current policy, no degree was conferred nor any honor awarded, unless financial obligations had been paid in full.[56] The first scholarship, one year's tuition in the collegiate department, was awarded to the valedictorian of Arkadelphia High School,[57] a procedure still followed.

The financial plight the college was to suffer was initially evidenced when subscribers failed to meet their first installment pledge (June 1, 1890) in the amount of ten percent; nevertheless, a contract for the building was let.[58] In summer months preceding the opening, entertainments and socials were given for benefit of the college. In July an ice-cream festival was held, and Mrs. Charles C. Henderson sponsored an entertainment at the opera house.[59] The opening week an oyster supper was given at the Spence Hotel, but attendance was poor. That same week a dime social was hosted at the mayor's home; the cake and lemonade sales netted only twelve dollars,[60] a far cry from the needed thousands. Despite this dismal financial outlook, the determined supporters would not let their optimism wane as they anxiously awaited the fall meeting of the Little Rock Conference of the Methodist Episcopal Church, South.

The conference met in Monticello, December 3–8, 1890; as agreed, the board of education presented the issue of Arkadelphia Methodist College to the group. Before submitting its resolution, however, the board defended its earlier action. It stated that following "mature and prayerful considerations of all related questions"[61] concerning the offer of the Arkadelphia citizens to give the college to the conference, the board had unanimously accepted the generous proposal, with provision that the courses of study would be equal to those of Ouachita Baptist College.[62] Upon submitting the question for vote, the board went on record stating:

> We desire to reaffirm our loyalty to our connectional schools [Vanderbilt, Hendrix, and Galloway], and state that our action is based upon what we conceive to be an absolute necessity in order to save the interest of our church in Southwest Arkansas.[63]

This commitment became the prime basis for support of the college throughout its entire existence under church control.

Though agreement had been made by the conference merely

six years earlier to maintain only two colleges, the issue was debated for more than two hours.[64] The delegates were strongly reminded of the staunch resolution, concerning relocation of Hendrix College, which had recently been adopted by the Arkansas
Conference:

> If the Conferences were not satisfied with the action of the
> Board of Trustees [Hendrix], we recognize that there is no room
> for dissent, since the whole matter was committed by the three
> Conferences to the Board with plenipotentiary powers.[65]

Sectionalism apparently became a major issue when delegate after
delegate reminded the group that each of the other conferences
had a college within its limits, that both were north of the Arkansas River, that the only degree granting institution south of the
river was Ouachita Baptist College, and that need for another existed. It was further emphasized that neither of the Methodist
schools was co-educational. When the vote was taken, three-
fourths of the delegates favored acceptance of the institution,[66] thus
Arkadelphia Methodist College was recognized by, and placed under the direction of, the Little Rock Conference. For the next
thirty-nine years, therefore, the stream of higher education fos-
tered by Arkansas Methodism flowed in three channels rather than
two as designed by the leaders in the last half of the decade of the
1880's.

With official conference acceptance and strong local patronage
the college ended its first term with a promising outlook. A simple
ceremony on February 4, 1891, marked the opening of the spring
term which began in the recently completed east wing of the building. At this time supporters in the conference were reminded that
now they had no reason to send their sons and daughters to Virginia and other states, for they could obtain a good Christian education within the conference.[67]

Recalling the opening year, ninety-nine-year-old Mrs. R. B.
Thomas, *nee* Birdie Holloway, a member of the first senior class,

recounted in 1971 that it was "strictly school work, no clubs or fraternities, and very little social activity." [68] But there were organized in 1890 two literary societies, Gamma Sigma for men and Philosophic for women.[69] "Dating was limited only to older girls, and then only on special occasions." [70] But then, as now, there were young ladies willing to chance meetings with the opposite sex. On one occasion "President Jones interrupted his class to apprehend two girls he saw sneaking away, no doubt to have dates with Ouachita boys. Catching them, he personally escorted them back to their rooms." [71]

Although the class schedule was rigorous, recreation hours were provided from 4:30 to 7:30 p.m., Monday through Friday; all day Saturday to 7:00 p.m.; and from 4:00 to 7:00 p.m. on Sunday. While the students were at greater liberty during these hours, "habitual loitering on the streets, or parading them, or riding on public vehicles," was considered "highly improper," and subjected a student to discipline, which could lead to suspension or expulsion.[72]

But the first year was not without its lighter moments. The faculty gave lectures and musicals which were open to the public. There were student debates and oratorical contests, but most activities took place at Grayson Hall, the opera house in downtown Arkadelphia. It provided the major attractions: hometown productions and semi-monthly band concerts were held there. In late January, 1891, students crowded into the theater to hear the Harvard University Quartet.[73] One event excitedly awaited was May Day celebration. On that day, the rules were suspended and the co-educational aspect of the college became a social reality. Business houses closed and the townspeople and students from both colleges enjoyed an outing and basket dinner at "the bluff" overlooking the Ouachita River.[74]

The most outstanding activity of the year was graduation week. The work with brick and mortar had progressed steadily, but not rapidly. Time for the first annual commencement came and the auditorium was not completed. The students, determined to have a grand occasion, ingeniously devised a temporary tarpaulin roof and interior decorations. Greenery and student works of art covered the unfinished walls. All was prepared, but the night before the activities a heavy rainstorm prevailed, and the wind, not waiting for the scheduled performance to "lift the roof," proceeded without assistance to wreck the improvised setting.[75] Among students making an anxious dash to save their drawings from ruin was Charles Richardson, who later became a noted Arkansas artist.[76] Despite dampened spirits, long before the hour for the program to begin the auditorium was packed with visitors, including Charles C. Henderson, soon to be appointed to the board of trustees.

The activities which were scheduled to last four days began Sunday morning, June 7, with the commencement sermon delivered by the Reverend M. B. Chapman of St. Louis; the baccalaureate sermon was preached that night by the Reverend H. W. Brooks of Hope. Monday, Undergraduate Day, an art exhibit and concert were held. On Tuesday, College Day, the Honorable Clifton R. Breckenridge, Representative in Congress from the Second District, addressed the student body and guests; an elocution recital was the evening function. Graduation Day began at 9:30 a.m. Wednesday. Each of the six graduates presented an essay; and merit medals sponsored by the trustees, teachers, and friends were given to outstanding students. The climax was the conferring of degrees. Four young ladies, Lena Crow, Mamie Crow, Susie Dyke, and Birdie Holloway, became the first graduates when they were awarded the Mistress of English Literature degree by President Jones. Certificates were presented to two women who had completed the business course. The activities ended with the address to the graduates by the Reverend H. M. Whaling. The flowers on the speaker's platform were a gift and tribute presented by the senior class of Ouachita Baptist College.[77] The following week, the Methodist college graduates bestowed like recognition upon the

Baptists. This simple presentation ceremony observed by every graduating class since is the oldest tradition of the college. Thus Arkadelphia Methodist College, conceived in the minds and hearts of the town's citizens and brought into existence through their self-sacrifice and unrelenting work, concluded its initial session.

The college's second year, which began September 2, 1891,[78] coincided with a number of significant changes in the town, all which enhanced the growth and development of the institution. That year witnessed the coming of electric lighting,[79] electric streetcars, six daily trains, a city water system,[80] and the town's first telephone exchange. The college was one of thirty initial telephone subscribers, and the original "hello girls" were Lena and Mamie Crow,[81] recent graduates of the school. The Arkadelphia Cotton Mill, though destined to be discontinued before the end of the decade, was then the only cotton mill in the state; three stories high, it contained seventy-four Lowell looms and 3,000 spindles valued at $60,000. Owned and operated by home people it "furnished employment to scores of worthy and needy children." [82] Lumbering, however, with a daily payroll of more than $300, was rapidly replacing cotton as the foundation of the economy.[83] And with a population of 2,455 [84] the town on the Ouachita was maintaining its traditional place as an industrial center.

Equal strides had been made in educational pursuits. Three new institutions had opened within the year. Pleasant Hill Baptist Church, a local Negro congregation, had instituted the Arkansas Industrial Institute and College for blacks,[85] and the African Methodist Episcopal Church had removed Bethel Institute (Shorter College) from Little Rock to Arkadelphia.[86] In addition to these two Negro schools, J. F. Draughon had opened a business college,[87] which functions today in Little Rock. In April, 1892, plans to remove the Presbyterian Synodical College from Batesville to Arkadelphia were announced, but last-minute efforts on the part of the Batesville citizens prevailed, and Arkansas' oldest denominational institution of higher learning remains at the location of its founding.[88] The Presbyterians founded Presbyterian Industrial School for Negroes in Arkadelphia in 1896.[89]

College interests had succeeded in obtaining a special legislative act prohibiting the sale of liquor for a ten-mile radius,[90] and Arkadelphia which had spent more than $98,000 on college buildings and hosted forty professors proudly proclaimed to be the "Athens of Arkansas."[91] And one newspaper in Texas, a state seldom acknowledging anything outside its borders as being "bigger or better," referred to Arkadelphia as "the educational center of the Southwest."[92]

Enrollment for the second year, 1891–1892, reached one hundred by noon on opening day,[93] and that number grew to 164 by the end of the registration period, an increase of twenty-two over the first year. Four students were preparing for the ministry, and twenty-one children of preachers were receiving free tuition.[94] Five students were non-residents of Arkansas.[95] To accommodate the increased enrollment, the faculty was enlarged by three. The most notable addition was a librarian, Eddie Featherston, who also served as college stenographer.[96] In spring of the first year, friends of the Reverend John McLauchlan, chairman of the board of trustees, and of the college contributed books and money for the establishment of McLauchlan Library.[97] Of the bound volumes collected, historical writings, especially those dealing with the ancient world, dominated,[98] illustrating the classical spirit prevailing within the liberal arts curricula. Periodicals were considered an important department in the library. Each faculty member was required to subscribe to at least one journal or magazine relating to his subject area and to place it in the library for the use of all.[99]

To prevent extravagance, a uniform for women students was adopted, inaugurating a feature of the college which continued until 1920. The first uniform consisted of a long-sleeved, high-necked white blouse, a tie, and a floor-length gathered skirt of a dark color.[100] (Eighty years later, 1971, a number of co-eds appeared on the same campus in floor-length attire only to be reminded by the administration that such was inappropriate and dangerous, although the women's dress code permitted any fashion except swim suits or bare feet.[101])

To a large extent the records of the early literary societies, Gamma Sigma and Philosophic, provide an insight into student life. Almost every collegiate was a member of these societies, forerunners of the present social fraternities, and their weekly meetings afforded some diversion from an otherwise rigorous schedule. Publication of the first student journal, *Methodist College Magazine*, resulted from their efforts. The initial edition, edited by Burris Head, appeared in October, 1891, and consisted of thirty-two pages. Its format was a basic compilation of essays and articles on education and religion, not limited to student authorship. A section on campus activities was also included and likewise provided additional information on student life during the first decade. The magazine continued, with slight name changes, through the 1898 session. The original subscription rate was one dollar per year,[102] but by 1894 it had been reduced to fifty cents.[103] To encourage circulation, the staff offered a one hundred-dollar scholarship, effective September, 1894, to the person securing the greatest number of cash subscribers. If five hundred subscriptions were credited to the successful contestant, a bonus of one year's board was included.[104]

Debate and oratory were an integral part of the curriculum, and students in all English classes were required to participate in one of these activities the first day of each school month.[105] It was in this area that the college entered its first competition and introduced the original school colors, cream and pink,[106] before the adoption of the now familiar "red and gray." In November student representatives joined with other Arkansas collegiates to form the state oratorical association.[107] Annual contests and debates were held, and special trains carried cheering sections accompanied with bands and other fanfare to support the participants. In 1895 the contest was hosted by the college, but most were held at the Capitol Theater in Little Rock. Arkadelphia Methodist College never captured the coveted gold medal, but rivals Hendrix College and Ouachita Baptist College did.[108] Yet throughout the "Gay Nineties" interest in debating remained keen and provided a spirit of rivalry not surpassed until the coming of inter-collegiate sports.

To the trustees' embarrassment, in the fall of 1891 the structure was still incomplete and construction had halted. To induce the contractor to continue the job, the board secured a loan to pay back-wages and finance roofing. They urgently requested that all subscribers make prompt payment by November 1.[109] Work recommenced November 3, and President Jones announced that the trustees had made arrangements to finish the building, hopefully by commencement.[110]

The most significant event of the year occurred in December when Charles Christopher Henderson was appointed to the board of trustees,[111] a position he held for nearly thirty-two years until his death in 1923. It would be difficult to assess Henderson's influence on the life of the institution. His imprint is great, however, and he is properly referred to as "the Savior of the College"[112] for its very survival is a credit to this extraordinary man.

Charles Christopher Henderson was the son of John and Margaret Reed Henderson, both natives of North Carolina. His mother, Margaret Mahalia Reed, was born in 1827 and at the age of twelve moved with her parents, Blencoe Wadsworth and Majories Ellis Reed, to Waldron, Arkansas, in Scott County. The exact date of her marriage to John Henderson is unknown, but it was before 1846. With his young bride Henderson lived in northwestern Arkansas where he pursued the occupations of carpentry and millwrighting. It was there in Lafayette Township in Scott County that Charles Christopher, the third of eight children, was born March 17, 1850. Sometime between that date and 1851 the family moved to nearby Hackett City, a village in Sebastian County, and Charles' uncle George Walker Reed, brother of his mother, moved to Arkadelphia where he came to operate a successful general merchandise company and to acquire reasonable wealth.[113]

When Charlie, as he was called by his family, was about fourteen, his father died; and the young man was compelled to seek employment to aid in the support of the large family. Their adverse economic circumstances were increased by Federal raids into that section of Arkansas during the Civil War. During those years the Reverend H. G. Hopkins, a Methodist minister, and his wife resided in the Henderson household and exerted Christian influence on the young man.

With the conclusion of the Civil War which had left Waldron prostrate, Charles Christopher Henderson's aunt Rebecca Reed Moles and her husband Jacob Cooper Moles moved to Arkadelphia in 1865; approximately five years later Charles' mother Margaret joined her sister and brother George in Arkadelphia. For a number of years Charles Christopher was employed by a St. Louis livestock commission; and in 1879 while in the service of that firm, the "Captain," as he had come to be called traveled to Arkadelphia where he was given the opportunity to manage the estate of his aunt Mrs. Jacob Cooper Moles and to obtain financial backing from his affluent uncle George Walker Reed. Impressed by the thriving town and sensing economic opportunity, Henderson, a tall, twenty-nine-year-old man with deep-set eyes and a mustache, began a successful career which he pursued in a determined manner.[114]

Approximately one year following his arrival, Henderson commissioned Hiram J. Allen of Texarkana to construct him a suitable home.[116] It was to this dwelling that he brought his bride, the talented Laura Bell Hall of New Orleans, in September, 1880.[117]

Near the turn of the century the house was enlarged and re-
modeled into the commodious two-story frame residence located
at the corner of Henderson and Tenth streets. This stately house,
shaded by large trees and surrounded by a fine iron fence, provided
an appropriate setting for the man of many and varied interests.

Henderson, a religious man and active member of the Methodist
Church, became one of the most prominent laymen in the South.
A member of the board of stewards and a long-time superintendent
of the Sunday school, in 1906 he was a lay-delegate to the Methodist General Conference, South, and in 1907 served as chairman of
the building committee for construction of the First Methodist
Church.[118] Mrs. Henderson shared her husband's religious convic-
tions, and it was in this atmosphere that they reared three children,
Laura, Margaret, and Harry.[119]

Henderson advanced through stages of commercial prestige
until he was a well recognized financier. For a time he operated
a dairy; then he was a cotton broker. But his real success began
when he entered the lumber and sawmilling business, which led to
railroading and banking interests. In partnerships with W. W.
Brown, R. W. Huie, W. E. Barkman, Dr. J. R. Dale and Dr. J. S.
Cargile,[120] all who served as trustees of the college, Henderson became a major stockholder in the Arkadelphia Lumber Company
and the Nashville Lumber Company, and a co-owner of Brown-
Henderson Improvement and Timber Company,[121] the last indicative of a nomenclature soon to be identified with the college
that they came to direct.

To reap the rich timber reserves of the virgin forests in southwest Arkansas, these flourishing industries built a number of railroads. Henderson was associated with ten; the first, a short line
established in June, 1883, had a name whose length almost rivaled
its 140 miles of rails—Ultima Thule, Arkadelphia, and Mississippi
Railway.[122] The major track, incorporated in 1906, was the Memphis, Paris, and Gulf Railway, which was to extend from the

Tennessee city through Texas to a point on the Gulf of Mexico. Predominantly owned by Henderson, Brown, Barkman, and John H. Hinemon (then serving as president of the college) it provided a nationwide outlet for an area having great potential in fruit-bearing orchards and serviced Murfreesboro recently crazed with diamond fever, but the principal incentive for building the railway was the Nashville Lumber Company.[123] In the first decade of the twentieth century, Henderson entered another enterprise. In 1905 the Elk Horn Bank, which had been organized in 1884, elected him its second president, a position he held until 1916.[124]

Although an active member of the Republican party [125] Henderson was accepted by the society of the antebellum town. His civic interests were manifested in a number of charitable enterprises, such as child welfare, Y.M.C.A., and Y.W.C.A. He and Robert B. F. Key, also a loyal friend of the college, purchased twenty-seven acres of land adjacent to the campus and conveyed it to Arkadelphia for a city park.[126] But it was Mrs. Henderson who first became actively involved with the Methodist college. When the movement to establish the institution was initiated Henderson himself was less than enthusiastic, but his wife sponsored activities to raise funds for the school and enrolled as a special student in art during the first session.[127] With a cautious eye the Captain observed the activity associated with construction of the educational center rising in the great expanse on the north side of his estate. He soon caught the zeal shared by his family and neighbors and began to labor for the institution's highest development.

The remainder of the year was but a footnote, but, as promised, the building was nearing completion and the June commencement week exercises were held in the recently completed chapel. Electric lighting gave additional luster to the activities scheduled in that hall which were concluded with the conferring of five degrees.[128] D. R. McDonald and W. W. Rice became the first male graduates when they received Bachelor of Philosophy degrees.[129]

CHAPTER V

The Troubled Years

THE troubled years of the 1890's marked the nadir of Arkadelphia Methodist College and the beginning of Henderson College. From 1892 to 1894 the institution was under lease to President Jones; the latter year it was sold to him. Jones continued to serve as president until 1904, except for a two-year period (1897–1899) during which he took a leave of absence. Arkadelphians and the Methodist denomination never lost confidence in the college, and throughout the remainder of the decade patrons and church leaders sought means to return it to Methodist ownership. In 1902 Charles Christopher Henderson provided the financial resources for restoring title to the church, but the next two years were scarred by a conflict of interests between the president and the benefactor which resulted in Jones' departure in 1904.

One hundred fifty students enrolled during the week that the school began its third year,[1] fourteen fewer than the preceding session; even so there was much jubilation, for after a two-year delay the entire building was ready for occupancy. The Victorian edifice rose four stories and was flanked with two three-story wings. Containing over a million bricks[2] and crowned with a clock tower, it was an imposing structure with a frontage of 166 feet and a depth of ninety-two. Known simply as "the college," it housed the academic facilities and provided boarding accommodations for 125 women. The central section contained administrative offices, the library, reading rooms, study hall, society halls, parlors, and some boarding rooms; the fourth floor housed the women's gymnasium. The president's family apartments, the dining halls, kitchen, and boarding rooms filled the east wing. The west wing contained the concert hall which featured an inclined floor with four hundred opera chairs, and recitation and music rooms on the upper two floors.[3] The building was lighted by electricity and gas, supplied with hot and cold water, serviced by an elevator,[4] and heated with wood until 1903.[5]

Carpets of floral designs complimented two parlors sparsely furnished with plush chairs and horsehair sofas. From tall windows hung floor-length lace panels topped by heavily-draped cornices.[6] Most impressive of all was the entrance hall, with its grand stairway (used only on formal occasions) and massive paintings, among which was a fine copy of Rosa Bonheur's "Horse Fair." [7] Each carpeted boarding room contained a lavatory with hot and cold running water and was conveniently located near a toilet and bathtub.[8] The classrooms were adequately equipped, especially the science room with its "full and very fine line of physical and chemical appliances" which had cost $2,000.[9]

With an additional $6,000 expended on furniture and fixtures and construction costs for the building exceeding the estimate by approximately $10,000, the investment totaled $52,750,[10] almost twice the amount pledged. How the trustees proposed to pay for the structure and furnishings posed an embarrassing question.

This situation resulted in President Jones' financial involvement beyond his original contract which provided that he only assume operational expenses of the school. It had been necessary that he advance more than $7,000 to clear a debt incurred by purchase of equipment.[11] The board had experienced grave difficulty in collecting partial payment of the $30,000 pledge, and it was completely unrealistic that they could now ask for an additional $22,750. In an attempt to erase the fiscal deficit, the trustees agreed to lease the college to Jones for ten years for the sum of $10,000.[12] In its annual session in December, 1892, the Little Rock Conference approved the trustees' action and reaffirmed its loyalty to the college, but it failed to make provisions for the school's monetary rescue.

When the conference met the following year (December, 1893) the financial report of the institution revealed dismal, if not acute, findings. Two mortgages were held against the school: the first, $11,000, by Arkansas Building and Loan Association; the second, $3,000, by the contractor. And the total indebtedness had increased to $25,800.[13]

The trustees assembled at 3:00 p.m., Monday, June 11, 1894, for their fourth annual session, but it was no ordinary meeting. Great difficulty in managing the indebtedness had been encountered, and after careful consideration of proposals to alleviate the distress, the trustees concluded that entrusting complete financial control to President Jones was the most acceptable alternative. Realizing the necessity of placing title in Jones' name to give the needed business credit for such an undertaking, they agreed, although somewhat ruefully, to sell him the property for $25,000, provided that he consent to "save the school to Methodism." The transfer was executed by Board Chairman McLauchlan and Secretary McDaniel on December 10, 1894.[14] Examination reveals that saving the school for Methodism actually meant retaining a board whose members were to be appointed by the Little Rock Conference and vested with authority to select the president and faculty. The action taken by the trustees verified their control of the institution, as they did not seek approval from the conference before entering into the transaction; too, they wisely retained jurisdiction of the school for themselves. They did submit these proceedings, however, to the conference for approval and endorsement.

The delicate issue concerning sale of the college was brought before the delegates of the forty-first session of the Little Rock Conference convened at Prescott, December 13, 1894. The group received the report with mixed emotions. The growth and development of the institution had been gratifying, and with a current student body of 185, of which 155 were in the collegiate department,[15] its success in providing Christian education in southwestern Arkansas could not be questioned. The demand for the school had also been shown by the fact that, though the patronage from the first had been satisfactory, it had in no way interfered with the other schools under Methodist control in the state.

The question of the trustees' authority to sell the property without instructions from the conference was then tendered to the presiding bishop. In reply to the query, he stated that the trustees could act only by consent of the body whom they represented.[16] It should be recalled, however, that the charter empowered the board with full responsibility, one which was as valid when an unpopular decision was reached as when a popular one was made. Finally, the Reverend J. R. Cason, Pastor, of Lakeside Church, Pine Bluff, introduced the following resolution:

> *Whereas*, The citizens of Arkadelphia have been unable to pay the debt which they incurred in building the College in accordance with the proposition under which the Little Rock Conference accepted the Arkadelphia Methodist College; and
> *Whereas*, The institution is highly valuable to the Church, and ought not to be lost to Arkansas Methodism; therefore,
> *Resolved*, That we authorize our Trustees to sell the property to President G. C. Jones, as arranged by them and him; and that we will recognize it as our co-educational College, and encourage our people to patronize it; *Provided*, That the Conference shall not be called upon to contribute money to its support; *and provided*, That its President and Faculty shall always be selected by a Board of Trustees appointed by the Little Rock Conference.[17]

The resolution was adopted, and for all practical purposes, Arkadelphia Methodist College became Jones College controlled by Methodist trustees. Ironically, the presiding prelate of the con-

GEORGE CHILDS JONES
First President of the College, 1890–1897, 1899–1904

JOHN HARTWELL HINEMON
President, 1904-1911

GEORGE HENRY CROWELL
President, 1911-1915

JAMES MIMS WORKMAN
President, 1915-1926

CLIFFORD LEE
HORNADAY
President, 1926–1928

JAMES WARTHEN
WORKMAN
President, 1928–1929

Top—Student body of Arkadelphia Methodist College on Dress Parade in 1907.
Bottom—The Cadets about 1910.

Top—The Military Band about 1910
Bottom—Co-eds Boating on the College Lake in the 1890's. Nettie McGhee,
Ollie Goodlett, Florence Karuss, Fannie Ross, and Marie Mathews.

Top—A view of the Main Building shortly before the Fire in 1914.
Bottom—The Ruins

Top—A silhouette of the Building in Flames on February 3, 1914.
Bottom—The make-shift Dining Hall was one of three temporary buildings
erected to house the College following the 1914 fire.

Top—Front view of the Charles Christopher Henderson house.
Bottom—Side view of the house.

ference session was Bishop Eugene R. Hendrix,[18] namesake of the institution Arkadelphians came to scorn.

Hendrix College opened on its new Conway campus in 1890, and from that time failed to surpass Arkadelphia Methodist College in enrollment. But the two colleges did share what had become a chronic ailment, no money. Hendrix College owed $20,000 by 1894, the year that Jones purchased the Arkadelphia school; and only the consolidated efforts of Arkansas Methodism saved the Conway institution. Throughout the decade the financial conditions of the two remained distressingly similar.[19]

The general public learned little of the transfer of ownership of Arkadelphia Methodist College from the church to Jones, and no public statement appeared until December 21, 1894.[20] Although the church had withdrawn all its financial support, control of the institution remained with conference appointed trustees, and patrons continued to refer to the school as "the Methodist college." Understandably, speed and secrecy surrounded the sale, for if the college were to open in September as scheduled, immediate action had to be taken, and the board in no way desired to endanger the future of the institution or injure the school's growing reputation.

From the time the college was leased to Jones until his two-year leave from presidential duties (1897–1899), the optimism expressed by the trustees for the general welfare of the college was fulfilled. The enrollment increased from 150 in 1892–1893, to 183 in 1893–1894, to a record high of 239 in 1895–1896.[21] The desire for continued growth was reflected in the college's instituting two new scholarship programs. In 1896 the school offered seven one hundred-dollar stipends, one to "a worthy young lady" in each district of the conference, and to encourage academic excellence, waived tuition for the student attaining the highest grade point during a session, the first honors scholarship.[22]

New courses of study complemented the increase in enrollment as did additions to the faculty, some who would spend the remainder of their lives in service to the college. Among such appointments was that in 1892 of Granville Goodloe as professor of ancient languages, a position he held with exception of a six-year interim until his death in 1911.[23] Born in 1857 near Forrest City, Arkansas, he was "a genuine son of the Old South, for which he showed his love by wearing its uniform in both life and death." [24] The young Arkansan was educated at Webb School (Bellbuckle, Tennessee) and Emory and Henry College where he was an honor student. In 1879 Vanderbilt University granted its first Master of Arts degree to Goodloe. While in Nashville, he was a classmate of President Jones and Ouachita Baptist College's first president, J. W. Conger. He was also the first president of the Y.M.C.A. at Vanderbilt and the faculty selected him to deliver the class oration at his graduation. A distinguished scholar in chemistry, Greek, and history, Goodloe held the chair of Greek at Wofford College for four years (1886–1890) and the same position at McTyeire Institute before coming to Arkadelphia.[25] During his tenure at the struggling, growing Arkadelphia institution he attained a reputation excelled by few associated with the college. Some called him peculiar, but his peculiarities were marks of his virtue. Commandant of the local Confederate veterans' association, he displayed the "Stars and Bars" daily before his door and "almost every morning sang 'The Bonnie Blue Flag.' " [26]

He kept his pupils alert in the classroom with keen, good-humored satires on student life, and his friendship for worthy students found expression in arduous labors outside the lecture hall. His tutoring sessions before breakfast and after supper for those who sought help in the classics or history became somewhat of a ritual.[27] Today Goodloe's memory is preserved through a men's residence hall, the second to bear his name. When constructed more than a decade ago, Goodloe Hall cost ten times the appraised value of the entire physical plant when he held the chair of ancient languages.

By 1894 the faculty numbered fourteen and had taken on a cosmopolitan flavor, as evidenced by appointments to the schools of music and natural and physical science. F. D. Baarz, a native of Leipzig, Germany, came as professor of piano and cornet. Nettie L. Kierulff, who held the Master of Arts and the Master of Music degrees, was directress of orchestral music and instructor of string instruments (violin, guitar, mandolin, and cello). And Florence Kierulff became the assistant in orchestral music.[28]

Letson Balliet, who held an engineering degree from Drake University, lectured in the natural sciences, thus enabling President Jones to concentrate his teaching efforts solely on mathematics. A notable addition to the faculty, Balliet instructed in chemistry and physics and served as director of laboratories.[29] An experienced chemist, metallurgist, mining and civil engineer, he was a member of the Des Moines Academy of Sciences, a former editor-in-chief of the *American Magazine of Natural Science*, and had served as chief engineer of Des Moines Umai Railway and as consulting engineer for the Oregon Gold Mining and Milling Company.[30] In 1895 the *Arkansas Gazette* announced publication of a new monthly magazine, *The Arkansas Technic*, to be under Balliet's editorship; the magazine was planned as a rival to *Scribner's, Harper's*, and *Century*.[31] In January, 1896, when the Arkadelphia municipal water and electric works burned, a severe loss to the college, he engineered the erection of an electric and water plant on the campus. Regarded as one of the best small facilities in the Southwest, this improvement made the college a little domain independent of the town. Concurrently, Balliet drafted plans for a steam plant to heat the building.[32]

During Balliet's two-year tenure, a short-lived but successful school of engineering was established.[33] This department had charge of the heating apparatus, electric and gas lights, and water supplies for the college. It also afforded firsthand experience of a practical nature to students pursuing such a profession. Announcement was made that a building would be constructed to house the new school and that it would be equipped with all the modern machinery necessary for programs in civil, mechanical, electrical, mining, and metallurgical engineering.[34] Before construction began, however, Balliet resigned to head a firm in Little Rock, and what was advertised to be "the best engineering school in the whole Southwest" [35] was terminated.

When the college opened in the fall of 1896 the faculty boasted a Harvard graduate, Roberta K. Borden, holding the chair of English, and two professors with degrees from the University of Chicago. Ida L. Duncan, a graduate of the latter, was appointed to the chair of history.[36] This was the first time a separate professor had been employed for each of the aforementioned disciplines and marked the beginning of a history department which maintains a reputation for being one of the best in the state. (The discipline of history is today headed by a University of Chicago graduate, Boyce A. Drummond,[37] one of three professors in Arkansas holding a Doctor of Philosophy degree in history from that university.[38])

Also in 1896 instruction was offered for the first time to preschool children when a kindergarten was begun; [39] (a nursery school is presently conducted by the institution). That year a normal class was initiated for those desiring to teach; [40] thus the college had been offering teacher education long before the state designated it as a center for that specific intention. Though currently the school is multipurpose, it graduates more students in teacher education than in any other area.

Following the Civil War, industrial growth accelerated the demand for business education. The final accolade of academic respectability was granted the field by the nation's universities; in 1881 the first academic college of business opened at the University of Pennsylvania.[41] Many, if not most, colleges followed with the opening of commercial departments, and during the same period private business schools began to appear. In 1896 I. W. Saunders merged his Arkadelphia Practical Business College (formerly Draughon's) with the business school of the college.[42] This school, the first in the college to operate on a twelve-month basis, then offered courses in shorthand, typewriting, copying, manifolding, duplicating, bookkeeping, and telegraphy;[43] and it boasted five typewriters.[44] To receive a certificate of graduation students had to attain a shorthand proficiency of 120 words per minute and an ability to transcribe thirty words per minute on the typewriter, and had to complete the sophomore class of the English degree curriculum.[45]

The graduation exercise of 1893 marked a milestone in the history of the college. Among the seven degrees awarded were the first Bachelor of Arts and the first two Master of Arts degrees.[46] Receiving the Bachelor of Arts degree was Mattie Stewart Hunt. The wording of her diploma, *Arkadelphum Methodisticum Collegium*, *Arkadelphiae*, *Arkansarum*, evidenced the classical course she had completed. The parchment document, signed by all members of the board and faculty, bore the institution's simple gold seal; without motto or insignia, the imprint gave only the name and location of the college. (This diploma was donated to the Henderson State College library in 1962.[47]) Robert B. McSwain and his wife Mary McKinnon McSwain, who was a member of the first faculty, received two of the four Master of Arts degrees ever conferred by the college;[48] the other two were granted in 1896 and 1897 respectively. Fifty-nine years would pass before another master's degree would be awarded; on August 3, 1956, Margie Lou Ballew received the first Master of Science in Education degree,[49] one of three graduate degrees presently conferred by the college. In 1895 Marion H. Brown earned the first Bachelor of Science degree.[50]

In keeping with the objective of promoting a Christian atmosphere, a Y.M.C.A., a Y.W.C.A., and an Epworth League (United

Methodist Youth), the only society open to both sexes, were organized in the third year.[51] All students were encouraged to become active members, and the "Y" groups distinguished themselves by sponsoring the first secular speakers on the campus.[52] That same year, Delphian, a second literary society for women was formed.[53]

An unusual student activity during the period was the promenades. Three times each week the girls in uniform dress lined up and filed down the city streets in twos under faculty supervision, attracting much attention. The residents often inspected the processions from windows, porches, and lawns.[54] The men, not to be outdone by females, retaliated and introduced "the severest epidemic that ever struck Arkadelphia," bicycling! [55]

To enhance the campus' natural beauty and to provide additional wholesome, supervised recreation, a lake covering more than half of the left front campus was built and equipped with skiffs. It was used by both students and faculty, and upon a few rare winter occasions it served as a skating rink. The lake became a favored place for meditations on problems of love or hard tasks, but near the turn of the century it became a breeding place for mosquitoes and consequently was drained and filled in.[56] It was not greatly missed, however, for to take its place a fish pond surrounded by ferns and caladiums was constructed in the center of the campus. The settees and benches on the concrete walk around it replaced the lake's banks as the place for special thoughts.[57] The class of 1921 rebuilt the fish pond, adding a fountain to the center. These continued to provide a place for relaxation until the mid-sixties when for some unknown reason both were filled in and the pond was cemented over.

The event receiving the greatest attention in the boarding rooms was "suspension of the rules," which occurred only two or three times per year. On these occasions young ladies were allowed conversation with, and escort by, approved gentlemen; at all other times college regulations prohibited such. Though permitted to talk with males in classroom situations, the fair sex was segregated from them on all other occasions. The girls were marched in twos to the auditorium for school programs and were returned in like manner.[58] Only two minutes between classes provided little opportunity for fracture of the rules.[59] Shortly after Jones obtained college ownership he contemplated changing the school from co-educational to female;[60] with such restrictions, the girls probably would have noticed little difference!

The most elegant evening in Arkadelphia Methodist College's history was the Jones' eleventh wedding anniversary celebration in January, 1896. The grand stairway was decorated with evergreen garlands and provided a suitable setting for the thirty-four-piece college orchestra. Five hundred guests attended the lavish reception and supper; the menu cards were printed on linen.[61]

For over a year Jones searched for a suitable man to assist him in his work and to relieve him and his wife of some of their excessive responsibilities.[62] At the 1897 commencement the trustees announced that he had secured the services of the Reverend Cadesman Pope. Jones leased the college to Pope for a two-year period (1897–1899), during which Jones assumed the title of vice-president and continued his professorial duties.[63]

A man of culture and a successful educator, the Reverend Cadesman Pope was widely known in Southern Methodism. He held the Doctor of Laws degree, but the time and place it was conferred are unknown. Born in Pike County, Georgia, June 21, 1837, Pope entered the ministry there in 1858 and remained active in the church until shortly before his death April 8, 1932. No stranger to Arkadelphians, the Reverend Pope had previously served two appointments as minister of the town's Methodist church. For twelve years before coming to Arkadelphia Methodist College, he held the presidency of Millersburg (Kentucky) Female College.[64]

As acting president of the Arkadelphia institution, Pope was

responsible for all current expenses and conducted the daily devo-
tionals, lecturing on the Bible and "evidences of Christianity." His
son, Olin C. Pope, a Cincinnati Business College graduate, headed
the business school and served as bursar. His daughter, Elma M.
Pope, a graduate of Millersburg Female College and Cincinnati
Conservatory, joined the music faculty. His wife managed the
domestic aspects of the college and served as dining halls super-
visor, as had Mrs. Jones before her.[65]

A distinguished faculty addition during Pope's administration
was Erwin Schneider, director of music.[66] A native of the former
German duchy of Nassau and a descendant of a well-known musical family, Schneider had studied under the bandmaster for the
Duke of Nassau, the conductor of the Royal Opera, Berlin, and
had concluded his musical education under the royal music director at the State Music School of Prussia.[67] Before coming to
Arkadelphia Methodist College Schneider had spent several years
teaching music in various Southern female colleges, the last thirteen
at Dr. Price's College, Nashville, Tennessee.[68] His orchestral concerts were greatly popularized when he introduced the xylophone
to Arkadelphia musical audiences.[69] (Schneider as a non-combatant
had witnessed the capture of French Emperor Napoleon III at the
significant Battle of Sedan in 1870 which resulted in the fall of the
Second Empire and the unification of Germany.[70]) Laying the
foundation for a fine music department he served as music director
until 1903 when he was replaced by his brother Carl J. Schneider
who continued the tradition. Another notable addition was Jennie
Brown, principal of the art department. Miss Brown was graduated
from the Montreal and Ontario Schools of Art and had studied
abroad. She held diplomas from six different departments of the
latter school.[71] The most unusual course offered in her department
was taxidermy, taught by Charles L. Reynolds.[72]

The greatest news item during Pope's tenure, and indeed of the
nineties, was the Spanish-American War. Four students, three who

served as officers, represented the college in the 1898 conflict, the first of five in which her students have participated.[73] Aside from better economic conditions which enhanced the institution, the real meaning of the "splendid little war" was hardly recognized.

In compliance with contract stipulations, Pope vacated the presidency in June, 1899.[74] Having reviewed the college's progress under Pope, noting the good enrollment and admirable internal management, the trustees expressed their gratitude:

> We heartily endorse the management of the school in all its departments, and commend the President and his Faculty as in every way peculiarly fitted for their high position, and the school as the very best in all the land.[75]

All anticipated the time when the institution would be unencumbered and again the conference's property.

With Pope's departure, Jones began his final tenure as the college's chief administrator, and the institution entered into its concluding years as Arkadelphia Methodist College. This five-year period (1899–1904) brought continued progress and prosperity. In 1903–1904 the enrollment, representing eleven states, was an impressive 250,[76] an increase of one hundred over that when Jones had presided over the first session thirteen years earlier; and the faculty had increased from ten to nineteen.

References in early catalogues to such terms as "department" and "school" were inconsistent and irregular. But by 1903 "school" had been deleted and all course offerings were classified under "departments;" and three new departments: dressmaking; gymnasium, including fencing and rowing; and artistic photography had been instituted. In introducing the latter, the catalogue stated that Arkadelphia Methodist College was the only school in the South and one of few in the United States offering such instruction. Discussing the merits of photography and its acceptance in both literary and scientific worlds, it emphasized that talented students could earn two to three thousand dollars a year in that profession and that to meet high standards only a limited number of applicants would be accepted. The department of music now offered instruction in wind instruments and maintained a band, in addition to the string orchestra; the business department added telegraphy to its program; and the English department absorbed the former school of reading into its courses.[77]

The faculty of 1890–1904, unlike those of many church colleges, was neither restricted to its Methodist denomination nor composed exclusively of southerners. Though provincial, it ranked high among those in Arkansas and should not be judged on the basis of degrees and scholarly productivity alone, for the professors of that era were confronted with the dual task of providing quality instruction and maintaining professional standards in an educational frontier. Though none held the Doctor of Philosophy degree, most had completed their Master of Arts degrees at respectable universities, notably Vanderbilt; and those few educated in distinguished midwestern, eastern, and foreign centers of learning provided awareness and erudition which added a great deal to the academic atmosphere of the young college.

As evidenced by the rigid merits system, discipline was of chief concern to President Jones, and the records of his administration do not indicate any serious breach of conduct. In part this can be attributed to the age of the male students and the absence of college housing for them until 1903. In this period of the college's history, it was not uncommon for men twenty-five to thirty years old to be in school, for higher education in Arkansas was only beginning to gain impetus. In 1910 an article appearing in the student newspaper revealed that the majority of the men attending the college during the Jones years were that age,[78] and viewing the class composites adds validity to the point.

The student body, however, must have been doing what it could to disturb the rest and quiet repose that President Jones so earnestly desired. The college magazine reported an unauthorized nocturnal town venture by "about half a dozen boys" who narrowly escaped detection by a pursuing professor.[79] And in 1902 the *Southern Standard* reminded its student readers that the president was "as tight as Dick's hatband this session and don't you forget it." [80] According to the paper, Jones held weekly disciplinary meetings, and once a month the board of trustees and faculty in joint assembly reviewed students who had received excessive demerits and advised them about "some other school that might suit them better than Arkadelphia Methodist College." [81]

The majority of the students worked off excess energy in physical activities approved by the authorities. Two male baseball teams, the first nine and the second nine, played regularly in intramural competition and against local opponents. Basketball teams were organized for the women, and both sexes participated in lawn tennis. In 1900 the cadet corps from rival Ouachita Baptist College entertained on the Methodist campus with "beautifully executed drills." [82] But one type of precision footwork was not permitted: President Jones stated that "dancing was a good recreation for dogs and monkeys, but not suitable for young ladies," and the more religious girls replied, "Amen." [83]

While a lyceum series brought speakers and performing artists to the campus, the town's opera house remained the center for the major touring attractions. No spectacle seems to have surpassed the 1901 performance of *Quo Vadis*,[84] unless it was the public hanging of a rapist witnessed by more than three thousand persons; ironically, the culprit's name was John Wesley! [85]

During the first fourteen sessions, hundreds attended; of these, 101 earned degrees (4 M.A.'s, 11 B.A.'s, 46 Ph.B.'s, and 31 M.E.L.'s), and 123 received certificates of graduation, the majority in music and business.[86]

Throughout the entire life of Arkadelphia Methodist College, total cost per session for boarding students remained the same, a remarkable fact when one takes into account the school's financial

THE METHODIST YEARS, 1890–1929 71

plight. According to the 1903 catalogue this was primarily attributed to the additional endeavors of the president, the faculty, and their families. Too, servants could be procured from the antebellum town for "less than half the city rate."[87] It was also emphasized that the college's location in a farming community likewise attributed to the low cost. Food for the student body, a source of perennial controversy in any age, was available for minimal prices even for that day: the very best beef and pork could be purchased for from four to six cents per pound; butter, fifteen cents per pound; eggs, ten cents per dozen; and potatoes, forty cents per bushel.[88]

Separate dining halls were maintained for men and women; the president and his wife supervised the women's, and a senior professor the men's. Food was served family style, with a faculty member presiding over each table. Whether the menu was appealing or not is questionable, but students did anticipate mealtime, for throughout the maintenance of separate dining rooms, stewards somewhat surreptitiously passed notes from the men to the women.[89]

If one became ill from indulging too freely in the food served on the first floor he could always apply for help in the infirmary, one of the most comfortable rooms in the building. It was supervised by the matron, and parents were assured that the sick would receive all possible care and attention. Beginning in 1894 all boarding pupils received free medical services.[90] The college was boastful of the town's healthful location, and throughout the fourteen years of Arkadelphia Methodist College there were no student fatalities, a statistic which the institution advertised. But the college was not without death. In 1895 a member of the music faculty died,[91] and in 1896 the decease of Board Chairman the Reverend John McLauchlan occurred.[92] Between 1893 and 1902 President and Mrs. Jones experienced personal tragedy with the deaths of three infant children.[93] Also, the twentieth century had only begun when the English world lamented the passing of Queen Victoria; in a lengthy tribute to her, Professor Goodloe expressed her death's impact on the college.[94] And in September, 1901, the students mourned the assassinated president of the United States, William McKinley.

The physical plant underwent a number of improvements. The two-block long campus grounds were graded, landscaped, and fronted with a wrought iron fence. That fence entwined with roses and honeysuckle and gracing the spacious tree shaded lawn of today's main campus is the sole surviving landmark of Arkadelphia Methodist College. In 1902 Vice-President J. S. Hawkins originated the movement which resulted in the city's constructing a concrete sidewalk linking the Methodist college and the Baptist college with each other, their respective church buildings, and the town.[95] Board Chairman the Reverend W. F. Evans liberally contributed to the $2,000 project.[96]

A small building to house the kitchen was constructed to the rear of the dining rooms, and was equipped with "the latest appliances and utensils." [97] In 1902 the *Southern Standard* announced preparations for erection of a $15,000 men's dormitory,[98] but these plans were not implemented for a number of years. The first college-operated housing for men, which did open the following year, was a former private dwelling,[99] reminiscent of the first residence hall for women.

By Jones' final year, the value of the buildings had increased to $75,000, and the scientific apparatus was appraised at $3,000. The library had grown from a mere collection of donated books to more than one thousand well chosen volumes.[100] In 1904 an unusual announcement concerning the library stated that "under certain limitations students will have access to these books!" [101]

The college's first memorial, given by the 1897 graduating class, was a stained glass window to ornament the entrance hall. Appropriately, it honored the late Reverend John McLauchlan, "Father of the College." [102] Following that precedent, each graduating class thereafter left a gift to their alma mater. Among these were book cases for the library (1900), electric chandeliers for the main foyer (1901) and concert hall (1903), and a gate and arch bearing the institution's name and founding date, to complement the iron fence (1902). Eighteen years later the gate and arch were relocated and replaced with the now familiar brick entrance pillars.[103]

Jones, continuing to hold title, subject to the conference's wishes, was prepared to retransfer the property to the church immediately upon alleviation of the indebtedness. Emphasizing that every school in the state labored under debts held in different ways, he reported that his school's $35,000 deficit was less than that of any other Arkansas college,[104] especially the two Methodist institutions. Galloway College had suffered a series of perils; in 1896 the failure to collect $10,000 in subscriptions had been accompanied by a cyclone's unroofing the main building and the collapsing of the heating plant.[105] Ironically, while its leaders were pleading its financial cause before the conference in 1898 word was received that the entire facility had burned.[106] Likewise, Hendrix College had experienced continued monetary distress, and patrons were toiling to free the Conway institution from its plight; [107] even the Arkadelphia district of the conference, struggling to save "its" college, was assessed $100.[108]

For several years friends of the Arkadelphia college exerted efforts to release the school from Jones' proprietorship, but there was opposition to the church's reassuming title. By default, Jones' ownership had returned state Methodism to its earlier two-college plan, and opponents desired to take full advantage of the situation preventing the meager revenues desperately needed for Hendrix and Galloway colleges from being shared with a third institution.

They believed it in the best interest of both church and education that no endeavor to return Arkadelphia Methodist College to church possession be pursued.

But the 1898 and 1899 Little Rock Conference minutes revealed anticipation for the title's reversion. In April, 1900, Board Chairman the Reverend W. F. Evans, agent of the Twentieth Century Fund in the conference initiated a subscription campaign for liquidating the debt and reconveying title to that body.[109] Former adversaries reluctantly endorsed the move, and opposition to the college was defeated in November, 1900, when the conference unanimously reaffirmed allegiance to "our co-educational college," recommended the school to its people as worthy of patronage and support, and hoped for an early retransfer of title.[110]

By fall, 1901, the total indebtedness was reduced to approximately $35,000, with $11,000 in outstanding debts. President Jones proposed that in return for a lease, he would surrender his $20,000 interest and deed the property to the conference, if the trustees would provide liquidation of the balance.[111] The board assented and presented the proposal to the conference at its November session. That group, by strong majority vote, accepted the proposition, with the understanding that the encumbrance was not to be paid by the conference.[112] The trustees successfully fulfilled their commitment when one of their number, Charles C. Henderson, agreed to donate $10,000 and Arkadelphians pledged nearly $5,000.[113]

In July, 1902, the trustees announced that all indebtedness had been liquidated and that they held a warranty deed conveying the college property to the church. In addition, they extended the public an invitation to attend a dedication ceremony at the school on July 15.[114] Throughout the months of July, August, and September, articles praising the philanthropy of Henderson and Jones, the generosity of Arkadelphians, and the unique financial status of the institution appeared in the church's official weekly newspaper,

Arkansas Methodist.[115] The following year, the trustees displayed their appreciation of Henderson by electing him their chairman, a position he held until 1922.[116]

In accordance with the agreement, the trustees executed a seventeen-year lease with Jones, as advised by presiding Bishop Charles B. Galloway. The lease was designed to guarantee the continued services of Jones as president, thereby giving permanency to the management and confidence to the people.[117] But as recorded in the May, 1902, board minutes, Jones, while desiring to retain the presidency, requested permission to sublet the college to Vice-President J. S. Hawkins when the new lease became effective. For the first time, the trustees declined acceptance of a recommendation from Jones, but they did re-elect him president.[118] Recalling the original agreement with Jones when employed in 1890, the trustees were again offering him facilities to conduct a college and manage its financial affairs.

Denied permission to sublease, Jones sold two-fifths interest of his lease, for an undisclosed price, to Business Professor J. E. Wootton. The trustees disapproved his action and convened in special session, the first in the board's history, April 15, 1904. At that time Chairman Henderson submitted a report concerning the relationship existing between the trustees and the president, emphasizing the unsatisfactory condition of their compact. The executive committee, which earlier had sought solution to the discord, reported that Jones had consented to sublease for $3,000 his interest to the trustees for two years, granting them option to purchase said interest any time during that period. They added that J. E. Wootton had agreed to convey his two-fifths interest to the trustees for $600 per annum on the same basis. The ten members present of the fifteen-member board voted unanimously to accept the proposals.[119] In a second special session, April 23, Henderson announced that transactions had been concluded, that the board possessed full and complete control of the college property, and that hereafter the school would be administered by three members of the board, to be known as the committee on administration.[120]

For fourteen years George Childs Jones and Arkadelphia Methodist College were synonymous, but both became history at the 1904 annual commencement. Jones concluded his tenure by presiding over that ceremony, and following performance of the "Captain C. C. Henderson March," the trustees announced that they had "unanimously and enthusiastically resolved: 'That the name of Arkadelphia Methodist College be changed to that of Henderson College.'" [121]

CHAPTER VI

The Progressive Years

THE institution's fifteenth annual session, its first as Henderson College, began September 6, 1904. The next seven years, the time of the college under that appellation, were ones of upturn, reorganization, and growth in numbers, resources, educational competence, and faculty and student morale. The trustees abolished the office of president,[1] and George Childs Jones departed to become vice-chancellor and professor of chemistry at Epworth University (Oklahoma City University).[2] Then the trustees elected from their number the committee on administration and created the position dean of the faculty to regulate curriculum and disciplinary procedures. The committee on administration, consisting of Charles C. Henderson, Eli H. McDaniel, and John H. Hinemon, executed the educational and monetary policies of the trustees, meeting monthly to audit and review all financial accounts. But the direct operation of the school was exercised by Hinemon, chairman of the committee, he and his family occupying the presidential apartments.[3] Chief Administrator Hinemon wisely prepared and guided the development of the school. The college's need was the strengthening of its foundation and superstructure, and he responded to that need.

John Hartwell Hinemon, third executive officer of the college and the first not an ordained minister, was born near Somerville, Tennessee, November 1, 1862. Educated in that state, he received the Master of Arts degree from the University of Nashville (George Peabody College for Teachers). After a short term as superintendent of schools in Union City, Tennessee, he came to Arkansas in 1887 and for more than forty years was intensely involved in educational activities and achieved national recognition. Before assuming the direction of Henderson College, he taught in Monticello for eight years where the citizens constructed a school in his honor, and for seven years he was superintendent of schools in Pine Bluff. In 1902 he was elected State Superintendent of Public Instruction and continued to hold that office for two years while serving as the chief administrator of the college.[4]

An active member of the Methodist Church, he was appointed to the college's board of trustees in 1903,[5] a position he uniquely continued to hold even while chief executive of the school and for a number of years thereafter. In 1906 the trustees reinstituted the office of president, and Hinemon, not quite forty-four, was unanimously elected to fill that position. At that same session of the board, he was also selected to the trustees' powerful three-member executive committee.[6]

In April, 1906, while supervising the college Hinemon appeared in his capacity as superintendent of public instruction before the United States House Committee on Public Lands in support of the Brundige Bill providing for donation of an additional section in each township in Arkansas to the public school fund.[7] That same year he was personally credited with securing additional legislation that increased taxation for Arkansas schools, the amendment authorizing such then known as the "Hinemon Amendment" to the state constitution. The United States Commissioner of Education recognized Hinemon's efforts as "the beginning of the educational renaissance in Arkansas," and referred to Hinemon as the "Horace Mann of the South."[8] Students and faculty were pleased that Hinemon rejected solicitations to seek the governorship in 1907 and 1909, but they recognized that such overtures to a president of an Arkansas college were unprecedented.[9]

Bringing additional honor to the college and the state, Hinemon served as president of the State Teachers' Association and wrote its constitution. He was on the board of directors of the National Education Association and was vice-president of that organization. Three-time delegate to the Democratic National Convention, he served a term as committee member on rules and business and as a presidential elector in 1908.[10] Three-time delegate to the General Conference of the Methodist Episcopal Church, South, he was appointed by the bishops of that denomination to the Educational Commission of the Church and as a lay-delegate to a Methodist World Conference. Active in civic affairs, he was also Grand Chancellor for Arkansas of the Knights of Pythias.[11]

Assisting Hinemon was Professor J. H. Witherspoon, dean of the faculty and science instructor, the first dean the college was to have. He held the Bachelor of Arts degree and the Pharmaceutical Chemistry degree (Ph.C.) from the University of Tennessee. For eight years he had served as principal of Pine Bluff High School where he was associated with Hinemon. The two were in complete accord as to the future of the college.[12]

Their intentions were evident in a new statement of purpose set forth in the 1904–1905 *Catalogue:*

> This School is operated upon the belief that the true purpose of education is to give symmetrical training to the mental, physical and moral powers, to stimulate high and noble aims in life, to fit for useful living, and to so guide and direct the development of each individual as to secure the greatest possible capability of thought and action. . . .[13]

It was further stated that the courses in the curriculum were those considered the basis of true culture and education, that no attempt was made to cover the whole scope of human learning, and that "nothing is printed in our announcement for the mere purpose of swelling our list of studies." [14] In keeping with the religious orientation of the institution, patrons were advised that efforts would be made "both by precept and example to have the young people committed to the school's care embrace and follow the principles of Christian manhood and womanhood." [15]

The reorganization of the curriculum in 1904 to conform to minimum standards established by the General Board of Education of the Methodist Episcopal Church, South, was a major advancement. Henceforth, only two degrees, the Bachelor of Arts and the Bachelor of Science, were offered; the three-year programs, those of Bachelor of Philosophy and Mistress of English Literature were abolished.[16] Courses of study leading to the two degrees were clearly outlined and work was pursued from nine literary departments: English language and literature, pure mathematics, history and mental science, natural and physical science, Latin language and literature, Greek language and literature, French, German, and Bible. Having been established in 1903, Bible study remained an integral aspect of the curriculum, and the catalogues reminded that the department was not organized for the purpose of instruction in ecclesiastical dogma but to afford a better acquaintance with Biblical literature, Christian history, and evangelical principles, for the trustees considered proper knowledge of the Bible an essential part of a liberal education.[17]

A units system was adopted as the basis for determining promotion and graduation, each unit equivalent of seventy-two class hours per semester in a subject. Twelve units per year were the required study, and a student had to attain a seventy-five percent cumulative average on all studies to receive a degree, sixty percent being the minimum score allowing credit. To obtain a diploma a student had to successfully complete fifty-two units, including four of Bible.[18] The minutes of the Little Rock Conference cited that no institution in the state had higher standards for degrees than Henderson College.[19]

Under the new system, as the old, electives for degrees were permissible in the languages and were now expanded to allow option of two additional units. Though Latin was required of all, a student could select Greek or French and German as his second language.[20] For the contemporary collegiate, it is of note that these students were required four years study in Latin and Greek or four years in Latin and two years each in the mentioned modern languages. Certificates of proficiency were available in music, art, elocution, domestic science, a teacher's course, and business.[21] In 1906, however, the business department was terminated [22] and such courses remained absent for the next seven years. In 1905 and 1906 respectively the Bachelor of Arts degree program was expanded to include work in music and elocution, allowing completion of those course programs to substitute for Greek or French and German.[23] With exception of the language options and eight additional units of science for the Bachelor of Science degree, the outlines of study for both degrees were identical; [24] therefore, in 1908 the Bachelor of Science degree was abandoned, and the Bachelor of Arts degree awarded to all meeting requirements of either the classical or scientific courses.[25]

Revision of the curriculum and concentration on the new programs of study were rewarded in May, 1909, when the Trustees proclaimed that the institution then met the standards of the Carnegie Board and the church's General Board of Education to be classified as a grade "A" college.[26] After eighteen sessions, the struggle to become first class was seemingly achieved. Cognizant of the lack of an absolute endowment, but presumptuous that the recently acquired guaranteed fund could be substituted for such, President Hinemon appeared before the General Board's committee on classification to present the college's credentials, but to no avail. When that committee declined to allow the substitution and grant Henderson College the advancement in rank, President Hinemon called attention to the fact that both Hendrix and Galloway colleges had been granted such recognition two years earlier though neither possessed a $100,000 endowment and in their cases could not present the required number of full professors for attainment of "A" standing. For this apparently adverse discrimination, Vanderbilt University's Chancellor James H. Kirkland gave no satisfactory explanation. And there was little consolation for Henderson College in knowing that but for the endowment, "A" requirements were met; for the institution remained on the "B" list. The only positive outcome of Hinemon's plea, an unfortunate one for Arkansas Methodism, however, was Galloway College's reversion to "B" standing.[27]

Aspiration for new status effected a second curriculum change, the first major one in the institution's history. Henceforth, sixty hours were required for graduation, those to be taken from four areas, an hour equivalent of forty clock hours of recitation:

Language and Literature: English	6
Latin	
Greek	
French	
German	15
Pure Mathematics	6
Science	6
History, Social Science or Philosophy	9
Elective	18

Evidently, the most significant change was allowing a student to elect more than one-fourth of his total program; as many as six hours of the elective work could be in music, art, or elocution, and three had to be in Bible.[28] Beginning in 1911, in addition to the comprehensive examinations, a degree candidate also had to submit a thesis showing a respectable amount of originality.[29]

Throughout the years of the institution, admissions had been based exclusively on written examinations. The first revision in this policy occurred in 1905 when pupils from "schools of known merit" were accepted on certificate, all others still being required to take the examinations.[30] Desire for grade "A" recognition dictated another alteration in entrance requirements, the second within five years. Consequently, written examinations were discontinued and the trustees ordered that beginning in the fall of 1909 freshmen students would have to submit a certificate showing completion of fourteen Carnegie Units.[31]

Although the college was not a member of the Southern Association of Colleges and Secondary Schools, its admissions policies were identical to those of that agency. Likewise, it allowed an applicant to present ten attained units at the time of entrance with the remaining four, known as "conditions," to be removed before graduation, provided that three units of English and two-and-one-half of mathematics were satisfied.[32] Since a unit was credited only on work taken through a nine-month high school session, these requirements were indicative of Hinemon's endeavors in elevating public school standards in the state. The following year, 1910, the faculty compiled a roster of acceptable "accredited" high schools. This indicated that certificates issued by these institutions were accepted at face value toward meeting the new entrance requirements. The performance of students from these schools determined whether their institutions would remain on the approved list.[33]

The first statement pertaining to transfer students appeared in the 1910 *Catalogue*. It stated that an official transcript showing grades of credit and evidence of honorable dismissal from the institution last attended was mandatory. These students also had to meet Henderson College's regular entrance and graduation requirements.[34]

As could be expected, these new regulations raising admissions requirements adversely affected the enrollment. The era had opened with the matriculation of 171 students; the number increased to an all-time high of 333 in 1908. Implementation of the revised standards marked a reversal when in 1909 of 242 students enrolled only ninety-six were admitted to full collegiate standing. During the last session under Hinemon, the total number had dropped to 217.[35]

Throughout his administration, Hinemon was fortunate in securing capable academicians. The literary faculty though never passing fifteen in number was composed of qualified personnel. With few exceptions, that body for the 1904–1905 session, like the administration, was new. Notable among the group was John Milford Williams, professor of Latin, an 1898 Phi Beta Kappa graduate of Vanderbilt University. After having served Henderson College for three years, the last two as dean of the faculty, in 1907 Williams was elected president of Galloway College (the Methodist female institution in Searcy), a position he held with distinction for twenty-four years.[36]

The first alumni to teach in a literary department assumed the chair of history in 1909. Farrar Claudius Newberry, one of the college's most loyal and distinguished graduates and one of Arkansas' most illustrious sons, replaced his former instructor, Cora Belle Wilson, professor of history since 1904, when she took leave to complete the Master of Arts degree at Columbia University.[37] Upon her return the following year, he assisted her and also taught higher mathematics.[38] Without question, he was a product of the institution he returned to serve. Living across from the college on Henderson Street, at the age of five he entered the primary department of its academy and was enrolled in the institution until he was awarded the Bachelor of Arts degree in 1906. Before his twenty-first birthday, he had earned the Master of Arts degree in history from Vanderbilt University where he received Phi Beta Kappa honors. After lecturing two years at his Arkadelphia alma mater, he accepted a one-year appointment in history at the University of Arkansas. Admitted to the bar in 1912 and elected to the Arkansas Legislature in 1915, he wrote and introduced the bill which resulted in state-wide prohibition.[39]

That same year Newberry became associated with Woodman of the World Life Insurance Society. Rising through its ranks, in 1943 he was elected president of that Omaha, Nebraska, company.[40] Retiring from that position in 1956, he returned to Arkadelphia where he and his wife (stepdaughter of former Board Chairman the Reverend A. O. Evans) rebuilt his boyhood home, "Homeplace." [41] With their deaths, in 1969 the spacious Georgian house and his personal papers were bequeathed to the institution, the house to serve the presidents and the papers to aid historians. The trustees memorialized Newberry shortly before his death when they named a multi-million-dollar dormitory Farrar C. Newberry Hall. From an historical view his greatest service to Arkansas was an outgrowth of his retirement, for in those years he devoted himself to collecting and researching primary materials and writing articles on Arkansas history, especially Clark County and its personages.

Two other men of distinction, both now deceased, joined the faculty during the Hinemon years, Robert Thomas Proctor and Benjamin Smith Foster. Born in Madison County, Alabama, on March 6, 1884, Proctor came to the chair of Latin in 1907 and for forty-one years remained in teaching and administrative positions. He attended Webb School, Trinity College (Duke University), and the University of Chicago where as a Phi Beta Kappa he received both the Bachelor of Arts and the Master of Arts degrees.[42] From 1907 to 1916 he taught Latin; for four years, 1916–1920, he instructed in Latin and history and sometimes Greek; beginning in 1918 he also assumed the duties of registrar. He continued in that position and was sometimes an assistant in history until his retirement, July 1, 1949. In addition to these duties, he often served as coach of the "Dragons," the junior varsity football team.[43]

Foster, affectionately known as the "Grand Old Man of Henderson" and "Godfather of the College," [44] arrived in 1908 from the presidency of Young Ladies College, Franklin, Kentucky, to assume duties as professor of English and as bursar. Already fifty-three, he spent his final seventeen years of teaching at this Methodist institution. He was born February 1, 1855, near Lebanon, Tennessee. Cumberland University awarded him the Bachelor of

Arts degree in 1876, the Bachelor of Laws three years later, and the Master of Arts in 1880. A pioneer in women's education, he and an associate established the female division of his alma mater where he lectured until assuming administration of the above Kentucky college.[45] In addition to professorial duties, in his third year at Henderson College he was appointed registrar; he held that position until 1918 when he was elected dean of the faculty, the administrative post he was holding at the time of his retirement in 1925. Filling the chair of Bible from 1913 to 1923, at intervals during his tenure he also taught philosophy, education, psychology, history, and social science.[46] In 1916 a grateful board of trustees conferred on him the school's loftiest honor, the Doctor of Laws degree: the only one the trustees ever conferred upon an inservice professor of the college.[47]

From the beginning of his employment it was apparent to all that a remarkable man was in their midst. He was a popular instructor and students sought him for counsel. One, now a Methodist bishop, stated that he took Professor Foster's courses because "he inspired all his students to strive for the highest that is possible. . . . and above all lived a true life." [48] Another, a later president of the college, remarked that "Of all that I received at Henderson (my wife included) I count as great a treasure as any, the principles of life that the beloved Dr. Foster gave to me and reinforced in my mind so that I shall never forget that life is not for self, but for unselfish service to others." [49]

Married in 1886 to Anne Stark McDaniel of Arkadelphia, he purchased her ancestral mansion, "Magnolia Manor" shortly before his election to the faculty.[50] Presiding regally over the antebellum estate and the clasroom, he exemplified the philosophy he taught. His death in 1927 signified the passing of that order of gracious men of a bygone century, for he was the last of such stature affiliated with the institution.

An unpleasant issue facing Henderson College during Hinemon's administration was negotiating purchase of the lease held on the institution's property. It should be recalled that when former President Jones redeeded the property to the church in 1903 he received a seventeen-year lease; that he subsequently sold interest in this lease to Professor J. E. Wootten; and that with his departure in 1904, he and Wootten sublet their leases to the trustees, granting them option to buy the contracts within two years.

Meeting in special session, in late December, 1904, the trustees discussed means to secure the compacts and appointed from their number a five-member committee to arrange a loan of $30,000 for obtaining settlement.[51] At their regular meeting the following May, this committee, propitious of an early adjustment, reported some progress but requested additional time to complete the transactions.[52] Representing the trustees, Chairman Henderson purchased Wootten's lease for $5,250 in August, 1905.[53] Shortly thereafter, Henderson and Jones, unable to agree upon their respective interests in the covenant, became involved in a law suit.

This legal maneuver prompted the trustees to remove the property entirely from the hands of the litigants. Consequently, in special session, in February, 1906, the trustees, with one dissenting vote, resolved to ask the court to appoint a receiver for them in the interest of the church and prayed for the court to appoint President Hinemon as the receiver.[54] In chancery court held at Mena, Arkansas, February 20, 1906, Chancellor J. D. Shaver granted their request and appointed Hinemon receiver.[55] This action in no way referred to the solvency of the institution but was pursued so that the school could not be interrupted while the litigation was pending.

At the regular meeting of the trustees in May, 1906, Chairman Henderson, who had been authorized to take such legal steps as he deemed necessary to obtain an equitable settlement in behalf of the board, reported he had not been able to purchase the lease at what he considered a reasonable price.[56] Another year elapsed before the former president and the college's principal benefactor resolved their conflict. At the regular session of the board of trustees, May, 1907, Chairman Henderson reported he had purchased the disputed lease from Dr. Jones at the cost of $18,000,[57] and an unfortunate episode in the college's history came to a close.

Mortgaging the college property to Metropolitan Life Insurance Company of New York provided the monies for settlement of the affair, but produced a $30,000 indebtedness against the physical plant now valued at $100,000.[58] To aid in alleviating the debt, in 1907 the Little Rock Conference, which had earlier authorized the mortgaging of the property, permitted the trustees to place a financial agent in the field to secure contributions for the school.[59] At that same session the General Board of Education gave $509.17 to the college.[60]

Two years later, the Little Rock Conference, appropriately meeting in Arkadelphia, resolved that its ban of 1894 barring the institution from financial aid was null and void, and assessed itself $1,000 for Henderson College.[61] Thus the school, which had existed exclusively on its own receipts and gifts since 1894, received its first fiscal aid from the conference; the amount was still $500 less than the assessment for Hendrix College, but no assessment was made for Galloway College.[62] The educational theme of that session like that of most was Hendrix College, not Henderson College, and the benevolent delegates raised an awesome $56,000 for the Conway institution. Following this display of generosity, the Reverend W. F. Evans, financial agent for Henderson College requested permission from presiding Bishop Hendrix "to gather a few crumbs for Henderson as we go along." [63] His pleas were answered with pledges in the amount of $5,000, prominent Arkadelphia residents being the principal donors.[64] Then to the astonishment of all present, the Reverend Evans announced that Henderson College was free of debt, for not only had he been successful in amassing funds to cover the mortgage but also had received pledges and cash gifts amounting to an almost unbelievable total of $66,912.25.[65]

In essence, the trustees themselves virtually paid the mortgage debt; for seven, including the president of the college, gave $27,-200 [66] of the needed $30,000. Noteworthy among these gifts were two of $10,000 each, one from Chairman Henderson, the other from Walter William Brown; for they foreshadowed the institution's third cognomen.[67] In addition to their payments on the mortgage, six of these same men pledged $16,000 of a $21,600 guaranteed fund to cover emergencies occurring within the next five years.[68] Though the large gifts stand forth, the hundreds of small donations exemplified acceptance of the college and the mission that it was fulfilling in southwestern Arkansas and Methodism.

In 1911 the six men who had pledged the guaranteed fund were called upon to honor their commitments. At the trustees' regular session, May 23, however, Chairman Henderson moved that the college's securities, his gift of four hundred shares of Nashville Lumber Company stock be entrusted to Elk Horn Bank to assure extension on the $12,500 in notes bearing their signatures held by that bank. In accepting his proposal, the trustees consented that should said notes not be paid, that the bank could sell the securities.[69] Chairman Henderson, and Trustees Robert B. F. Key and Walter E. Barkman were then serving as president, vice-president, and cashier of Elk Horn Bank.

During this era the tuition of fifty dollars remained unchanged; but increases occurred in board rates, and the total cost per session rose from $160 in 1890 to $190. Beginning in 1909 additional assessments were made, among them a two-dollar library fee, a fifty-cents-per-month charge for electricity if a boarding student chose to study in the privacy of his room and not the study hall, and a three-dollar payment for use of the bathrooms.[70]

Another change in student expenses occurred in 1904 when the trustees abolished all scholarships and withdrew those already in effect.[71] Ministers' children were still accepted tuition free; however, they now had to pay full charges for room and board and any other incidentals.[72] Though the trustees eliminated scholarships, three years later Chairman Henderson, pledging $100 for himself and $100 for his son Harry, and Trustee H. L. Remmel, also pledging $100, generously provided an annual loan fund for needy students.[73] Trustee W. K. Ramsey gave additional financial aid in 1909 when he established an annual loan sufficient to support a male student throughout his degree program, the amount to be re-paid upon graduation in reasonable installments at six percent. Robert B. F. Key, also a trustee, made the same provision for a young lady.[74]

A visible change in the institution's character was expansion and renovation of the physical plant. Three acres of land were added to the campus, and additional landscaping accentuated its natural beauty. A tree-planting ceremony which became a tradition was instituted by the senior class of 1906; each class member partici-pated by placing a shovelful of dirt and repeating some appropriate verse. At the close of the ritual, the senior president presented the shovel to the junior president, symbolizing the transfer of senior power.[75] That tree and those of later classes, some appropriately designated by small stone markers indicating the year of planting, line the main walk of, and graciously shade, the present front campus.

The main building underwent its first major refurbishment in 1904 when more than $3,000 was expended.[76] According to the *Southern Standard*, the college then had "some of the prettiest water closets and bathrooms in the state." [77] That same year addi-tional housing for men was obtained when a large house on Wilson Street was occupied; the residents christened it "The Barn." In 1909 an eleven-room house, where Evans Hall now stands, was ob-tained for the president; also, twelve five-room cottages, located across Twelfth Street from the president's home, were secured for men's housing.[78] That same year Key Hall, the second major building, was occupied.

In 1907 Robert Benjamin Franklin Key, a trustee from 1901 to 1913, presented the college with a $20,000 gift for erection of a building to house the music department.[79] Born in Butts County, Georgia, June 14, 1848, he came with his family to Clark County, Arkansas, at the age of eight. He early engaged in grist milling and ginning, but his fortune was accrued from lumbering which he pursued for more than thirty-one years, owning and operating a number of major saw mills, notably at Keyton and Delight. His retirement in 1907 was accompanied by his gift to the college. His last years in Arkadelphia were spent in the house he erected in 1906; the two-story Victorian residence later served as the chapter house for Sigma Phi Epsilon Fraternity. A Mason and a philanthropist, Key was interested in education. The father of fourteen children, he reared to adulthood and educated thirteen, including two orphans; except for his two eldest and two youngest, all attended Henderson College to which he gave continual financial aid. His fondness for the school is evidenced in the names of his twin sons: James Henderson and Albert Brown. A director and vice-president of Elk Horn Bank, in 1918 he moved to Florida where he continued in banking until his death in 1931.[80]

With eager alacrity, the trustees accepted Key's gift, the first and last of such consequence in the history of the institution, for Key was the only person to ever give a building. Construction on the three-story brick structure began July 18, 1907, but before it was completed, the funds were depleted and once again Charles C. Henderson came to the rescue, furnishing the money to finish the undertaking.[81] Connected to the main building by a covered walkway extending from the second and third floors, the new building, fittingly named Key Hall, housed more than the music department; expression, art, and domestic science occupied the first floor, dormi-

tory rooms and apartments for the music faculty the third.[82] Music
utilized Key Hall until 1964 when that department moved into the
new fine arts center, which remains nameless, and the former building was razed.

Plans for two other major buildings were announced. One was
to be the William K. Ramsey Memorial Hall to honor the vice-
chairman of the board of trustees who died in 1910. Ramsey, a
wealthy Camden businessman, had liberally contributed to the college for a number of years.[83] This building was never erected. The
other, an alumni hall, fared somewhat better. The idea for this
facility originated with the alumni association, which had been organized in the second year of the institution and from 1900 had
been holding annual banquets at the college.[84] Their desire was to
have a building all their own, erected by their own endeavors and
money. The first step toward realization of this goal came when
the class of 1906 donated $100 for the project and memorialized
following classes to do likewise.[85]

Then, in 1909 the athletic association, in need of a gymnasium,
joined the alumni in a joint project to construct one building which
would serve both purposes. On March 29, 1910, the ground break-
ing ceremony for what was to be the first alumni hall in the state
was held, and during commencement week in May, the dedication
conducted and the cornerstone laid. The building was to be of
Greek Revival order; and according to the student publication, the
ground floor would contain lockers, dressing rooms, and showers
for the athletes and storage space for athletic equipment; the main
floor, a large meeting room for the Y.M.C.A., a trophy room, and
the gymnasium, "large and commodious, which can be used also
for the alumni banquets;" the upper floor, halls for the literary societies and the amphitheater of the gym.[86] The two groups raised
slightly over $3,000 and students and faculty contributed labor.[87]
But only the foundation had been completed when construction

halted, and it was not until the late 1920's that the ground floor was partially completed to serve its intended purpose. The building stood incomplete until 1938 when with W.P.A. aid a modified one-story version for classroom purposes was erected on the front section of the foundation. On May 23, 1938, exactly twenty-eight years to the day of the original dedication, the building was named to honor Robert T. Proctor, the only professor involved with the original effort who was still connected with the college at that time.[88] The completion of the building by the state literally symbolizes that the present institution rests upon the foundation of its Methodist predecessor, and in 1974 that foundation is the only construction remaining from the Methodist era.

One structure built in 1907 was the First United Methodist Church, patterned after one in Colorado which Charles C. Henderson admired. Though not on the campus, it played a significant role in the religious and social life of the school. Chairman Henderson and President Hinemon headed the building committee, with several other trustees also serving. Their donations to this project, like those to the college they served, were notable. One of two large stained glass windows, the one depicting Christ blessing the children, and the rosewood chancel were among Chairman Henderson's gifts; the other window, a reproduction of Raphael's "Crucifixion," was given by Trustee Robert W. Huie.[89] Two smaller windows were given by Trustees Murry and McDaniel; Achilles O. Evans, also a trustee, was the pastor. Unless parents or guardians made requests to the contrary, all students were required to attend Sunday morning worship services at this church,[90] thus accounting for its size. (On October 14, 1973, the building was deconsecrated and the congregation moved to a new sanctuary. The windows and chancel were among its many fixtures incorporated into the new structure. The present minister, the Reverend John Pershing Miles, is seeking to reemphasize the relationship between the local congregation and the college and is attempting to recover certain pieces of furniture from the school and to place them in the new library-conference room.)

A peculiar phase of the college program which had a profound impact on student life was military drill which had been initiated as early as 1895 and made permanent during the Hinemon years. The 1895–1896 *Catalogue* listed "Military Tactics" in association with physical education and carried the statement that "Plato has spoken of a man as being lame whose mind was developed to the disparagement of his body." [91] Two years later a class composite showed a cadet group wearing West Point-style uniforms. Announcements for 1903–1904 informed the prospective student that:

> For the first time in the history of the College, real military tactics will be introduced, for the sole purpose of securing better discipline, and positive results in physical development, correcting evil habits and creating good ones.[92]

They also stated that the West Point cadet uniform had been adopted for all men students.[93]

President Hinemon, like former President Jones, wholeheartedly believed physical exercise was necessary for full development. Beginning in 1905, drills were held before morning class periods, five times per week. Students were required to purchase their own uniforms at a cost of twelve dollars, but their rifles of Spanish-American War vintage were provided free of charge; the cadets were required to keep them spotlessly clean.[94] The first commandant, Major W. L. Floyd, a graduate of South Carolina Military Academy and Harvard University, also taught French.[95] Drills were conducted according to the United States Army manual though the program was in no way government sponsored. Students who cut classes were required additional drills, and those guilty of infraction of drill rules, mainly talking in ranks, disobedience to officer's commands, tardiness, and absences, were punished by hours of solitary marching.[96] Assisting Major Floyd was Major Drew Luten, honor graduate of Kentucky State College,[97] who the next year instituted regular drills for the women students. These "gray ladies," who marched without rifles, were required to dress in ground-length gray skirts, white blouses, dark masculine ties, gray jackets, and hats resembling mortar boards.[98] This program was compulsory for the women for only that year; however, this uniform remained their official school dress, and they, like the men, were required to wear this military costume on all public occasions. At one such gathering in October, 1909, a historic one for Arkadelphians, their appearance prompted remarks from United States President William Howard Taft when he commented upon their attire, especially the young ladies' "academic hats." [99] In 1908 the trustees voted to make the military feature of the school permanent.[100] In his annual report to the trustees the following year, President Hinemon, who took the rank of colonel, reported that the department had been conducted with very little friction. Hinemon's successor, however, continued the military program only one year.[101]

The literary societies and "Y" groups begun in the first years of the institution remained the core of student associations, and during the first decade of the twentieth century the former inaugurated what have become two lasting mirrors of student activity, an annual and a newspaper. In 1905 *Star*, the first yearbook, appeared under the editorship of Farrar C. Newberry. It is said that the name *Star* was derived from the fact that the yearbook's publication represented "a new star in the Henderson galaxy;" the first copies sold for two dollars.[102] Approximately three years later, *The Oracle*, the student newspaper, made its debut on October 6, 1908. First published bi-monthly and under the editorship of Edgar L. Dean, it sold for ten cents a copy or one dollar per year.[103]

A number of new organizations appeared and vied with the older groups for membership. The Chafing Dish Club, a women's

society begun in 1905, provided opportunities for young ladies interested in haute cuisine.[104] A Glee Club, the second co-educational
group, formed in 1907.[105] Two years later the student newspaper
editorialized that participation among males in the literary societies
was no longer one hundred percent and commented that those who
had failed to join either of them were "either uncaring for the
largest and best or too indolent to work for it." [106] The men had,
however, found diversion in three new clubs in 1908: Young Men's
Democratic Club to debate the Young Republicans, and the Minis-
terial Club providing "closer fellowship among the preacher boys
and interchange of ideas and sympathies." [107]

The first alma mater song appeared in 1905. Written by Gordon
Lockhart, it was sung to the tune of "My Old Kentucky
Home." [108] From its chorus it is learned that the school colors had
become the now familiar red and gray. Four years later the songs
"H-E-N-D-E-R-S-O-N" and "Henderson, Henderson, Grand Old
College Name" became popular on the campus.[109] In 1910 an *Oracle* editorial challenged students to compose an original work of
music and words so that the school could have a distinctly Henderson song.[110] Such was not achieved, however, until 1929 when
James W. Workman, the last president of the Methodist years,
wrote the present alma mater: "Alma Mater Henderson."

While the local opera house had fulfilled an important role in the
cultural life of the early institution, its position lessened when Henderson College joined with Ouachita Baptist College in providing
a lecture and artist series on the campuses, each student being required to purchase a ticket for the events. The artists were of national reputation, but many of the speakers were regional and their
topics reflected that the section was still looking backward. In 1910
alone three lectures concerning the South of the past were delivered, one by a former governor of Mississippi, James K. Vardaman,
"The Great White Chief." [111]

Beginning in 1904, at the time of registration each student was required to sign the following contract:

> I do hereby contract with the Henderson College that so long as I shall remain a student of the College, I will endeavor to comply cheerfully with all its regulations in all particulars, and I agree not to deface or injure, by writing or otherwise, any of its furniture, books or other property. Moreover, if I should by accident do damage to any property of the College I hereby agree to report it promptly to the Dean, or in case it should be dormitory property, I agree to report it to the Governess, that it may be properly assessed and that I must pay for or replace the same.[112]

And from 1905 forward, in addition to the above contract, students were compelled to take the following pledge: "I pledge my word of honor that I will not be absent from my premises at night without permission of authorities." [113] Continuing a rule instituted in the first session, students were discouraged to be on the city streets except for business purposes. Apparently this regulation was obeyed, for in 1908 the *Oracle* commented about the townspeople's frequent remarks that the young men of Henderson College were seldom upon the streets and that when they did appear they were properly attired and practiced excellent deportment.[114]

Although social fraternities were nonexistent, the young ladies formed several ad hoc societies. The girls residing in the dormitories grouped themselves according to floors under such descriptive names as "Paradise Alley, Scalowag Hall, Morning Side, and the Key Hall Midnight Terrors." [115] Whereas the modern co-ed relies on the hot plate or "orders out" for an after hours snack, the girls of these groups depended upon chafing dishes to prepare midnight feasts. Although cooking in the rooms was prohibited, a recognized club requiring its members to have access to a chafing utensil enabled them to circumvent that rule and prepare food in their rooms. Never revoking the regulation, the administration came to accept this infraction as a "forbidden pleasure." [116] Social events were usually group functions, and one activity anxiously awaited was the annual Junior-Senior Picnic, at which the former entertained the "astute and dignified ones." [117] This outing alternated between the bluff overlooking the Ouachita River and the green meadows of the Caddo River Valley.

Despite some laxity in restrictions the catalogue still reminded its readers that neither teachers nor students were permitted use of the college telephones during school hours, that women students were discouraged to dine at hotels or public restaurants, that strangers to the president who desired to call on young ladies had to present letters of introduction, and that the president reserved the right to terminate attendance of any pupil whose conduct or influence was detrimental to the college.[118]

One activity soon surpassed all others: intercollegiate sports. The Henderson College Athletic Association was organized in 1904, and during that first year fielded only a baseball team.[119] The following year witnessed the launching of intercollegiate track and football teams. The coach for both was Mathematics Professor J. Burton Webster. On April 28, 1906, the track team, consisting of only five men, captured sixty of 108 points to win the first annual Arkansas State Athletic Association Track Championship, an honor that future teams maintained until 1911 when the University of Arkansas defeated Henderson College by three points. The *Southern Standard* reported that had not Henderson College's star been absent from the meet because of illness, the school would have no doubt retained its position.[120]

The sport which eventually drew the largest and most loyal following was football. Although the *Southern Standard* mentions an Arkadelphia Methodist College football team as early as 1896, the school's first intercollegiate team was not organized until 1905. The first game, a contest with Arkansas Military Academy, was played at West End Park in Little Rock on November 18, with the

Academy winning 15 to 5. Articles in both the *Arkansas Gazette* and the local press emphasized the unpleasant effects of the unseasonally warm weather that Saturday afternoon, reporting that both teams were forced to ask for time repeatedly and that the spectators fared but little better. The college yearbook in relating the story of the first season only names the individual team members and states that the game with Arkansas Military Academy was a credit to the institution.[121]

The 1906 season was opened with a coveted 26–0 victory over Hendrix College. This game, the initial one for the Conway eleven, began what was to become the oldest athletic rivalry during the Methodist era.[122] The following year, a significant one for the varsity team, marked the arrival of the first full-time coach and the beginning of the traditional game with Ouachita Baptist College. James R. Haygood, famed Vanderbilt University quarterback, assumed the position of coach in 1907. An engineering student at the Tennessee institution from 1904 to 1906, he was employed as a civil engineer by the Louisville and Nashville Railway before coming to Arkadelphia.[123] Known as "Smiling Jimmy," he served as coach and athletic director, with exception of two interims, until 1925. In his first four years he guided his teams to as many state championships. Although he coached a number of first place teams, he never had a perfect season, a record still unachieved by a Henderson coach in 1973.[124] In 1934 the college recognized Haygood by giving his name to both the first gymnasium building and the improved football field. Fittingly, when Henderson State College occupied the present ten thousand-seat stadium in 1968, the trustees transferred the name Haygood from the old to the new.

The "Battle of the Ravine" also began in 1907 when on a Monday afternoon in mid-October Henderson College met Ouachita Baptist College on the home field and defeated her arch-rival 22–6, scoring four touchdowns and kicking two goals. The Ouachitonians sportingly entertained the victors with a postgame reception.[125]

The following year the team traveled to Fayetteville in a private pullman car where in their opening game they suffered a 51–0 loss to the University of Arkansas,[126] spoiling an otherwise perfect season. This year also brought initiation of receptions in the parlors by the young ladies for visiting football teams, properly chaperoned of course.[127] One honor bestowed upon the football team, and one which would be rejected by today's standards, was the annual smoker. The first one was held at "Cottage 5," in December, 1908, and each player, as he arrived, was offered a pipe or cigar by "Mose," the Negro attendant. This ritual preceded an oyster supper.[128] The next year the "Reddies" again opened their schedule with the University of Arkansas, this time losing 24–0; [129] but in November of that season, they won acclaim in Arkansas by playing highly ranked "Ole Miss" to a 12–12 tie in Arkadelphia.[130]

Throughout the years the teams have been known as "Reddies." Several stories persist as to how the name originated, but no doubt it came from the color of the jerseys worn by the first football team. Early editions of student publications refer to the players as "Red Jackets" and at other times as "Red Men." The initial edition of the *Oracle*, October 6, 1908, contains a story that Nellie Hartsgeld had the honor of naming the football team the "Red Jackets" and received an annual pass to the games. By 1908, however, the scribes were referring to them simply as "Reds." A plausible explanation for the evolution to "Reddies" is that it fitted into pep songs and yells better than the shorter and more blunt "Reds." In later years well-meaning sports writers have called the teams "Redskins," "Indians," and "Big Red," but the name "Reddies," apparently originating from the red of the red and gray school colors, has stuck and the teams therefore remain without the traditional mascot.[131]

Student admission to home games for the first three seasons was twenty-five cents, but in 1908 the price for tickets was increased

one hundred percent to fifty cents, accompanied by the explanation "as the team grows so do expenses." Disgruntled collegians
were informed that the University of the South (Sewanee) required each student to pay a ten-dollar fee each year for football
tickets.[132]

At the same time that the coach and his teams were bringing
regional attention to the small Methodist college, Greek and German Professor Jesse C. Rapp was laboring unceasingly to bring international recognition to the school by conducting a series of
European tours for its students.[133]

For seven years (1904–1911) President Hinemon administered
Henderson College; his service to the institution was inestimable.[134]
When he assumed office, the school was a somewhat unusual one.
It had been a personal college, reflecting the ideas of George C.
Jones and complicated by the attitude of official Methodism. Hine-
mon's long effort was to make the college complete in its structure
and competent in its operation. With this purpose his success was
the success of Henderson College.

With the college's affairs in a prosperous state, Hinemon submitted his resignation to the chairman of the board in February,
1911. On April 4 in a special session the trustees refused to accept
it and reelected him president. Further considerations were held
during the month of April when it became apparent that Hinemon
would not continue as president. On May 23, 1911, the trustees reluctantly accepted his resignation, effective July 1, and granted him
salary and use of the president's house until that date. Shortly
thereafter Hinemon returned to Little Rock to become superintendent of the State School for the Blind.[135]

In his final report to the Henderson College trustees he made his
valedictory:

> . . . there has been a kind of evolution in the character and
> quality of our student body. Seven years ago, our students were
> . . . boys and girls poorly qualified for college work who came

to Henderson for a year of polish or finish without any serious
purposes in life and with no intention of taking a full college
course. Only about twenty percent of the student body returned
the next year. Such has been the change in the tone of the student
body that each succeeding year has brought an increase in the
number who returned after one year in college and the number
of those who intend to continue from year to year has grown to
such an extent that our latest report shows that, of the whole number now in school . . . less than a half dozen announce their
determination not to return. . . . This is . . . a most wholesome
and satisfactory condition for, after all, the most powerful influence in building up a school is the active work of the old students.
From a body of students utterly lacking in college loyalty we
have developed . . . [a] most devoted and enthusiastic body of
students . . . and, whatever, we may say of other phases and
features of our work, this loyalty and love on the part of our
graduates and students is the most valuable asset of Henderson
today.[136]

Although Hinemon resigned his position as president, he remained
a member of the board of trustees until 1920. It was in the latter
capacity that he moved that "the name of Henderson College be
changed to that of Henderson-Brown." [137]

The issue of the name change had first been presented to the
trustees on May 25, 1910, when Chairman Henderson advanced a
motion to include the name of Walter William Brown, his business
associate and the school's recent liberal contributor, with that of
his own in the institution's title. Henderson's request came just
one day following Brown's election to the board to fill the vacancy
created by the death of his father-in-law, William K. Ramsey.[138]

Walter William Brown was born May 19, 1868, in Camden,
Arkansas, the son of Emma Leake and George Brown. Unlike
Charles C. Henderson, he was born to a prosperous family. The
only male in three children, he attended the local schools, was
graduated from the Webb School in Tennessee, and was a student
at Washington and Lee University from 1887 to 1889. Returning

from Virginia he married Marian Ramsey, member of another prominent Camden family. The father of one child, Anne Zalinda, he was active in various civic organizations and was chairman of the board of trustees of the town's First Methodist Church. In addition to his numerous railroad and timber interests with Charles C. Henderson, he was president of Ouachita Valley Bank.[139]

On motion of R. B. F. Key, the trustees rejected Henderson's plea, but the following year in April, 1911, shortly before Brown's forty-second birthday, they unanimously honored retiring President Hinemon's motion and proclaimed the institution to be Henderson-Brown College.[140]

CHAPTER VII

The Rise of the Phoenix

THE trustees brought as successor to President Hinemon, George Henry Crowell, vice-chancellor and dean of Epworth University (Oklahoma City University). The first person possessing a Doctor of Philosophy degree to be employed by the college, he began his term of office June 1, 1911.[1]

A native of North Carolina, Crowell had been born February 7, 1865, in New London. He earned the Bachelor of Philosophy degree in 1892 from the state university at Chapel Hill where he was graduated with honors. Three years later he completed the English theological course at Vanderbilt University (1894–1895), and he received the Doctor of Philosophy degree from Central University, Indianapolis, in 1907.[2] A Mason and a man of scholarship, he had also traveled extensively in Europe, Canada, and the United States. A professor of history and economics, Crowell had held teaching and administrative positions for fifteen years in the public schools of North Carolina before assuming duties at the Oklahoma college where he remained for three years before coming to Henderson-Brown College. Well-known in Southern Methodist educational circles and an ordained minister, he had served as chairman of the Board of Education of the West Oklahoma Annual Conference and was received into the Little Rock Conference in 1911, following his arrival in Arkansas.[3]

In negotiating with Crowell the trustees offered a salary of $2,000 and use of the presidential house, or a salary of $1,650 and use of the presidential apartments in the main building, including board.[4] He chose the house and $2,000. For his installation, the trustees followed the old and dignified custom of formal inauguration and in the presence of Bishop James H. McCoy invested Crowell as the fourth president of the institution on November 1, 1911.[5]

Crowell began his tenure on a note of optimism, for the college was free of debt and its future prospects seemed brighter than at any time in the past. The physical plant was valued at $125,000,[6] and plans for expansion were being formulated. Too, the trustees would soon seek conference approval to bond the college property to the Elk Horn Bank in order to obtain $6,000 to finance completion of the Alumni Hall and $14,000 to erect a boys' dormitory.[7] With the college solvent, the Little Rock Conference was assessing itself $1,500 for Henderson-Brown College, the same as for Hendrix College. The following year, 1912, the conference requested that the trustees offer the school as joint property to the White River and Arkansas conferences, to bring in additional revenues and to gain state-wide support.[8] After two years of negotiations, the trustees were still unable to reach agreement with the other two conferences, and the proposal was not effected until 1920.

Assisting Crowell as dean was Robert Clinton Rhodes, son of Trustee James Clinton Rhodes. Dean Rhodes, an alumnus of the class of 1906, held the Master of Arts degree from Vanderbilt University and had been assistant professor of biology at the University of Mississippi for three years before returning to Henderson-Brown College.[9] (He later received the Doctor of Philosophy degree from the University of California, Berkeley; studied marine biology at the University of Chicago; and, while head of the biology department of Emory University, achieved national recognition.)

The faculty began its climb to academic excellence when Boyd Ashby Wise, a Phi Beta Kappa graduate of Johns Hopkins University (1905) and the college's first professor to hold the Doctor of Philosophy degree, came to the chair of Latin in 1913. Born in Stephens City, Virginia, July 7, 1874, Wise, an alumnus of Randolph-Macon Academy (Front Royal), received the Bachelor of Arts and Master of Arts degrees from Randolph-Macon College in 1897 and 1898 respectively. Assuming an educational career, he taught in the Front Royal Academy and was a fellow for two years while pursuing the Doctor of Philosophy degree at the Baltimore institution. Before joining the faculty of Henderson-Brown College, he had held positions in Latin and English at Millsaps College, Emory College (University), and Richmond College (Virginia). A teacher of note, Wise was also the first member of the faculty to achieve inclusion in *Who's Who in America*.[10]

Any illusions of harmony that President Crowell may have held in the early months of his association with the trustees were clearly dispelled when he met with the board at its regular session concluding his first year, for he barely survived a vote of confidence and was reelected by the fifteen-member board by only two votes.[11] Until this period in the institution's history, the trustees, though granted full and complete control by the charter, had seldom interfered with the president's execution of policy and had dictated neither selection of the faculty nor salary schedules. But in the regular session, May, 1912, they made their first move toward establishing minimum and maximum wages for all officers and teachers of the college, resolving that henceforth upon nomination by the president, salaries for all personnel had to be stipulated. The trustees set the salary for full professors at $855, with those for others ranging from $405 to $600, all including board. The dean, who also held teaching responsibilities, received $1,500.[12]

The next year with respect to hiring of the professor of Bible, the trustees requested that the president ascertain in advance of employment whether or not the prospective teacher adhered to the views and theories of the "higher critics," emphasizing their belief that the higher criticism of the Bible, subjecting it to the test of historical knowledge, was beyond the domain of the college's work.[13] To assure compliance with the trustees' ruling, President Crowell submitted his own name for the position. They accepted and also elected Professor Benjamin S. Foster to assist him in the newly established Chair of Bible and Sunday School Pedagogy.[14] At that same meeting in 1913, the board resolved that it would grant only one honorary degree during any year and conferred that year's recognition upon Trustee the Reverend Achilles O. Evans, who held a theological diploma from Vanderbilt University.[15]

Later in 1913 President Crowell informed the Little Rock Conference in his annual report to it that at the beginning of the fall session Henderson-Brown College had reorganized its teaching force into a college faculty and a high school faculty, separate and distinct from each other, and that for the first time the faculties of the academy and college were not basically composed of the same individuals. The college instructors numbered eight; the arts, six; the high school, five.[16] With this reorganization the primary grades of the academy were discontinued. Although this implied that the state had made progress in bringing fundamental education to a larger number of its people, it indicated the scarcity of secondary schools and the distressing educational conditions in Arkansas.

The first regional effort to raise the educational level in the South was made in 1895 when the Southern Association of Colleges and Secondary Schools was formed to establish entrance requirements among colleges and universities. One of the major goals for the group's organization was to prohibit institutions of higher learning from operating academies, and the association refused membership to any school maintaining one.[17] When the association formed, only six institutions qualified for membership; by 1913 that number had risen only to twenty-eight, and no Arkansas college was included.[18] Church school education was improved in

1896 when the Southern Methodist Church created an educational commission to set standards for its institutions, and it was this body which most directly affected Henderson-Brown College's policies. This commission refused the institution "A" standing because of insufficient endowment, thus giving stimulus to and reason for the campaign which had been launched with conference approval in 1912 to obtain a minimum $100,000.[19]

With only a nominal endowment Henderson-Brown College was continuing to operate on its own receipts and the meager assessment from the conference. The failure to collect amounts pledged in earlier financial campaigns placed the institution in pecuniary stress, and by late 1913, it was the same familiar story: the college was carrying a heavy indebtedness, this time in the amount of $22,000.[20]

The trying times plaguing Crowell reached a climax in the early hours of February 3, 1914, when fire completely destroyed the main building. Around 5:00 o'clock, James B. Garrett, superintendent of buildings and grounds, discovered a small blaze in the kitchen adjacent to the structure.[21] No one knows how the fire originated, but according to newspaper accounts it was thought that it began in the storeroom and that it must have been caused by defective wiring. Immediately upon detecting the blaze, Garrett sounded an alarm on the college bell. From the very start, the scene was marked by the coolness of those in charge of the dormitories. Girls in the rooms located on the second and third floors were marched from the burning building in military-like fashion under the direction of the resident women teachers. Although there was much excitement among the girls, there was no panic; no lives were endangered, nor was there any report of injury during the evacuation. So hurried was the departure, though, that some young ladies were clad only in their night clothes, a condition which, no doubt, caused the matrons as much alarm as did the flames.[22]

The ringing of the college bell and the firing of shots brought hundreds to the scene of the blaze rapidly reaching uncontrollable magnitude. The men students of both Henderson-Brown College and neighboring Ouachita Baptist College, assisted by citizens of the town, manned the school's fire fighting equipment in an attempt to quench the flames, but soon turned full attention to saving Key Hall from the expanding fire. Delayed arrival of the Arkadelphia Fire Department prompted a number of the men to enter the blazing structure to remove the young ladies' trunks and personal valuables. This action was the first serious risk of life in the holocaust which had reached spectacular proportions. In dramatic fashion, as the men labored, great bursts of violent, blue and green tinged flames enveloped the lofty tower of the majestic structure; and as the last hero escaped, all hopes of saving the building vanished. In the illumination from the fire the students could be seen standing in groups, all dismayed and many crying aloud as they watched their college crumble.[23]

Afterwards it was learned that the salvage lines formed by the students and friends had been successful in saving the trophies of the teams, more than a dozen pianos, and the entire library consisting of over three thousand volumes.[24] Later, several ironically humorous incidents were recalled: Men students staggering under the weight of heavy boxes and trunks were reminded, "Be careful, don't mar the grand staircase!" One young lady threw her crystal perfume bottles out the window and came out carrying a pair of stockings. A teacher tossed down her prized mirror and carried a feather pillow. A local preacher retrieved a chafing dish and left the girl's Bible beside it to burn.[25]

There were those among the spectators who falsely predicted that this would be the end of Henderson-Brown College, but before the smoke had cleared from the ruins, optimistic ones were formulating plans for continuing the session and for erecting temporary buildings on the campus. As news of the disaster spread,

Governor George W. Hayes tendered use of a national guard tent to serve as a chapel, and Ouachita Baptist College generously offered facilities. The roomless co-eds were welcomed into homes of residents near the campus,[26] a courtesy which represented Arkadelphia's love for the college. The girls continued to room in the private dwellings until they occupied their new quarters in early 1915.

The day of the tragedy a large crowd met at the Methodist Church where President Crowell informed them that the year's work would continue in temporary wooden structures and that permanent buildings soon would replace the destroyed one. He also announced that classes would resume the next day in his own home and in the town's churches. The encouraged gathering contributed over $2,000 in cash to implement construction of the intermediate quarters.[27]

If there were anything of a redeeming nature associated with the devastation, it was the solidification of student loyalty to the institution. President Crowell pleaded with them not to leave; as a result, they assembled in the pine grove near the ruins and not only pledged their determination to remain but also gave more than $1,000 to the rebuilding fund. Consequently, only the day of the catastrophe was lost from recitations, and of nearly three hundred enrolled, only one male and six females left school.[28] Rallying to the support of their alma mater, the students cleared the ruins, salvaging more than 150,000 bricks for reuse.[29] And from this time forward, "Reddie Spirit" grew to mean more than enthusiasm for athletic events.

Exactly one week from the day of the fire, supper was served in the make-shift dining hall, complete with wall separating the women from the men. The following day, the fourteen-room classroom and administration building was occupied; only three weeks later the auditorium was in use.[30] In these rough, unpainted structures the life of the college continued almost undaunted. Partitions affording some degree of privacy divided the recitation area into stall-like rooms but contributed to a confusion of tongues, leading students to dub it "the Tower of Babel." The barn-like auditorium accommodated such spectacles as a recital performed by a young lady in white formal dress seated at a grand piano on a stage of unfinished lumber. But elegance had not altogether disappeared, for Trustee Walter E. Barkman and his wife opened their nearby antebellum mansion to the girls on Sunday afternoons.[31]

The trustees assembled in special session February 17, 1914, to discuss the financial status of the institution and proposals for rebuilding. They faced a major crisis, for after reviewing the liabilities held against the college, the financial officer presented the dismal report that the $45,000 received from insurance lacked $194.75 covering the college's outstanding debts. Following a lengthy and frank discussion of the issue, a motion prevailed to proceed at once with the difficult task of constructing permanent buildings. Reminiscent of action taken at the first session of the board nearly twenty-five years earlier, the trustees appointed a building committee to employ an architect to draft plans for appropriate structures to house the college.[32]

Reconvening the following day the trustees instructed the committee to consider designs for five structures instead of a single massive building: one unit to contain the administrative offices, twelve to sixteen classrooms, an auditorium, and "other necessary compartments;"[33] two to serve as dormitories, one to accommodate 125 women, the other, the same number of men; another unit to house the kitchen and dining rooms; and the fifth to contain the new power house and laundry.[34]

The first order of business of the trustees' April session was the election of a president for the coming year. After discussion, they reelected Crowell to his position and also charged him with the additional burden of serving as financial agent to conduct the campaign to secure construction funds.[35] Realizing that raising money

is a difficult task requiring endless time and energy, President
Crowell who had been recognized as an outstanding speaker by the
University of North Carolina immediately embarked upon his
duties to secure $100,000. Canvassing the state in the following
months, he in a forceful manner made a dramatic appeal for his
cause, pleading with all to join in "this noble service to the young
men and women of Arkansas." [36] His office was deluged with letters of sympathy and encouragement. One from a New Orleans
business firm contained a donation and the statement of hope "that
a new college will rise Phoenix-like from the ashes and be one that
your city can be justly proud of." [37] The Methodist churches
throughout Arkansas held "Henderson-Brown Days," and those
in Little Rock alone undertook to raise $10,000 for the cause.[38]

In the meantime architect Jim Blainsdell drafted plans for five
buildings, but his proposals were altered to include only two
structures: one large building to house the administrative offices,
classrooms, auditorium, and women's dormitory; another to contain the kitchen and dining rooms. The estimated cost of these two
buildings was $71,000. The executive committee awarded A. O.
Campbell the contract on June 13, 1914,[39] approximately two
weeks before events in Europe led the world into war.

Work on the new facilities began immediately, but halted a
few weeks later when funds were depleted; for although Crowell
had secured pledges for the construction costs, he had encountered
great difficulty in collecting them. Approximately $40,000 was
needed to finish the projects. Following entreaties from Trustee
Robert W. Huie, the contractor in a philanthropic spirit offered
to complete the buildings, financing one-half himself, provided that
Huie and his associates would assume the remaining half. His
proposal was accepted, and Trustees Huie, Henderson, Key, and
Barkman underwrote the deficit.[40] Through the united efforts of
these men the structures were built; and for their faith, loyalty,
and patronage, these trustees who also had rescued the institution
on previous occasions came to be known as "The Big Four."

The 1914 session of the Little Rock Conference listened attentively as President Crowell related the salient facts concerning the dilemma of Henderson-Brown College. He reported that he had succeeded in collecting $20,274.38, all of which had been applied on construction, leaving an unpaid balance of $51,425.62. The institution held unpaid subscriptions amounting to $36,526.62, leaving a balance of almost $15,000 with no promise of guarantee.[41] The conference's pessimism for the school's future was attested in the collection of a mere $28.75 from the special offering taken to help alleviate the crisis.[42] But realizing that the college had to be funded, the conference resolved that through its presiding elders and pastors an attempt would be made to secure one dollar from each member of their several districts and charges.[43] The General Board of Education supplemented the conference's $1,500 assessment with a grant of almost $900.[44]

The Little Rock *Arkansas Democrat*, the state's leading afternoon daily, was holding a coupon contest unrelated to the church's fund raising campaign, offering the winner a prize of $500. Enterprising supporters of the college organized a group effort and entered the winning number of votes in Henderson-Brown College's name and gave the much needed prize money to the depleted school treasury.[45]

Of the many contributions to the college during this trying period there was one gift of unusual merit, for it came not from a prominent financier but from an endeared member of the staff. James Benjamin Garrett, discoverer of the fire, gave his entire life's savings of more than $5,000, assuring construction of temporary quarters and continuation of the college. Known to students and faculty simply as "Dad," Garrett had been superintendent of buildings and grounds since 1901 and continued in that capacity until his death in 1944 at age ninety. At his own request, his noble sacrifice received no publicity and remained unknown even to his family until his death, his stated reason being that he did not wish to worry his wife. Of distinguished Virginia lineage, he had been born near Arkadelphia, on October 22, 1853. As a young man he pursued the carpentry trade throughout Arkansas, returning to the town of his birth in 1900 so that his three children could obtain a college education. During his long years with the institution, he completely dedicated himself to its success, and though in failing health during the last years of his life, he could be seen daily on the campus observing and making sure that everything went well at his beloved Henderson-Brown College. Upon his death, its state college successor, mindful of his unselfish gift and service, had his body lie in state at the school and several years later named a dormitory Garrett Hall in his honor.[46]

With the new buildings practically completed the trustees proclaimed a holiday to recognize those who had faithfully and earnestly aided in the work. They designated November 12, 1914, as the date to celebrate and invited the townspeople to join in the activities, for the rebuilding was indeed the result of community effort. Most of the Arkadelphia merchants closed their firms and joined the more than one thousand persons attending the festivities which were very like unto an old-time "singing and dinner on the ground affair" so characteristic of early Methodism. Victory addresses were the order of the afternoon, with former President Hinemon and Bishop H. C. Morrison being the principal speakers. Throughout the program a note of triumph prevailed, for those assembled had proved their determination and won victory over gloom and despair left by the fire.[47]

The formal dedication, however, was held appropriately on February 3, 1915,[48] the first anniversary of the disaster. Following a short program the college hosted an open house and welcomed visitors to inspect the new facilities which had cost $80,000, excluding furnishings and equipment.[49] Again, as with the original building, the trustees over-expended their resources. The main building, henceforth to be called "College Hall," was of classical mold. The three-story red brick structure was 166 feet long and

116 feet wide. The front entrance was from the second level and was reached by wide, sweeping stairs, the bottom two having been salvaged from the original building. The ground floor contained the college's first basketball gymnasium with gallery seating for four hundred spectators and other rooms. The second floor housed administrative offices, the library, classrooms, formal parlors, and the largest college auditorium in the state, seating more than eight hundred. The third floor was the women's dormitory; these rooms, containing oak furniture, each had a lavatory, large closet, and two outside windows. Only two girls were assigned to a room. The entire building was heated with steam and lighted by electricity. Fire escapes led from every corridor, and water hoses placed in accessible locations lessened the chances of a repeat of the earlier misfortune.[50]

The Dining Hall, of the same architecture, was located nearby. Consisting of separate eating areas for men and women, it seated 260 persons;[51] a faculty member still presided over each table. The kitchen, equipped with natural gas, was supervised by Malichi Smith, who had been employed by the college in 1903 and remained in that capacity until 1948. Smith was the first person to contribute to the rebuilding fund when he gave his gift of twenty-five dollars.[52]

The room attracting the most attention from the visitors was the one set aside in College Hall as a memorial to Laura Lee Henson, a young co-ed who had survived the college fire only to die as a result of another. Ten days following the festive celebration marking the near completion of the buildings, the eighteen-year-old girl received severe burns when her clothing caught fire from the flames of a gas heater in the home where she was residing, awaiting occupation of the new dormitory facilities. Three days later she died; her death was the first among boarding students in the college's history.[53] Her family and friends provided the room's furnishings, and the college placed a marble tablet bearing an inscription written by her brother John, who was also a student at the college:

IN MEMORIAM
Laura Lee Henson
Student
Henderson-Brown College
Born February 1, 1896—Died November 25, 1914
Dedicated to her by the College and her loving friends.[54]

This room became the center of campus religious life; daily worship services were held there, and Christian organizations, especially the Y.W.C.A., used it for meetings. It also assumed the role of an interdenominational chapel; it was there that the first Roman Catholic mass was said in Arkadelphia and that the Protestant Episcopal Church of the town was reorganized. This sanctuary maintained by the college until the building was razed in 1964 perpetuated the memory of Laura Lee Henson. (When College Hall was demolished, the plaque and other memorabilia were carelessly discarded. Only the steps salvaged from the 1914 fire were preserved.)

Much student activity revolved around the new auditorium. A few months following the first transcontinental telephone call in the United States, Governor Hays, who had aided the college earlier, chose the new facility to introduce the Southwestern Telegraph and Telephone Company's new invention, "The Loud Talking Telephone," to the state. From his office in Little Rock, March 22, 1915, the governor addressed a capacity audience for twenty minutes with the first speech to be delivered over long distance lines in Arkansas.[55] It was also here that on May 8 the students assembled to hear the grim announcement of the sinking of the *Lusitania* the previous day. In early June the hall was the setting for commencement exercises marking the twenty-fifth anniversary of the college. Commencement week was, in reality, a "homecoming," for scores who had attended the institution returned for alumni activities, but only seven young men and women joined their number as graduates.[56] The honor student, who received a Bachelor of Arts degree, was Nila Embree (Nila Turner); she returned to her alma mater as a member of the English faculty in 1930 and taught that subject until her retirement in 1965.[57]

Although President Crowell's leadership and determination should be credited as major forces in keeping the institution open, during his four-year administration some trustees yearly made efforts to remove him from office.[58] He lacked the grace and finesse of President Hinemon in obtaining his ends; and from the beginning of their association, Crowell and the board had experienced discord over the strictness of rules and regulations governing both faculty and students. In tactless manner he admonished the trustees for being overly influenced by Ouachita Baptist College and insisted that they should set their own rules and exert a more progressive philosophy. One major disagreement between them was an outgrowth of the board's insistence on continuing the policy of maintaining separate dining rooms for men and women in the new dining hall.[59]

A progressive leader, Crowell was reproved for being "too big for Henderson-Brown College and beyond his time for Arkansas educational ideas." [60] When in prolonged special session in mid-May the trustees created a board of control, it became apparent that the fifty-year-old president's employment was coming to a close. This board, a direct affront to the president, was granted plenary power: it possessed jurisdiction over the management of the school's affairs; full authority over all members of the faculty, from the president down; and the right to employ or discharge any member as it saw fit. The implementation of any of Crowell's ideas was doomed when the trustees determined that the school "shall continue on its present basis." [61] After deliberation they did reelect him president,[62] but approximately one month later Crowell tendered his resignation. The board, without a dissenting vote, accepted, but published the usual resolution of appreciation for his services.[63] On this note, the trustees and Crowell severed their relationship. Departing Arkadelphia, Crowell served as Field Manager for the Junaluska Assembly and Kentucky Wesleyan College before being named president of Logan College in 1917.[64]

CHAPTER VIII

The School with a Heart

O N June 15, 1915, the day that President Crowell resigned, the trustees conferred the degree of Doctor of Laws on James Mims Workman and elected him president of Henderson-Brown College, his term of office to begin immediately.[1]

Son of the Reverend James J. and Mary Sullivan Workman, he was born March 8, 1867, in Greenville, South Carolina. Workman received the Bachelor of Arts degree in 1889 from Wofford College, where he had studied under Professor Granville Goodloe. Active in fraternal organizations, he was a Mason, Knight of Pythias, Oddfellow, and Woodman of the World. Following his graduation from Wofford College, he became a field secretary for the Young Men's Christian Association, and that work brought him to Little Rock, Arkansas, where he was general secretary for that group. Ordained in 1894 by the Methodist Episcopal Church, South, he became influential in Arkansas Methodism, holding pastorates at Benton, Crossett, Malvern, and Little Rock's Winfield Memorial Church, then second largest in the state.[2] He was minister at the last when elected chief executive of the Arkadelphia institution.

The first president with an Arkansas background, Workman accepted the position at the solicitations of Trustee the Reverend Achilles O. Evans and Trustee the Reverend Thomas D. Scott, who advocated that only a more urbane and familiar personality could obtain the moral and financial support necessary to save the institution.[3] The trustees had selected Workman to perform a miracle, for although the college had fine new buildings, it was

119

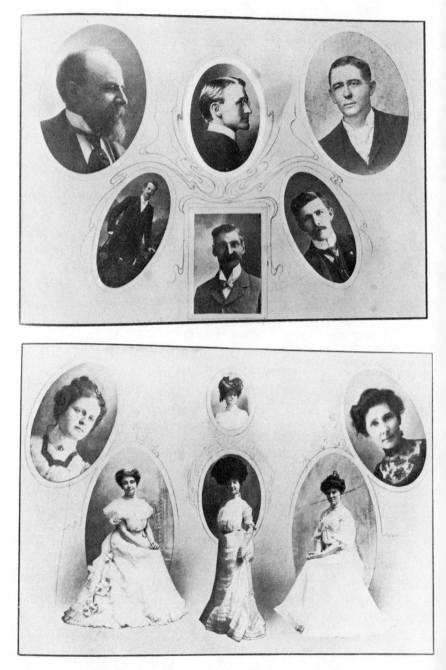

Members of the Faculty in 1903.

BOYD ASHBY WISE
Professor of Latin, 1913–1916
Phi Beta Kappa and Ph.D. degree from
Johns Hopkins University. First member
of the faculty to hold the Ph.D. degree.

FREDERICK HARWOOD
Professor and Head of the Music Conservatory, 1913–1946. A pianist of national reputation, Harwood served eight
presidents.

BENJAMIN SMITH FOSTER and the Chair used by him for forty years. Professor of English and Bible, he also taught a wealth of other subjects and served as Bursar, Registrar, and Dean of the Faculty. A member of the faculty from 1908 until 1925, he was affectionately known as the "Grand Old Man of Henderson" and was the only inservice professor to ever receive the Doctor of Laws degree from the College's Board of Trustees.

ROBERT THOMAS PROCTOR Professor of Latin, History, and Greek, 1907–1949. Phi Beta Kappa, University of Chicago, he was Registrar from 1918 until 1949 and often served as coach of the junior varsity football team.

Top—The first Reddie Football team to win the coveted State Championship. Coach Haygood wearing his Vanderbilt sweater is the first person (Left) on the second row.

Bottom—A picture of the 1922 Turkey Day classic between the Henderson Reddies and the Ouachita Tigers. The games between the two rival colleges began in 1907.

Top   A view of College Hall shortly after construction in 1915. The building
was razed in 1964.
Bottom   The First Goodloe Hall. Built in 1920 on the site now occupied by
Haygood Gym, the building burned in 1928.

THE JAMES E. BARKMAN HOUSE.

Built in 1860, it was the home of Trustee Walter E. Barkman and is now the Panhellenic House.

gravely embarrassed by the heavy indebtedness incurred in constructing and furnishing them and was in need of a minimum $110,000 to survive.[4] Accepting this challenge, Workman began what was to be an eleven-year administration, the second longest of the Methodist years and the third longest to date.

His wife, Elizabeth Thornburgh, was a native Arkansan and held the Bachelor of Arts degree from Galloway College.[5] Highly respected by the students and townspeople, she graciously presided over numerous social and civic affairs and throughout her husband's tenure filled the chair of religious education (Sunday school teacher's training). From 1924 to 1926 she was also dean of women.[6] The Workmans were parents of six children, three girls and three boys. Their sons all graduated from the school; and one, James Warthen, later followed in his father's footsteps as president of Henderson-Brown College.[7]

Shortly after assuming office, President Workman convinced Trustee the Reverend Evans, chairman of the executive committee and the school's field agent, to resign his pastorate of the Arkadelphia Methodist Church so that he could devote his entire livelihood to the college's pressing needs. The following summer (July, 1916), the Reverend Evans, President Workman, Bishop James H. McCoy, and the educational secretary of the Southern Methodist Church conducted a two-week campaign. For the first time, statewide sympathy for Henderson-Brown College was aroused.[8] The Reverend Evans' efforts were achieving worthy ends when terminated by his sudden death, May 23, 1917.[9] Again, Workman found himself in charge of the financial straits until another leader could be obtained.

Through coincidence, the president secured Evans' successor. The Reverend James E. Congdon, pastor of the Presbyterian Church, Benton, then doing field work for the Red Cross, came to Arkadelphia to meet with President Workman in an effort to organize a local chapter. Workman's influence, however, led Congdon to assist in the fund raising campaign for the college. It was this noted Presbyterian minister who was solely responsible for amassing more than $38,000 in only three days for the Methodist institution.[10]

In 1916 H. Grady Smith, another man long associated with the financial affairs of the college, became bursar. With exception of a leave for military duty during World War I, he gave forty-nine years of valuable service as business manager and in 1938 also served as acting president. Two years following his 1965 retirement, his abilities and knowledge of the institution were called upon again when he was appointed to the board of trustees, a position he held until 1974. The first campus building costing more than one million dollars, a high rise dormitory, was named in his honor in 1966.[11]

Despite the accomplishments of the Reverend Evans and the Reverend Congdon, the financial situation remained critical, and legal action against the college was in the formulative stages. When the Little Rock Conference met in December, 1917, Bishop E. D. Mouzon called upon Trustee Robert W. Huie, Jr., an Arkadelphia attorney who that year had succeeded his father as a member of the board, to inform the delegation of the impending crisis. Huie stated that $56,000 of the debt incurred from the rebuilding program had been secured by a first mortgage; but that the balance of $60,000 was unsecured; that a contractor's suit had been filed; and that postponement had been granted for the final time. He further noted that unless cash in the amount of $110,000 were on hand by April 4, 1918, judgment would be entered and the property placed for sale by the sheriff. If this transpired, the college would be sold for the mortgage value, and the balance would become a debt against the conference.[12] Bishop Mouzon implored the conference to save the school and persuaded the young lawyer to accept the responsibility of conducting the campaign to raise the necessary money.[13] Attorney Huie arranged for a ninety-day absence from his office and enlisted the aid of the Reverend Congdon for the same period.[14] In brief, between January 31, and April 1, 1918, these men succeeded in securing from more than four thousand people a total of $125,000 in subscriptions, and of that amount collected over $100,000 in cash.[15] Two years later, the appreciative trustees conferred the Doctor of Divinity degree upon Calvinist crusader Congdon in recognition of his Christian service in overcoming the crisis.[16] They also incorporated into their minutes a resolution of thanks to Trustee Robert W. Huie, Jr., for his faithful labors in the campaign.[17]

The year that the college suffered its disastrous fire and was all but lost by the Little Rock Conference, the 1914 General Conference of the Methodist Episcopal Church, South, was likewise confronted with a serious educational dilemma: its relationship with Vanderbilt University. The Nashville institution, founded by Southern Methodism in 1872, had been the most potent force in the educational awakening of the post-bellum South and had enriched Henderson-Brown College from its beginning in 1890 by numerous teachers and administrators who had been educated there. That year, however, Vanderbilt University became independent of the church; and the General Conference directed that Arkansas Methodism, one of Vanderbilt's original supporters, adopt the recently established Southern Methodist University as its connectional university.[18]

At that same session, the General Conference on petition from the conferences themselves authorized the merger of Arkansas and White River Conferences and thus restored the Arkansas Episcopal area to its 1854 status of only two annual conferences. The new administrative unit assumed a name appropriate for its geographical position, North Arkansas Conference.[19]

With alleviation of the recent financial crisis, friends of Henderson-Brown College, realizing it imperative to obtain support of all Arkansas Methodism, urged the trustees to negotiate immediately with the North Arkansas Conference and offer them the college as joint property and responsibility.[20] The trustees agreed to tender co-ownership of "their" college, provided that no restrictions be placed upon its sovereignty nor their prerogative to operate it as a college "of whatever grade and classification they may deem advisable." [21] Following deliberations, the North Arkansas Conference proposed to accept on condition that it be allowed to name seven trustees. The existing board conceded this point; and by unanimous vote, November 28, 1920, Henderson-Brown College achieved acceptance from the other conference.[22] Financially the college benefited from joint ownership, for in 1921 both conferences assessed themselves $4,000 each for the Arkadelphia institution, and from 1922 forward $5,000 each; [23] thus until 1929 the combined efforts of Arkansas Methodism operated three degree-granting institutions.

Henderson-Brown College's charter was duly amended to state that the board would consist of fifteen members: seven to be appointed by each conference and one, appointed by the Alumni Association, to be confirmed by both conferences. This revision permitted retention of only seven members of the existing board, and the election of their successors was that body's final action. On March 1, 1921, the school took unto itself a new board of trustees. From the previous membership there remained W. E. Barkman, H. C. Couch, C. C. Henderson, R. W. Huie, Jr., and the Reverends J. L. Cannon, R. W. McKay, and J. A. Sage. The North Arkansas Conference's representatives were the Reverend J. J. Galloway, the Reverend J. H. O'Bryant, W. P. Jones, W. T. Martin, Will Pyles, T. Y. Ramsey, and J. P. Womack,[24] who later became the first state president of the institution. Through the alumni's appointment of Leslie Goodloe, member and secretary of the board since 1914,[25] the Little Rock Conference retained the majority of the trustees.

From its creation in 1890 the board of trustees had always had prominent ministers among its number, and its lay membership roll often read much like a "who's who" in Arkansas financial circles. The new board maintained this tradition. Charles Christopher Henderson, trustee since 1891 and chairman from 1903, continued in that position, although he had moved to El Paso, Texas, in 1913 to assume additional banking responsibilities. In failing health, at age seventy-two, he resigned his office in 1922, but remained a trustee until his death, June 4, 1923. At that time, the board incorporated into its record a fitting resolution in memory of the man who had been a namesake and savior of the college.[26]

Harvey C. Couch, member of the board since 1916, replaced Henderson as chairman and held the position until the state assumed control.[27] Born August 21, 1877, the son of a Methodist minister, Couch became Arkansas' utility magnate, and perhaps did more than any other person in bringing to the state the conveniences and comforts of modern civilization. Sensing that the future of the state lay in and that a fortune could be made from utilities, he instituted telephone service to rural communities in Arkansas and Louisiana and built the first hydro-electric plant in the state. He sold the former to Southwestern Bell Telephone Company and while residing in Arkadelphia developed the latter into Arkansas Power and Light Company. Before his election as chairman of the college's board, he was president of his own company and like ones in Mississippi and Louisiana, chairman of the board of Louisiana Gas and Fuel Corporation, and a vice-president of the Southwestern Division, National Electric Association. He was a director of the Chase National Bank of New York and of numerous ones in Arkansas. A Mason and Methodist, he was also a trustee of George Peabody College for Teachers and Arkansas State Teachers College (State College of Arkansas).[28] Without question, his position on the board added prestige to Henderson-Brown College.

Among other noteworthy appointments to the board were those

of lumber giants Adam Trieschman (1917–1923), his brother John W. (1925–1929), and Fred Dierks (1926–1929). Two other appointees were Harmon Liverwright Remmel (1905–1911) and his wife, Elizabeth Cameron (1926). Remmel, one of the foremost businessmen and financiers of Arkansas, was associated with Couch in developing hydro-electricity; and the oldest such dam in the state, located on the Ouachita River approximately twenty-five miles north of Arkadelphia, bears his name. It was his influence as a Republican which had earlier brought United States President Taft to Arkadelphia.[29] Mrs. Remmel, of prominent New York background and an active member and supporter of the Methodist Church and its charities, holds the distinction of being the only woman ever to serve on the board during the church era; in fact, she was the first woman to serve as a trustee of any Arkansas college.[30]

The trustees' concern for capitalism and its future during the "Red Scare" of the twenties was evidenced when they directed that "the president shall from time to time have lectures by big businessmen of the state before the student body." The first address was delivered by former Trustee Remmel. He praised the opportunities for economic and social mobility found within the American system, and commented that he had personally known eight presidents of the United States and had entertained two, Theodore Roosevelt and William Howard Taft, in his Arkansas home.[31] Likewise, the professional interests of the lay members of the board were evident in their recommendation that beginning in fall of 1926 the science department would add reforestation to its course offerings.[32] The catalogues for 1926 and succeeding years, however, do not indicate that the course was instituted.

Mindful that the first obligation of the college was to provide quality education, the trustees and the presidents worked endlessly to achieve that goal. Since the curriculum had been made to conform to first-class criteria in 1909, concerns from that time centered on strengthening and expanding the existing program. During Crowell's four-year administration (1911–1914), only minor changes occurred. Total hours for graduation increased from sixty to sixty-four, and the Bachelor of Science degree, which had been abolished in 1908, was reinstituted in 1912.[33] With return of the science degree program, requirements for the Bachelor of Arts degree were altered; interestingly, requisites for men and women differed. The girls were required three hours fewer of math but had to take nine hours of domestic science (home economics), resulting in the allowance of only eighteen elective hours for women but twenty-four for men. In 1915 these changes were revised so that degree requirements would be the same for both sexes.[34]

New courses were begun, and others dropped. In 1912 sociology was added to the social sciences;[35] the following year, two new departments appeared: pedagogy (education) and home economics. The department of pedagogy was the organization of the teachers' course into a systematic approach. Home economics, taught from the first year of the college as special courses under such names as fancy cooking, domestic science, and domestic art, was divided into two areas of concentration: cooking and sewing.[36] In 1923, however, this department, along with the art department, was abolished by the trustees, the stated reason being that these funds were needed to strengthen the literary offerings.[37] Courses in modern languages were expanded in 1918 to include Spanish,[38] and from time to time Italian was also taught. In 1920 the first assault on the classical languages occurred. Although four years of Latin remained required, a student could no longer offer Greek as his second language. For this requirement he had to render either four years' study of one modern language or two years each in two. And from 1920, catalogues carried the statement that Greek would be taught only if student demands merited it.[39] Beginning in 1923, students pursuing the Bachelor of Science degree were no longer required study in any foreign language.[40] (In 1973 the Division of Sociology in the School of Education began offering an alternate plan for the Bachelor of Arts degree allowing students the option of a foreign language or twelve hours of directed studies.)

In addition to the Bachelor of Arts and Bachelor of Science degrees, in 1921 two new degrees were granted: Bachelor of Music and Bachelor of Oratory.[41] Institution of these programs marked academic acceptance of two departments which had been a part of the curriculum since the founding of the college. Though in the early years these areas were non-literary, in 1905 and 1906 respectively, music and elocution began their emergence into academic echelons when work in the two was accepted toward the Bachelor of Arts degree.[42] In 1912 the school of fine arts, consisting of art, elocution, and music, was organized, and in 1921 the degree programs in the latter two were offered. It was in this area that the school obtained membership in its first national scholastic fraternity. On October 27, 1923, a chapter of Phi Kappa Delta, an honorary society in recognition of high standards in forensics, was installed, the first for any Arkansas college.[43] And students pursuing the Bachelor of Music degree were required to pass the State Music Teachers Examination.[44] In 1924 weekly programs from the conservatory were broadcast over station W.O.K., courtesy of Chairman Couch's Arkansas Power and Light Company.[45]

Another expansion of the curriculum, one that was to become a permanent feature of the college, also began in 1921 when the first summer school opened in June of that year. Although I. W. Saunders had established a summer school in 1896, it was a private enterprise of the professor and its courses of study were business alone. From time to time teachers' courses and "preacher's institutes" had also been held, but in 1921 summer school became a coherent part of the educational program. Under the direction of Professor Benjamin S. Foster, the first session began June 3. A faculty of seven offered courses in art, English, history, Latin, mathematics, philosophy, science, and music (piano, violin, theory).[46] (The summer school functions today as an integral part of the college.)

To emphasize the religious character of the school and to honor retiring Professor Foster for his seventeen-year service, the longest in the Methodist era, in June, 1925, the trustees established the Benjamin Smith Foster Chair of Bible,[47] the only endowed chair in the school's history. To arouse interest in and support for the $50,000 endowment campaign, the college published two brochures: *The Bible and the Schools* and *Doctor Benjamin S. Foster: A Great Teacher.* An anonymous friend offered $25,000 toward the goal, provided that the church match his pledge. To meet this challenge, Bishop Sam R. Hay and seventy-five ministers, meeting on the campus September 15, 1925, announced that a public offering would be taken October 4 in the Methodist congregations throughout the state.[48] This collection provided only slightly more than $15,000, but before the year's end, the challenger's gift had been bestowed upon the fund. Ironically, the chair established to perpetuate Bible study lasted but three years, for it was abolished when the state assumed control, although courses in Bible were taught from time to time until the fall of 1935.[49]

Significant additions to the faculty and staff complemented the curricular improvements. With few exceptions they constituted one-man departments, and hosts of students bear witness to their broad and deep educational and cultural philosophies. All are remembered as teachers of extraordinary influence, but a number of them deserve more than passing reference, for they made the college their careers and provided continuity from the Methodist years well into the state years.

In 1911, the year that the school became Henderson-Brown College, Mary Sue Mooney joined the faculty and taught until her retirement in 1944, serving under six presidents. A native of Tennessee, she held the Master of Arts degree from Bellevue Collegiate Institute and the Master of Laws degree from Memphis Conference Female Institute. Throughout her tenure she taught English and sometimes mathematics, and from time to time she was dean of women. In unprecedented action the trustees adopted a resolution in 1919 recognizing Miss Mooney as a valuable asset to the college, emphasizing her strong influence as a Christian example in building character among the women students. While teaching in the school she continued her own studies at the University of Chicago and also received the Bachelor of Science degree in 1925 and the Master of Arts degree in 1928 from George Peabody College. A contribution of her scholarship was the editing of the life and reviews of her friend, Mary Noailles Murfree, the noted Tennessee local colorist who wrote under the penname Charles Egbert Craddock. In 1933 a women's dormitory, the first building erected after state assumption, was named in her honor, and when the college observed its semicentennial in 1940, the commemorative volume published for the occasion was dedicated to her.[50]

There were two others who served the English department; both were graduates of the institution. An alumnus of the class of 1913, Percy Winfield Turrentine assumed his post as assistant professor in 1920. Having studied at Harvard University for three years (1914–1917), receiving the Master of Arts degree in 1917, he returned to his alma mater where he remained for thirty-four years, most of that time as head of the department. He later received the Doctor of Philosophy degree in English from Harvard; upon his retirement in 1954, the trustees made him professor emeritus of English.[51] Professor Turrentine was further honored in 1960 when a new residence hall was given his name. In 1925 one of his former students was appointed assistant in English. Ellen Boulware Martin (Ohls), a member of the class of 1921, had received the Bachelor of Arts and the Bachelor of Oratory degrees and had done graduate work at the University of Oklahoma; she later received the

Master of Arts degree from Tulane University. In the final years of her tenure, she was alumni secretary; after forty-two years of recurrent employment at the institution, she retired in 1967.[52]

In the foreign languages the tradition of effective teaching was continued by David Porter Holmes and Mildred Sherrod. Teacher of Latin and French, Holmes came in 1920; he held the Bachelor of Arts degree from the University of Arkansas and the Master of Arts degree from the University of Chicago. With Holmes' retirement as assistant professor of languages, following twenty-eight years at the college,[53] Latin's prominence decreased and within ten years that language was dropped from the curriculum.[54] Mildred Sherrod joined the faculty in 1923 as assistant professor of French. Born in Tuscumbia, Alabama, she received the Bachelor of Arts degree from Athens College and the Master of Arts from Tulane University and studied at the University of Dijon and under private tutors in Paris. Maintaining her studies and seeking to improve her classroom techniques, she spent several summers in study at various prominent American universities. When she became professor emeritus in 1966, she ended a notable career of thirty-five years at the Arkadelphia institution.[55]

In 1913, one year following the organization of the school of fine arts, Frederick Harwood came to head the conservatory of music. He occupied that position for thirty-three years, during which time he served eight presidents until his retirement in 1946. Born in Lehi, Utah, February 1, 1880, he entered the University of Michigan at the age of fourteen and studied for three years; he then attended Combs' Broad Street Conservatory, Philadelphia, and earned the Bachelor of Music degree. Having studied under renowned teachers in the United States, he spent the year before coming to Henderson-Brown College in France studying under Isador Phillipp, director of the Paris Conservatory. A pianist of national reputation and a composer of note, in 1928 he was elected to the National Music Advisory Board and employed to teach for several years in the summer sessions of the Chicago Conservatory.[56] He brought with him his wife, Dora Sellard, a graduate of Hardin College (New Mexico) and his former pupil; she taught violin until her retirement in 1959.[57] Together, this distinguished couple gave the college seventy-nine years of first-rate music instruction. In 1933 the honorary Doctor of Music degree was conferred upon each of them by the Bouguslawzki School of Music, Chicago.[58] Under Harwood's direction the music conservatory came to be recognized as perhaps the most distinguished part of the college. Interestingly, at times during the Methodist years Harwood's salary exceeded the president's, for he not only received a fixed income but also fifty percent of the fees paid by his piano students.[59]

The music conservatory's faculty increased as did its enrollment, and in the final year of church administration it numbered six. Among them were two women, both teachers of piano and both graduates of the college with the Bachelor of Music degree. Lois Smith (nee McNabb) who had also studied at Bush Conservatory, Chicago, and other music schools came in 1923. Wife of Bursar H. Grady Smith, she headed the music department from 1950 to her retirement in 1969.[60] The forty-six year services of Dora Harwood and Lois Smith currently stand as the longest unbroken tenures in the classrooms of the school. In fall, 1928, Mae Whipple who had received the Bachelor of Music degree in 1927 and the Bachelor of Arts degree in 1928 from Henderson-Brown College, began instruction in piano. She later studied at Chicago Musical College and Julliard and earned the Master of Music degree from Gunn School of Music and the Master of Arts degree from Columbia University. A charming lady of perpetual youth, Mae Whipple, with her forty-five years of service, is the senior professor. Her eighteen trans-Atlantic crossings constitute another record for the faculty.[61]

Olin Eli McKnight came to the chair of education in 1924. Born in Alabama, he had earned the Bachelor of Science degree from George Peabody College in 1916 and the Master of Arts degree in 1920 from Columbia University. Before coming to Arkadelphia, he held positions in the public schools of his native state and taught at Birmingham-Southern College; when elected to the Henderson-Brown College faculty, he was holding the chair of education at Millsaps College.[62] McKnight, who advanced to full professor in 1948, became increasingly interested in Arkansas history. He was author and co-author of several textbooks currently used in the public schools system; among them are: *A History of Development of Arkansas*, *Living in Arkansas*, *The Arkansas Story*, and *A History of Arkansas*. An active member of the faculty for thirty years, he was director of teacher placement at the time of his death in 1955.[63]

Since the founding of the college the department of science had consisted of only one man. In 1920 that position was filled by Charles Aylmer Evans who had earned the Bachelor of Arts and Doctor of Medicine degrees from Vanderbilt University in 1897 and 1902 respectively and had done additional graduate work at Tulane University. From 1902 until 1916 he practiced medicine, but in 1916 he entered the teaching profession. During his first year at Henderson-Brown College he taught astronomy, biology, botany, chemistry, geology, and physics, and was also in charge of the premedical course instituted in 1919.[64] A respected member of the faculty for twenty-one years, he retired in 1942 with the rank of professor emeritus.[65] To honor him, "one of Henderson's great teachers," a classroom building erected in 1951 was named Charles Aylmer Evans Hall.

In his second year, Professor Evans was joined by Matt Locke Ellis, valedictorian of the class of 1921. Following a summer's study at Southern Methodist University, he returned as assistant in science, teaching physics for two years. But Ellis' real interest was philosophy; and the young Arkansan, who had been born in 1901, spent the next ten years alternately teaching at the college and continuing his graduate study in that field at Yale University, receiving both the Master of Arts (1925) and the Doctor of Philosophy (1933) degrees. From 1933 to 1935 he was professor of philosophy in the new Henderson State Teachers College, and in 1934 was named dean. The following year he departed to become professor of philosophy and director of the library at Hendrix College. In 1941 he was recalled to the institution as president, the position he held until 1945 when he was elected president of Hendrix College. Fulfilling that office until 1958, he resigned to resume teaching philosophy there; he remained active in that capacity until 1972. A productive scholar, he is author of numerous publications, including *The Idea of God in the Philosophy of Aristotle* and *John Dewey's Theory of Value*. His leadership was recognized in 1950 when he became the first Arkansan to be president of the North Central Association of Colleges and Secondary Schools.[66] Student and professor at the Methodist college; professor at, and dean and president of its state successor; professor at, and president of the merged Methodist institutions: his career covers the gamut of Henderson State College's history.

Improvement of the library, necessary for development of a first-class college, did not keep pace with the progress of the faculty. The library was housed first in one room and then three in College Hall; like the dining hall, it maintained separate areas for men and women. Until 1920 there was no card catalogue.[67] In 1921 Mrs. Robert W. Huie, Jr., the college's first professionally trained librarian, was employed. She had been a student at Baylor University and the University of Arkansas and had done special library work at the University of Illinois.[68] Laboring under difficult odds, Mrs. Huie competently guided the library from 1921 to 1933, the period of its first extensive expansion. She adopted the

Dewey classification system, and on October 5, 1921, the first book, Carl L. Becker's *The Beginnings of the American People*, was acessioned.[69]

As early as 1909 appeals had been made for individuals to "just give a book," but the decade of the twenties saw the first major efforts to increase the holdings. Several valuable private collections were donated, among them those of the Reverend Thomas D. Scott, the Reverend Charles F. Evans, and the Honorable George Thornburgh.[70] In 1925 Mrs. Huie organized a drive to obtain ten dollars each from five hundred people to make purchases.[71] The most unusual gift came from the class of 1925 who bought a $5,000 insurance policy on the life of the class president, Dallas Dalton, and made the library the beneficiary.[72] Also beginning in 1925, the trustees made yearly appropriations of $2,150 to the library.[73] Although during the decade of the twenties the library holdings were increased nearly threefold, from approximately 3,500 to almost 10,000 volumes, they were still considerably below the 1920 national average of 42,000. While nearly one-third of America's colleges failed to meet this standard, the school could take little comfort, for almost all were Southern institutions. Throughout the thirty-nine Methodist sessions, the library was substandard and remained inadequate to meet the needs of quality education; yet in Arkansas only the holdings of the state university and Hendrix College surpassed those of Henderson-Brown College.[74]

The name McLauchlan had early fallen into disuse, and when the school moved into its first library building in 1934, the name Huie was given to it. Fittingly, the name honored the family, as well as the woman, for Huie appeared on the trustees' roll from beginning to end of the Methodist era. (In 1968 Huie Library occupied its third building, a one million-dollar facility, and in 1973 contained some 140,000 bound volumes.)

Although no institution in the state held membership in a regional accrediting association, the college attempted to keep abreast

of its neighbors and constantly strove toward accreditation. Therefore, in May, 1920, the Arkansas college presidents met and, in
accordance with the requirements for obtaining membership in
the Southern Association of Colleges and Secondary Schools,
agreed upon the following seventeen requirements as the criteria
for being a standard college in Arkansas:

1. Entrance requirements.—Entrance requirements should be
not less than 15 standard high-school units as defined in the by-
laws of the Southern Association of Colleges.

2. Required for graduation.—The completion of college work
amounting to not less than fifteen 60-minute class periods per
week through four years of 36 weeks each.

3. Number of degrees.—The conferring of a multiplicity of
degrees should be discouraged. Small institutions should confine
themselves to one or two. When more than one baccalaureate degree is offered all should be equal in requirements for admission
and for graduation. Institutions of limited resources should confine themselves to undergraduate work.

4. Number of college departments.—The college should maintain at least eight separate departments in liberal arts and sciences,
with not less than one professor devoting his whole time to each
department. This shall be effective after 1920–21. Seven may be
allowed till that time.

5. Training of the faculty.—A properly qualified faculty should
consist entirely of graduates of standard colleges, and each head
of a department should hold at least a master's degree from a
university having a fully organized graduate school. Graduate
study and training in research equivalent to that required for the
Ph.D. degree are urgently recommended.

6. Salaries.—The average salary paid to members of the faculty
is an important consideration in determining the standing of an
institution.

7. Number of classroom hours per teacher.—Not more than
18 hours per week should be required of any teacher, 15 being
recommended as the maximum.

8. Number of students in classes.—The number of students in

a recitation or laboratory section should be limited to 30. A smaller number is desirable.

9. Support.—In addition to income from tuition fees, room rent, boarding halls, etc., the college should have a productive endowment of not less than $200,000, or its equivalent in assured annual income.

10. Library.—The library should contain, exclusive of public documents and periodicals, at least 5,000 volumes bearing specifically upon the subjects taught, and should have an appropriation of not less than $500 a year for permanent additions. The library should contain 7,000 volumes two years from the present time [May 5, 1920].

11. Laboratories.—The laboratory equipment should be sufficient for all the experiments called for by the courses offered in the sciences—sufficiency to be measured by the value of apparatus and equipment.

12. Separation of college and academy.—The college may not maintain a preparatory school as part of its college organization. In case such a school is maintained under the college charter, it must be kept rigidly distinct and separate from the college in students and faculty.

13. No subfreshman work.—The college may not maintain or provide for any classes except those for which college credit can be given in a degree schedule.

14. Proportion of regular college students to the whole student body.—At least 18 per cent of the students in a college should be pursuing courses leading to baccalaureate degrees in arts and science. The classification of students must be printed in the catalogue.

15. General statement concerning material equipment.—The location and construction of the buildings, the lighting, heating, and ventilation of the rooms, the nature of the laboratories, corridors, closets, water supply, school furniture, apparatus, and methods of cleaning shall be such as to insure hygienic conditions for both students and teachers.

16. General statement concerning curriculum and spirit of administration.—The character of the curriculum, the efficiency of instruction, the scientific spirit, the standard for regular degrees,

the conservatism in granting honorary degrees, and the tone of the institution shall also be factors in determining its standing.

17. Standing in the educational world.—The institution must be able to prepare its students to enter recognized schools as candidates for advanced degrees.[75]

At the request of the Arkansas Board of Education, a representative from the United States Bureau of Education made inspections of all the state's higher institutions for the purpose of determining those which could satisfy the above standards. Resultantly, Henderson-Brown College, along with four others—University of Arkansas, Hendrix College, Little Rock College, Ouachita Baptist College—was acknowledged as a college of the highest classification, or "A" grade. The four colleges were then accredited by the University of Arkansas.[76] In 1922 the school appeared on the Bureau of Education's compiled list of class "A" colleges.[77] The lack of sufficient endowment became the fundamental difficulty in maintaining this recently acquired recognition and for achieving acceptance into either the Southern or North Central association or approval from Southern Methodism's General Board of Education for first-class status.

Determined to achieve these goals, the trustees in their regular meeting in March, 1923, authorized a $400,000 campaign: $300,000 to be invested as endowment; $100,000 to be used to construct two buildings, a science hall and a library.[78] In pursuance of this plan, President Workman and Board Chairman Couch journeyed to New York City where they made application to the General Education Board (a John D. Rockefeller philanthropy) for a grant of $75,000, on condition that the college raise $225,000.[79] On their return, the trustees launched a state-wide campaign, dividing the state into ten districts; the headquarters of each area was managed by noted Methodist businessmen who were assisted by alumni. In June, 1924, the trustees contracted a professional fund raising organization in Chicago to control the project from

September 26 through December 31. Conducted under the slogan
"Serve and Save Henderson-Brown College," the campaign assumed a more emotional aura when Edward F. Trefz, former assistant to Herbert Hoover and first field secretary of the United
States Chamber of Commerce, toured the districts in the college's
behalf, passionately appealing to his audiences to choose "Bolshevism or Christianity." [80] The most concentrated effort was made
when all Arkansas Methodist businessmen were called upon to
devote the week of December 7 to the cause.[81] The largest single
contribution, $20,000, came from former Trustee Remmel; the
next, $10,000, from John W. Trieschman, soon-to-be trustee; and
plagued Arkadelphians gave in excess of $35,000.[82] But by the
closing date, the quota was still short by approximately $20,000,
and the deadline was extended one month until February 1, 1925.[83]
The extension period was directed by Trustee the Reverend J. J.
Galloway, who had been named executive secretary (financial
agent) of the college in 1922. Through his extensive letter campaign, within seventeen days an additional $20,000 was received.[84]
And by the end of the period the college, which but a few months
earlier had been without one cent of endowment, could boast one
of nearly one quarter of a million dollars. Five days later, President
Workman exuberantly proclaimed that Southern Methodism's
General Board of Education had granted the college class "A"
standing.[85] And two milestones in the college's history were realized.

Another advance toward obtaining membership in an accrediting
association was the abolition of the preparatory high school. This
action was finalized in May, 1925, when the academy, a feature
of the school since the opening session, was discontinued.[86] In the
fall of 1928 the dean of the graduate school of the University of
Arkansas, representing the North Central Association, recommended Henderson-Brown College for membership in that body,

but the school was only placed on the approved list, and full membership was not achieved until 1934.[87]

During the first years of Workman's administration the world was preoccupied with World War I, and although President Woodrow Wilson had enjoined neutrality upon the nation, one who peruses the Henderson-Brown College campus records and journals of 1914, 1915, and 1916 must be struck by total absence of reference to the conflict. By and large, the average Henderson student seems to have simply disregarded the events, but when the United States entered into the war in spring of 1917, this attitude changed severely and student editorials endorsed entry into the European confrontation.[88] Correspondingly, the campus assumed a military-like character when the trustees established a voluntary training unit.[89] In fall of 1918 the War Department replaced it with a Student Army Training Corps (S.A.T.C.) divided into two sections; collegiate and vocational, the former composed of collegiate students and the latter of non-collegiate personnel, some as young as nine years old. As privates in the army, the S.A.T.C. students received thirty dollars a month, room, board, tuition, and books. They were placed under strict military routine and were restricted to the campus except from Saturday noon until Sunday night.[90]

This program, which offered financial assistance, opened the doors of higher education to many Arkansas men; noteworthy among them was John Roy Steelman, who later became chief assistant to President Harry S. Truman. Steelman entered Henderson-Brown College in 1918 and was graduated with the Bachelor of Arts degree in 1922. Called to Washington, D.C., by the Franklin D. Roosevelt Administration, he advanced to the position of special advisor to President Truman. He refused an appointment as Secretary of Labor; nevertheless, as coordinator of White House operations, he was the only non-Secretary to attend Cabinet meetings and was regarded by some to be, if not in name at least in fact, Vice-President of the United States. Although Steelman progressed only to the rank of corporal in the S.A.T.C., the program provided him with the initial education that carried him to the White House as a key personality in both the Roosevelt and Truman administrations.[91]

In December following the Armistice, the S.A.T.C. unit was demobilized, but the collegiate group was maintained through May, 1919. Announcement was made that a voluntary Reserve Officers' Training Corps (R.O.T.C.) unit would be established. An army officer was assigned to Henderson-Brown College for the 1919–1920 term to organize and train such a group, provided one hundred physically fit male students would enroll.[92] Apparently this condition was not met, for it was not until 1936 that the college had a R.O.T.C. unit, when a compulsory program was begun. In 1972, however, the program was made voluntary.

The real effect of the World War was felt with the departure of 181 students, former students, and faculty members to the regular armed forces; volunteer or draftee, they were accorded the same recognition by the college.[93] Five students—Jerry Collins, Jesse Joyner, Robert Jackson, Jack Tidball, and Murray Moore— and a former football coach, James Crow, gave their lives, and on February 3, 1920, Henderson-Brown College honored her dead with an unusual memorial. Following a religious service, the student body assembled on the campus where they heard a former student and professor, Farrar Newberry, proclaim, "We build a memorial not of stone, not of bronze, but of the living tree—and this is symbolic of the service they performed for Henderson, France, and the world." [94] A tribute was paid to each of the six with the planting of that number of holly trees in a circle on the front lawn. Each tree was consigned a caretaker: four to the college classes, and one each to the academy and faculty.[95] This simple tribute prompted inquiry from the American Forestry Association, and the memorial trees were registered by that organization on its national honor roll.[96]

The students and faculty alike voiced concern for a lasting peace. President Workman and Professor Foster both made speeches advocating that the Versailles Treaty with its League of Nations be accepted without compromise. The student body overwhelmingly voted in the League's favor, with only one vote rejecting it, when they participated in the national intercollegiate referendum.[97] Professor Foster's son, Benjamin, was presented to Belgium's King Albert I in Washington, D.C., and the Henderson-Brown Y.M.C.A. later gave fifty dollars toward reconstruction in the king's country.[98]

Surprisingly the war years had no adverse effect on enrollment. Instead, the number of students increased to the extent that by the end of Workman's tenth year it had almost tripled, increasing from 135 in 1914–1915, to 255 in 1917–1918, to 310 (403 including the S.A.T.C.) in 1918–1919, to 341 in 1924–1925.[99]

One very pressing problem confronting the college was its physical plant which was inadequate for the growth envisioned by the trustees. In special session in December, 1919, the executive committee, reviewing the imperative needs of the school, recommended a $585,000 master plan for expansion: two dormitories, a new music conservatory, a science building, a president's house, and a long sought heating plant and laundry. The plan was adopted and a motion carried that they borrow $200,000 to erect a men's dormitory and an addition to Key Hall.[100]

This somewhat ambitious proposal was modified, and on April 20, 1920, they borrowed $30,000 from former Trustee John S. Cargile to construct the men's residence hall.[101] The two-story dormitory was constructed from the three barracks which the United States government had built on the campuses of Ouachita Baptist and Henderson-Brown colleges to house the S.A.T.C. participants. The trustees purchased the buildings, removed the two from Ouachita Baptist College to Henderson-Brown College, and joined the three units into one and veneered it with brick. This U-shaped structure was the college's first on-campus housing for men. It provided rooms for approximately one hundred, a library, and the college guest room.[102] Named in honor of the late Professor Goodloe,[103] it was located where Haygood Gymnasium presently stands and faced the recently completed "Broadway of America" transcontinental highway which separated the campus and the athletic field. (Reportedly Henderson-Brown College was the only college in the nation fronted by the highway.) A small infirmary cottage was built behind the new dormitory; a matron of "recognized ability" lived there and had charge of all who needed medical attention.[104] This arrangement continued intermittently until 1970 when the infirmary building was demolished.

In June, 1922, the trustees purchased the present southeast corner of the campus. The residence on that property was made into a home for the president, placing him in the shadow of the C. C. Henderson and W. E. Barkman mansions. (In 1936 this house was replaced with a new one constructed on the same location, which served until 1969 when the president occupied Homeplace. Now known as Henderson House, it is the college guest house and alumni headquarters.) The dwelling formerly occupied by President Workman was converted into a dormitory for senior girls and rechristened "Senior House." [105]

In April, 1923, Executive Secretary Galloway undertook a campaign to secure funds to build an addition to the music conservatory, by obtaining $1,000 contributions from various Arkansas towns.[106] The three-story brick annex to Key Hall was put into use in November, 1923; the dedication was held the following January, with members of the Key family present.[107] By coincidence the addition made the building resemble a key. With these improvements the value of the physical plant advanced to $335,-000.[108]

Complementing campus growth was the paving of city streets in 1926, bringing an end to perpetual dust and mud; the college financed the work on Henderson and Twelfth streets.[109] Also in 1926 the trustees granted Mrs. J. H. Bell permission to build an art building on campus and authorized that friends of the college be allowed to construct homes for professors on college property, such to be donated to the school.[110] Neither project was ever done, and no additional buildings were erected during the Methodist years.

The physical plant was augmented by acquisition of additional lands. The college acquired fifteen acres adjacent to and north of the original campus. These lands were used for orchards, vegetable gardens, pastures for the dairy herd and swine, and the poultry yard. The institution was the only one in the state, with exception of the agricultural schools, which supplied its tables from its own operations.[111] Because the spring session closed before harvest, the college maintained a canning factory which annually preserved more than three thousand gallons of fruits and vegetables. A small creamery provided dairy products.[112] By 1922 the financial status of the school made it feasible to discontinue maintenance of the cannery and creamery, and in June the trustees authorized President Workman and Executive Secretary Galloway to sell the dairy and swine herds and to rent out the pasture lands and barn.

The following year, former Trustee the Reverend Archelaus Turrentine deeded the college two acres adjacent to the north side of the campus and granted the school option to purchase his home-place when offered for sale.[113] The Reverend Turrentine, father of Professor Percy Turrentine, had served the college as trustee for a quarter of a century (1896–1921), voluntarily retiring when the board was reorganized. Like other Methodist ministers, he lived in Arkadelphia so that he could give his nine children a college education.[114] The college was also named beneficiary in several wills and thus received additional properties in various Arkansas towns.

In 1925, the final year of Workman's administration, Executive Secretary Galloway was empowered to sell all lands belonging to, or coming to the college, except the campus proper, the revenues to be credited to the endowment.[115]

During the first twenty-eight years of the school the fees for tuition and room and board remained basically constant, but beginning in 1918 the trustees authorized increments that considerably increased these expenses. That year costs advanced from $190 to $270 for men and $290 for women, with tuition being $70; this increase of $20 in tuition was the first since the opening session in 1890.[116] In 1921 these fees rose to $349 for men and $369 for women, and in 1925 to $360 and $370 respectively, with total cost for the academic session of 1925–1926 in excess of $400.[117]

To aid in defraying the rising costs of attending Henderson-Brown College a number of scholarships and a substantial loan fund were made available. From 1912 through 1918, eighteen tuition scholarships were given annually, one to a worthy student in each of the districts of the Little Rock Conference, and from 1918 onward one to the honor graduate of any high school.[118] Also in 1912 the Federation of Women's Clubs provided a music scholarship to a young lady; beginning in 1914 the United Daughters of the Confederacy provided a similar one.[119] With joint ownership, the college offered free tuition to any minister; the children of all ministers, living or dead; and all preparing for any Orthodox Protestant ordination. This liberal policy was perhaps too enticing, for in 1926 the college was expending nearly $9,000 [120] for such out of its meager conference appropriations of $10,000! Although student loan funds had been made available by trustees and others from time to time none exceeded the $21,000 E. O. Hamon Memorial Loan Fund given in 1922 by W. N. Hamon of Morrilton, Arkansas. The conditions of the loan stated that no student could receive more than $200 in any one year and no more than $600.[121]

Students attending the college had accustomed themselves to the semester system; but in 1908 this plan was modified to a quarter system, two quarters replacing one semester.[122] By 1919 the calendar was revised to include three terms during the academic year: fall, winter, and spring; this system continued into the state years until 1934 when the semester plan was reinstituted.[123] Beginning in 1904 Thanksgiving was observed as a holiday and a two-week Christmas recess was instituted. In 1905 Washington's Birthday was added to the list; and from time to time May Day was also celebrated.

For one year, 1913–1914, a six-day work week was followed: classes met from 8:00 a.m. to 1:30 p.m.; study hours from 2:00 to 4:00 p.m.; physical activity, including athletic practice, from 4:00 to 6:00 p.m.; and the day ended with a half-hour chapel service at 9:00 p.m.[124] The next year, the work week returned to its former five-day agenda; classes met Tuesday through Saturday with Monday being a rest day.[125] Likewise, this schedule was maintained well into the state years.

But the students found time and energy to engage in activities other than their studies. One academically related involvement was the student newspaper. In January, 1920, the *Oracle* joined with four other school papers to form the College Press Association of Arkansas in an effort to raise the standard of journalism among the colleges.[126] The *Oracle* received praise outside the state, but cross-ravine rival Ouachita Baptist College charged that it was copying its *Signal*.[127] The Henderson-Brown College weekly's editor keenly refuted the accusation, emphasizing that the Methodist paper had never resorted to printing the Sunday school lesson nor long dissertations from church papers.[128] In 1919 an *Oracle* editorial scathingly attacked Trustee Couch's Arkansas Power and Light Company for its "wretched service." Its author remarked that "not being Bolsheviks we are too considerate to call the company a crooked gang of grafters," [129] and advocated that the college should return to its former private electric and water system.[130]

The effect of the editorial on the electric service is unknown, but when Trustee Couch opened his first hydro-electric dam, he hosted a picnic at the site, provided automobile transportation for the entire student body, and personally conducted the students on tours of the facility. This time the paper praised Couch and reminded all to go, pointing out that it could well be the only "Dam Picnic" they would ever attend with approval of the Methodist Church.[131]

The opera house became aware of competition from a new diversion sweeping America, the motion picture. In 1914 students and faculty attended the opening of the Royal Theatre, Arkadelphia's first movie house;[132] a successor by the same name provides their counterparts entertainment today. On Saturday night, May 7, 1920, the first movies were shown on the campus: *No Story* by O'Henry, *The Brook* by Tennyson, and a two-reel comedy. These first films were provided through the generosity of the college Sunday school, on the assumption that they were ushering in a new educational era.[133]

Greek letter fraternities had their origin in the United States during the period when the classics dominated the college curricula. By the decade of the twenties they were about all that remained to remind Henderson-Brown College students of the language which had earlier been a dominant influence in their school. In addition to the debate societies and scholastic groups, a number of Greek letter social organizations began to appear. In 1919 Tau Beta Chi Delta, for women, organized and by 1926 had been joined by four others: Delta Alpha Chi (1920), Eta Beta Phi (1922), Tau Eta Alpha, and Omega Zeta Omega.[134]

There were also other social clubs to gain one's attention. The children of former students formed the Son's and Daughter's Club, and students from the same home towns organized. The men who were not privileged to live in Goodloe Hall formed the "Inmates of the Barracks," named appropriately for their housing. Besides the various language clubs, there was a chess club for men and women.[135]

Following the opening of the college's first indoor basketball court in 1915, a men's round ball team was formed. The Reddies closed their first season against Arkansas College on the new court, suffering a 43–13 defeat. The *Oracle* defended the team's poor showing by pointing out that the players had all been accustomed to playing out-of-doors and would have to adjust to inside conditions.[136] In February, 1920, the facility was the scene of the first intercollegiate basketball tournament to be played in Arkansas. That the team had become accustomed to its court was seen when the Reddies reached the championship game. They lost to Little Rock College, but placed three out of the five on that first All Tournament team.[137] The sport grew in popularity, and in 1922 three hundred seats were added to the gymnasium, bringing the total seating capacity to seven hundred.[138] (In 1972 the college occupied its fourth gymnasium, a two million-dollar, 3,400-seat coliseum.) The track team continued to win honors, and in May, 1920, sophomore Elbert T. Moody hurled the discus 124 feet and 1 inch, 12 feet beyond the state record and within 12 feet of the world record.[139]

In one movement Henderson-Brown College was current: the football craze that had engulfed the nation. Then, as now, however, there was opposition to the sport. The issue was brought before the Little Rock Conference in 1913 where it was charged that football was too costly, encouraged profanity and gambling, and was a detriment to Christian education. The conference resolved: "That we recommend that the Trustees of the Colleges under our control abolish inter-collegiate football from our policy and practice," for it was bringing censure upon the church.[140] Resolutions or no resolutions, football upheld its position as the number one sport; and President Workman, an avid sports enthusiast who had played in the first rugby game in Arkansas, gave the teams personal encouragement during his eleven-year administration.[141]

In 1913, the year the Little Rock Conference condemned football, the Henderson-Brown Reddies played their most rigorous schedule. In October alone they opposed three university teams: Arkansas, Vanderbilt, and Mississippi. They suffered only a 3–0 defeat by the University of Arkansas; became the first Arkansas team to play Vanderbilt University but lost 33–0; and fell 7–2 to the University of Mississippi, when Ole Miss spent the weekend in Arkadelphia, playing both Henderson-Brown College and Ouachita Baptist College.[142] To the disappointment of football fans the game with Ouachita Baptist College initiated in 1907, was cancelled by Henderson-Brown College because the town rival was not a member of the Arkansas Athletic Association and therefore was not bound by eligibility rules.[143] The following year, the contest was resumed, and for the first time the Reddies did not win, but the teams did play to a scoreless tie.[144] The next year (1915) the Ouachita Tigers achieved their first victory by a score of 34–7.[145] Traditionally played on Thanksgiving Day, the "Battle of the Ravine" soon became the major collegiate sports attraction in Arkansas. The revenues from these events grew to equal, and sometimes surpass, annual conference appropriations.[146]

The following years saw little improvement in winnings, and the season of 1919 was dismal. In November of that year arch rivals Hendrix College and Ouachita Baptist College massacred the Reddies. Despite a high-spirited send-off by the co-eds who were allowed to march to the rail station unchaperoned, the team lost to Hendrix College, their oldest gridiron rival, 128–0 in Conway, failing to make a first down in the game. On Thanksgiving Day Ouachita delivered a 66–0 defeat.[147] Following the Hendrix game, Coach W. E. Watson was relieved of his duties, and President Workman persuaded former Coach James Haygood, who had resigned in 1911 but had aided his various successors from time to time, to return on a full-time basis.[148]

The playing field and grandstand had deteriorated as had the team, and for several years the Reddies had been using the Ouachita Baptist College stadium for home games. With Haygood's return, the executive committee purchased from Trustee W. E. Barkman ten acres including land which he had allowed the college to use for its athletic field since 1905.[149] The gridiron was relocated, and in September, 1921, Coach Haygood and his football proteges began constructing a new grandstand to seat seven hundred spectators. The new field was first used for the Thanksgiving Day game with Ouachita Baptist College.[150] Again the two colleges maintained separate football fields within yards of each other, an arrangement which persisted until the decade of the sixties when both fields were relocated, still within sight of each other. For some undisclosed reason, even today the colleges refuse to share a stadium though they never schedule conflicting home games.

Return of alumni to the campus in association with football began in 1920. At that time Coach Haygood encouraged former members of the "H" Club, an association formed in 1918 for men who had won the college letter in any sport, to come back to the campus for the annual Thanksgiving Day game with Ouachita Baptist College. By 1922 "Homecoming" in association with the sport was evolving into a tradition. The first football homecoming queen (sponsor, as the honoree was called in early years) was named in 1923. Zoe Frederica Mintern, known to her friends as "Fred," was selected by the team to represent them in the festivities. The selection of the maids was left to her discretion; diplomatically, she selected three girls from each of the rival literary organizations, Philomathean and Upsilon Phi. Miss Mintern was crowned in a special assembly and not on the field, a policy which has become a fifty-year-old tradition; however, the queen, wearing a borrowed fur coat, and her maids, wearing team sweaters, were presented at the game.[151] During the homecoming activities the first Reddie Blankets were distributed to the entire football team. The red, gray-bordered blankets with *Reddie* down the center were donated to the players by boosters from throughout the state. The four senior squadsmen—Turner DeLoney, Hearin Harmon, Hal Norwood, and Horace Williamson—were allowed to keep theirs as tokens of appreciation.[152]

Another tradition linked to homecoming, the legend of the "Black Lady," began around 1912. The legend had its origin in a tale of love, death, and the supernatural told to the students by Professor Mary Sue Mooney. The story centered around a beautiful young Henderson senior girl who was betrayed by her lover, a Reddie athlete, for a freshman girl. In an aura of dejection, the heartbroken young lady jumped from "the bluff" to her death. Dressed in black, she returned the following year, and each year thereafter, during the week preceding the game, seeking revenge among the freshmen girls. (The tale, in its original form, had many of the same elements one would find in "The Harnt that Walks the Chilhowee" and other stories of Miss Mooney's friend, Mary Noailles Murfree.) An outgrowth of the legend is the yearly enactment by a senior woman of the revenant's stalk for revenge. Anticipation of the "Black Lady's" return which is accompanied by clanking chains and flickering candlelight eventually led to chaos in the women's dormitory. In later years, the "walks" have required close supervision by college officials.[153]

A pep club to promote "Reddie Spirit" was formed by the students in 1921. A new fight song, "That Old Reddie Spirit," was introduced by cheerleader Anna Lee Chidister in 1923. Sung to the tune of "That Old Time Religion" and affectionately known as "The Reddie Hymn," the words were composed by the Reverend Lewis Cannon, then pastor of the local Methodist Church. Reminiscent of the revival fervor of early Methodism and hopeful of renewing school spirit, the tune generated some controversy. The year that it was introduced, President Workman, fearful of offending some of the college's guests for the contest with Ouachita Baptist College, persuaded the cheerleaders not to use the song for that game. Despite admonition, the hymn was retained and has evolved into the most prominent music heard at Reddie football games.[154] Among those yell leaders who generated great zeal from the students for "That Old Reddie Spirit," criticism or no criticism, was Paul Vernon Galloway, who later became a prelate of the Methodist Church. Son of the Reverend J. J. Galloway, he was graduated from Henderson-Brown College with the Bachelor of Arts degree in 1926 and three years later received the Bachelor of Divinity degree from Yale University. In 1960 he was elected bishop and in 1964 was assigned to the Arkansas area, the position he held until his retirement in 1972.[155]

Despite the optimistic enthusiasm and rejuvenated spirit accompanying Coach Haygood's return, he failed to lead the teams to a single winning season, compiling only a record of twelve wins, twenty-two losses, and three ties. He did, however, improve the schedule by returning Vanderbilt University and adding Southern Methodist University. Though in 1923 he coached the Reddies to their first victory in seven years over the Ouachita Baptist College Tigers, it remained for his successor to return the Reddies to their former greatness. When Haygood's five-year contract expired in March, 1925, the trustees expressed their confidence in him by offering him a new one-year contract in the amount of $3,500. Haygood accepted but in June proffered his resignation. The trustees assented and named John Howell Rowland to the position for one year with a salary of only $1,250. Rowland held the Bachelor of Laws degree from Vanderbilt University and, like Haygood, had been an outstanding football player there.[156]

Because of age and failing health, for several years President Workman had wished to be spared the heavy duties as head of the college, but his desires to see his plans for the institution materialize were so great that he willingly sacrificed for the cause of the school that he loved. It was in this spirit of care and concern for the students placed under his charge that he gave the college its motto: "The School With a Heart In It." Used for the first time in the 1919 *Star*,[157] it soon appeared on the official letterheads and all other publications. In recent years, however, it has been altered to "The School With a Heart." On March 2, 1926, six days before his sixty-ninth birthday, President Workman tendered his resignation to the board of trustees, to take effect at the end of the session, or if no successor had been named at that time, not later than one year.[158] The success of his administration was evident: the enrollment had doubled; the indebtedness had been liquidated; a small but respectable endowment had been amassed; accreditation had been achieved; Henderson-Brown College had been accepted by state Methodism. Workman's personal qualities and abilities had earlier been recognized by his selection to *Who's Who in America* in 1922. In parting from the school, he gratefully thanked his faithful ally, the Reverend J. J. Galloway, for his help in making it possible for him to accomplish the nearly insurmountable task with which the trustees had confronted him eleven years earlier.[159]

CHAPTER IX

The End of an Era

B Y the middle of the 1920's it was increasingly apparent to many Arkansas Methodists that they could never develop all three colleges under their control—Henderson-Brown, Hendrix, Galloway—into superior centers of learning, and that re-evaluation of the church's educational system was imperative. For the next three years, 1926 to 1929, the respective institutions and the church were involved in deliberations concerning their destinies. During this brief period, Henderson-Brown College came of age, saw two presidential administrations, was abandoned by the Methodists, and was accepted by the state.

Ironically, the college entered into its final phase as a Methodist institution in an atmosphere of total optimism. Considerable delight greeted the announcement by the board of trustees that Clifford Lee Hornaday, president of Davenport College, Lenoir, North Carolina, had accepted the presidency.[1]

Hornaday had been born in Hemford, North Carolina, on April 5, 1879. He attended the public schools of Ridgeway, North Carolina, and entered Trinity College (Duke University) in September, 1896, where he received the Bachelor of Arts degree in 1902 and the Master of Arts degree four years later. At that Methodist institution he attained the high level of scholarship which allowed him to wear the key of Phi Beta Kappa. The second president of Henderson-Brown College not a minister, he had enjoyed a respectable teaching career. From 1902 until 1916 he taught at Trinity Park School, Durham; in 1916 he returned to his alma

153

mater, where as instructor in modern languages he attained the rank of assistant professor. From that position he was elected president of Davenport College in 1922, and he headed that institution until coming to Arkadelphia. He had also continued his education, pursuing work leading to the Doctor of Philosophy degree at Columbia University, which later conferred that title upon him.[2] The sixth president of Henderson-Brown College, he began his duties on July 1, 1926.[3]

In his inaugural address President Hornaday repeatedly emphasized his concern for academic excellence. He stated that all activities of the collegiate year would be centered around achieving that goal and that any inclined to conflict with that purpose would be modified or eliminated. He continued that to carry out the theme changes would be made in the physical equipment of the college with the library and laboratories, the "tools of our educational progress," being focal points for improvement. He announced that the library budget would be increased by $400, and that the dining hall and meal services would be placed on a more efficient basis. The new president further added that all improvements would be made with the end in view of obtaining full membership in the North Central Association.[4]

An unexpected advancement toward reaching that aim came on Christmas Day, 1926, when Board Chairman Harvey C. Couch gave the college $100,000 to be applied to the endowment fund. The donation, said to be the largest single gift ever made to any cause in Arkansas up to that time and the largest individual one ever to the college, was, at the donor's request, announced as anonymous. Other yule gifts amounted to $30,000, bringing the school's interest-drawing endowment to more than $360,000;[5] and the vision of a half-million-dollar one was becoming realistic.

Joyous occasions for the new president were few, and controversy plagued his two-year term of office. As a means of reducing operational expenses, he decreased the kitchen staff to two cooks and two dishwashers. Consequently, Malichi Smith, the endeared chief cook since 1903, quit; and the school newspaper defended the Negro's action.[6] This was the first evidence of discord between the students and President Hornaday.

The college's first involvement with the issue of racial integration came in November, 1926, in connection with the Young Men's and Young Women's Christian Associations. Women students at Henderson-Brown College joined with the Southwest Council of their group in incorporating into their policy the social equality of the black man in all instances. But the men students, along with their state association, declined to follow like procedure and, therefore, refused to hold the annual joint assembly of the two groups. While recognizing the need of social uplift of the Negro within certain limits, the male students called for such emancipation to be carried on gradually and cautiously.[7]

Concurrent with Hornaday's arrival, the state following the pattern of its Southern counterparts engaged in the virulent anti-evolution issue. Arkansas' solution to the dispute was unique, for it was the only state to defend Genesis by referendum. In January, 1927, the state legislature killed the prospect of any anti-evolution legislation when the senate tabled it. But in the spirit of Rousseau, its sponsors took the issue directly to the people; as expected, they overwhelmingly approved the statute.[8] The student weekly denounced the action as an affront to the integrity of the state and remarked that any restrictions on the presentation of materials for the advancement of knowledge was nothing more than a return to suppression and ignorance. Pleased that the law did not pertain to the institution, the editor concluded that there was no reason why both science and religion could not be advanced at Henderson-Brown College.[9]

That Hornaday's emphasis on scholarship had produced results was evident at the 1927 commencement exercise ending his first year, when fifty degrees were conferred, the largest number for any year of the Methodist era.[10] One *magna cum laude* graduate, John Paul McConnel, received a Bachelor of Science degree. A Rhodes Scholar alternate, he pursued a military career, and in 1964, as a four-star general, was named Chief of Staff of the United States Air Force.[11]

Early in Hornaday's second year, to extend the college's growing reputation and rapport with the general public, alumni and friends formed a Henderson-Brown Club in Arkadelphia as the parent organization to foster other such groups over the state.[12] Before the clubs could perform their intended service, they were called upon to assist with a building project.

The second disastrous fire in the school's history occurred on Friday night, February 17, 1928, when Goodloe Hall, the seven-year-old men's dormitory was destroyed by fire, a loss totaling $45,000. Fortunately, the majority of the residents were attending a basketball game on campus, and there were no fatalities nor injuries, but most of the men lost all their personal possessions. Forty-four of them were given temporary housing in the vacated academy building. The Huie family placed their Caddo Hotel at the college's disposal, and Ouachita Baptist College and townspeople also offered shelter. Merchants in Little Rock, Prescott, and Arkadelphia helped in outfitting the men with new apparel; and almost immediately, friends of the school began contributing to a rebuilding fund.[13]

But the most serious problem that the president confronted was a major misunderstanding between him and the students over their attempt to alter rules. With minor exceptions, the regulations had remained unchanged since 1890. Student unrest had actually begun during the Workman administration, and following World War I the *Oracle* commented that a suitable punishment for the German kaizer would be to place him under Henderson-Brown College boarding rules. It also recounted "10 of 10,000 college commandments," among them: "Thou shalt not talk to boys"; "Thou shalt not play the piano on Sunday"; and "Thou shalt not question any rule, regardless of how strict it may be." It later stated reasons why Bolshevism should be introduced on the campus.[14] In a school where men and women were segregated in the dining halls, library reading rooms, and on the campus grounds, the Jazz Age students took notice that Vanderbilt University co-eds had progressed from the shimmy to cheek-to-cheek dances, but that at Henderson-Brown College one couldn't even hold a girl's arm while escorting her through the halls;[15] and that Louisiana State University women were waging a fight for equal representation on the student council, while at Henderson-Brown College there was no student government.[16]

The most personal complaint that the women students presented concerned the dean of women and her intense supervisory role. College policy required her presence during all in-coming and out-going telephone conversations of the women and her reading of all telegrams delivered to them. Protesting this invasion of privacy as unwarranted and unnecessary, the students went on a one-day strike, refusing to attend classes. During that time students, faculty, and administrators debated the issues, and moderation prevailed. An editorial in the February 14, 1923, *Oracle* stated that "During the recent commotion the students secured several things that they have been wanting for some time." Among them were a student committee to cooperate with the faculty and a student social committee. There had long been a spirit of dissatisfaction with the social program, and with these changes the students had an opportunity to remedy the situation. The editor reminded the students, however, that they could accomplish nothing unless they were willing to cooperate with the administration. Although a student government association was not created, the co-eds were allowed to form a Women Students' Association Council.[17] Feeling that the young ladies had made much of the issue a personal affront to her, the dean of women resigned.[18]

There were no additional serious altercations during the remaining years of Workman's administration, but in February, 1928, during President Hornaday's second year the male students requested permission to petition the trustees to further relax the antiquated restrictions. Denied this approval, they threatened to leave school. Oddly, this new protest occurred but a few days short of the fifth anniversary of the earlier one. And as before, the students displayed their maturity and did not carry out their threat. Their calm reason was displayed in a student editorial entitled "Change—Not Revolution":

> Coming, as if blown in by the prematurely warm breezes we are having, there has swept over the campus a spirit of unrest, a disquietude, which has made itself manifest in more than one way. It is easily recognized as a spirit which makes for change, sometimes that we have wisely elected men to head our student body who are level headed and capable of managing and directing these streams of restless energy into the proper channels whose banks will hold their floods. That we are possessed of such leaders was recently made evident. It is also well that we have men at the head of our faculty who know how and in what manner to respond to such a spirit among a student body. It is unfortunate that there are, and always will be, those who when they feel the surge of this current of unrest give themselves completely up to it, drink lustily of it, and shout mightily, "Down with everything." We readily recognize this type of common anarchist and mob-minded revolutionist. Here is a man who misrepresents his followers; he brings disgrace on the cause they sponsor and, in general, creates an offensive stench. If this type is suppressed, a spirit of change usually makes for progress. If he is allowed to flout his red flag, we may never expect progress.[19]

It is apparent from subsequent editorials that the desired changes were not forthcoming. The collegians repeatedly pleaded for privileges for the women to be based on merit, not on class standing; and they appraised the administration that cooperation was of necessity a reciprocal action.[20] Their requests were still unheeded, and a short time later the situation reached serious proportions.

One late winter morning in 1928, before the daily assembly was called to order, Glenn Coker, president of the senior class, led a discussion concerning ways to bring their case before the trustees. When in customary processional fashion the president and faculty entered the auditorium, Hornaday assumed that he had discovered a plot to undermine his authority and accused the students of attempting to introduce a spirit of anarchy into the school. In an emotional tirade, he ordered them from the assembly hall and to classes, but not a single one obeyed. Then, as if rehearsed, several challenged not just their denial of petition, but also the regulations. One senior co-ed who spoke out was Amy Jean Greene, who became affectionately known as "the spirit of Henderson State College." (She returned to her alma mater as an instructor in 1945, and upon her retirement as an associate professor of education in 1972, the Alumni Association established a $10,000 endowment scholarship in her honor, the largest in the institution's history.)[21]

With direct confrontation eminent, the student body proclaimed themselves on strike, reassembled on the front lawn, and proceeded to violate, within reason, every rule. From the front steps of College Hall, President Hornaday declared the entire student body expelled; the men students, accepting his dictate retired to their boarding rooms and prepared to leave, forcing the president to rescind his decree.[22]

Further antagonism resulted from charges concerning excessive profits from the college book store operated by Hornaday's niece. Some students wrote the publishers of the required texts and obtained a list of suggested retail prices, which they posted. Reportedly, these two young men were Cyrus Richard "Dick" Huie and Comer Vann Woodward.[23] (Grandson of former Trustee Robert Huie, Sr., and son of Trustee Robert Huie, Jr., Huie is an established attorney and is currently the first Executive Secretary of the

Arkansas Judicial Department.[24] Woodward, one of the school's most illustrious alumni and an author and historian of national reputation, presently occupies the distinguished Sterling Chair of History, Yale University.)[25]

The situation improved but little, and on June 20, 1928, the trustees in special session accepted, without dissent, the resignation of Clifford Lee Hornaday, effective July 1. The local news release of Hornaday's resignation appeared on page four of the weekly *Southern Standard*, with other stories about the college printed on page one. The editor commented that the trustees gave no explanation of the resignation, nor gave any information at all. The implication is that it resulted from Hornaday's failure to exert effective leadership. So ended the tenure of the college's sixth president. Only forty-nine years old when he departed from Arkansas, Hornaday later achieved a creditable teaching career at Brooklyn College, Williams College, Hunter College, and Presbyterian Junior College, retiring from the last in his native North Carolina in 1958.[26]

At that same meeting the board unanimously elected the new chief administrator: the Reverend James Warthen Workman,[27] son of the former President Workman. The selection of Hornaday's successor exemplified the tendency to name outsiders during periods of prosperity but to elevate friends in times of stress. It also pointed out another phenomenon of the college's history, short presidential administrations.

The first native Arkansan and the first alumni to head the institution, Workman had been born in Little Rock, November 4, 1897. After serving as a second lieutenant during World War I, he received the Bachelor of Arts degree from Henderson-Brown College in 1919 (during his father's tenure). He continued his education at Yale University, obtaining three degrees: the Bachelor of Arts, 1921; the Bachelor of Divinity, 1923; and the Master of Arts, 1924. Also in 1924, as an ordained minister, he became the Southern Methodist Church's first Wesley Foundation director. He embarked upon this duty at the University of Arkansas where he was also professor of Bible. After serving there for three years, the year before assuming the presidency of Henderson-Brown College he accepted a similar position at the University of Oklahoma. An active member in Sons of the American Revolution and the Knights Templar Masonic Fraternity, the thirty-year-old president assumed office July 1, 1928, at the salary of $4,200.[28]

In negotiating with Workman to accept the presidency, Board Chairman Harvey C. Couch personally pledged that he would underwrite financial obligations incurred by the college for $250,000 for four years so that Workman could assemble a superior faculty to offer a first-class program.[29] In an earlier meeting, the trustees, as if they had some premonition of what the forth-coming year held for the school, directed that the college once again discontinue the Bachelor of Science degree, strengthen the liberal arts program, and emphasize teacher training.[30] Following the board's mandate and Chairman Couch's financial backing, the dignified young president went "on the road" in a used Stutz-Bearcat to interview prospective faculty members "to make Henderson go." [31] His efforts proved successful, for several professors holding Doctor of Philosophy degrees from distinguished graduate schools were employed. Heading the education department was Herbert W. Blashfield, New York University, who had formerly taught at Columbia University. The new head of the social science department was George Allen Hubbell, Columbia University; a former vice-president of Berea College and a president of High College (Kentucky), Hubbell was author of five books. The first female faculty member to hold the Doctor of Philosophy degree was Emma Gertrude Jaeck, University of Illinois, who had also studied at the universities of Berlin, Madrid, Strasbourg, California, and Chicago. She assumed duties as dean of women and head of the department of modern languages. Jerry Hall Service, Ohio State University,

joined the physics faculty; recognized in his field, he had conducted research for the United States Government and had contributed knowledge in his subject with fifteen published works. In
addition to these new appointments, Luther Orland Leach, who
had originally become associated with the institution in 1923, returned after receiving his degree from the University of Chicago
to head the department of chemistry and physics and to assist President Workman as dean of the faculty.[32]

The college began its thirty-ninth session, the final as a Methodist institution, September 11, 1928, with an enrollment of 240.[33]
To be of greater service to the town and Southern Arkansas, the
college also began a night school program; the classes met on Tuesday evenings and offered credit leading to literary degrees. Emphasizing teacher education, the first courses offered were principles
of education, methods in education, child psychology, and Bible.[34]

That the college had come of age and was fulfilling a vital educational role in Arkansas was not questionable, but as early as 1907
efforts to devise a plan to unite the three Methodist colleges were
advanced. In April of that year, at the request of Hendrix College
and Galloway College trustees, the board convened with them to
discuss their proposition to unify the schools. By unanimous vote,
the Henderson-Brown College trustees approved consolidation into
one institution with three branches maintained on the existing
campuses to be directed by a central board, each branch retaining
degree-granting power.[35] Then, in November, the Little Rock
Conference recommended that Henderson-Brown College be correlated with Hendrix and Galloway colleges and that an educational commission be appointed to expedite the matter.[36] One year
later, the conference, on advisement of the commission, recommended that Henderson and Galloway colleges be reduced to junior colleges, with Hendrix College invested with exclusive power
to confer degrees; Henderson-Brown College to be for males and
Galloway College to continue for females; and Hendrix College to

be made co-educational in the junior and senior years.[37] Although the plan was recognized as desirable, immediate opposition developed in Arkadelphia and Searcy. Henderson-Brown College students adopted a resolution imploring the administration and friends to do all within their powers to prevent implementation of the conference ruling.[38] As a result, the three colleges continued as separate degree granting institutions.

In November, 1926, however, the unification issue was revived when both conferences adopted resolutions asking Bishop Hiram A. Boaz to appoint a new commission to study the educational situation.[39] In February, 1927, Bishop Boaz, chairman of the commission, recommended a bold proposal to reduce all three to junior colleges and to create a three million-dollar university at Little Rock, with all four institutions managed by one board. With minor dissent, the trustees of the three colleges and the presiding elders of the conferences approved the bishop's plan.[40]

But the respective presidents and their students resisted the university scheme. And although Henderson-Brown College was not a member of the North Central Association, that body's immediate past president, J. D. Elliff, and its president, W. W. Boyd, both recent visitors to Arkadelphia, substantiated the school's objection by declaring that demotion of the college to junior rank would be a great misfortune to higher education and questioned the wisdom of such a move.[41] The controversial issue was debated throughout the summer; by fall the commission was convinced that the conferences were not prepared to endorse its proposal, and the plan was dropped.[42] The conferences did approve continuation of the educational commission and charged it with the duty of developing a more unified system, their report to be submitted to a called session of the annual conferences not later than March 1, 1928.[43]

On February 28, Bishop Boaz called the conferences into joint session in Little Rock where they received the commission's report that the schools be placed under one board of trustees consisting of thirty members, that Galloway College be continued as a four-year school for women, and that Henderson-Brown and Hendrix colleges be consolidated. Following discussion the delegates overwhelmingly rejected the proposal five hundred to six.[44] But in separate action they did vote to place the three institutions under one board, to consist of thirty members, twelve from each conference with the remaining six to be elected by those twenty-four.[45] The new board, to become effective in April, was charged with the difficult task of determining the futures of the three institutions and was instructed "to give immediate and serious study to the problem of consolidation of Henderson-Brown and Hendrix colleges." [46]

In the following days some significant events transpired in Arkadelphia. The Henderson-Brown College board elected to its membership Senator Joseph Taylor Robinson,[47] soon to be the Democratic party's candidate for vice-president of the United States. (Subsequently, he was elected to the new united board.) The trustees also took steps to maintain the college as a four-year institution in Arkadelphia. In keeping with that purpose, they revealed the unexpected news that they could guarantee an endowment surpassing $600,000, provided that the school remain at its present location. In a surprise move, a prominent local resident, A. J. Vestal, offered the college $100,000. Chairman Couch pledged double that amount and, in conjunction with Trustee W. C. Ribenack, agreed to give the returns from an additional $150,000 to the permanent endowment.[48]

Although only five Henderson-Brown College trustees became members of the united board, to the encouragement of the institution's friends, Harvey C. Couch was elected chairman of the group.[49] The major question confronting the new board was whether to merge Henderson-Brown and Hendrix colleges, or to operate them as one institution on two campuses with different purposes: one a liberal arts college, the other an industrial or self-help school. To aid them in their decision, they directed President Workman and Hendrix College President John Hugh Reynolds to study Park College in Missouri and Antioch College in Ohio. For further assistance, Southern Methodism's General Board of Education employed B. W. Brown of Chicago to make a scientific survey of the total situation.[50]

The presidents concluded that prospects of an industrial institution were worthy but not feasible, for their study revealed it more expensive to maintain such an institution than to continue operation of the two existing liberal arts schools. Brown's survey disclosed that, unless the church were prepared to expend considerably larger revenues on the current programs, consolidation was the only possible solution.[51] Convinced by these reports, on October 22, 1928, the central board voted twenty-three to three to recommend to the annual conferences that Galloway College be standardized as the senior college for women; that Henderson-Brown College and Hendrix College be consolidated into one co-educational school at one site; that the location of the consolidated institution be left to the discretion of the joint board; and that Galloway College and the consolidated college be placed under the same trustees.[52]

The board's recommendation was presented to both conferences in November. That the schools were to be merged was conceded, but "where" constituted an emotional issue. Alumni and friends emphasized that the combined physical plants represented a value of almost one and one-half million dollars.[53] President Workman and Chairman Couch both stated they believed that the best solution was to locate the united school on neutral territory.[54] The Reverend A. C. Miller, editor of the *Arkansas Methodist*, endorsed their position, but suggested that the Methodists negotiate with other Protestant faiths to build a great interdenominational university in Little Rock.[55]

The Little Rock Conference adopted the report as given, but the

North Arkansas Conference amended it to state that should the consolidated institution be located in a place other than Arkadelphia or Conway, there must be provided an adequate site and a minimum of two and one-half million dollars above the present endowments.[56] Although the conferences accepted, only slightly more than one-third of the delegates voted for the proposal, and Bishop Boaz was accused of exerting influence to the point of hypnotism over the assemblies.[57]

Both Arkadelphia and Conway began accelerated moves to secure additional funds and other enticements to assure continuance of their respective colleges. Both communities reiterated that they were not attempting to gain the consolidated institution but rather were engaging in public campaigns to preserve their existing schools, each the product of sacrifice and struggle since 1890.[58] The Arkadelphia Henderson-Brown Club, the parent organization of statewide alumni, became the most aggressive force in fighting the consolidation of Henderson-Brown and Hendrix colleges. In November, 1928, the group directed an extensive letter campaign corresponding with the chambers of commerce throughout the state seeking cooperation in opposing the plan.[59] They also wrote to alumni, friends, and prospective students urging their support in the movement and informing them that Arkadelphia and the club would work to the last to keep the college in the town. To aid the organization in this endeavor, Arkadelphia Business College offered the services of its students in preparing the letters and Henderson-Brown College paid for the stationery and stamps used in mailing them.[60]

Fully aware of the concerted efforts being waged in both communities, the trustees assembled New Year's Eve and officially approved the merger as endorsed by the conferences and announced inspection tours of the colleges in question to aid them in determining the site of the future school. When they visited Henderson-Brown College on January 17, 1929, they were received by the entire community, with the chamber of commerce serving as host. At that time, the town offered the enticing proposal of $300,000; of that amount $200,000 was pledged from citizens of southern Arkansas.[62] Conway made similar overtures. Despite cordial receptions given the trustees, both towns informed them that they were prepared to take legal action should the board attempt to invalidate the contracts made between the towns and the church when the properties were donated in 1890.[63]

Nevertheless, the following day without a negative vote, the trustees rejected the generous offers from both Arkadelphia and Conway. Much to the bishop's relief, they decided to locate the combined institution in Little Rock, on condition that the capital city provide an acceptable campus and two and one-half million dollars on or before March 15, 1929. To advance the proposed new facility, Chairman Couch and Trustee R. E. Lee Wilson pledged $250,000 each.[64] The trustees then directed the boards of Henderson-Brown and Hendrix colleges to return those properties to the respective towns.[65]

Led by Noel Adams, prominent Arkadelphians and friends of the college began immediate negotiations with political personalities offering them the attractive proposal to deed the entire physical plant and all equipment, including the library holdings, valued in excess of $350,000, in return for state control. Fortunately for the advocates the Arkansas General Assembly was in session and Senator Claude Rankin from Little Rock introduced the town's generous proposition (Senate Bill 179) to the solons for consideration. And House Floor Leader E. E. Alexander, representative of Mississippi County, led the fight in that chamber.[66] Within a few weeks, February 15, 1929, Arkadelphia was again entertaining dignitaries, this time the entire legislature. The legislators inspected the college facilities and were reminded that the state did not operate a degree-granting institution south of the Arkansas River and that now there was an opportunity to provide that needed service at no expense to the tax payers. Since the state operated but one teachers college, the lawmakers, sensing the need as well as the regional popular support for another, on return to Little Rock, enacted the necessary legislation to assume ownership of Henderson-Brown College.[67]

The bill to "establish a standard Teachers College at Arkadelphia, Clark County, Arkansas," was unanimously accepted by the Senate; passed by the House 52 to 20; and signed by Governor Harvey Parnell as Act 46, on February 25, 1929. Section II of the act provided for a seven-member board of trustees: three state officials—auditor, treasurer, and superintendent of public instruction—and four non-state officials, to be appointed by the governor, who was named ex-officio chairman. The superintendent of instruction was designated as the chairman. Section IX provided free tuition to citizens of the state, but denied entrance to persons not sixteen years old and those who would not give a written pledge to teach in the common schools of Arkansas for two years after graduation. Section XV provided that the conservatory could be maintained as long as it was "no expense whatsoever to the state." Act 351 of the same session appropriated $120,000 for the biennial period ending in 1931; and Henderson-Brown College became the responsibility of the state.[68]

The legislative action was greeted with jubilation for the college was to live and continue the mission it had long fulfilled in Arkansas. The college newspaper hailed the new ownership and somewhat mercilessly attacked the Methodist Church and its prelate. It stated that the time had passed when "some ecclesiastical dictator" could determine the school's policies and rejoiced that "Henderson [was] no longer an inmate of the Methodist orphanage, but a daughter of the State." [69]

Arkadelphia's immediate success in obtaining state control for her institution and the surprising failure of Little Rock to meet the trustees' stipulation for relocation of the consolidated Methodist school resulted in a drastic reversal of the united board's policy. Consequently, on March 12, 1929, those trustees rescinded their earlier decree and voted to retain Hendrix College in Conway as the "merged" institution under the name Hendrix-Henderson College,[70] a decision which only a few other than the hierarchy of the Methodist church accepted and one which inadvertently confirmed suspicions of slyness on the part of church leaders in the minds of some Henderson-Brown College alumni and friends. Nonetheless, with the matter settled for the church, Arkansas Methodism returned to its 1884 educational commitment to operate only two institutions of higher learning.

While students and town residents rejoiced, the faculty and administrative staff experienced anxiety over the uncertainty of their positions and futures with the state successor, a situation which remained unchanged until August when the new faculty was named.[71] In support of the personnel, the local members of the Henderson-Brown College board, led by Secretary Goodloe, drafted a petition asking the "governor and members of the 'Henderson State College for Teachers' board to retain the present faculty for one year." [72] With remarkable optimism they continued to serve and with alumni and students pledged loyalty to an institution whose very name was debatable. Members of the state legislature asked Henderson-Brown College Club members to suggest a name for the college under its new standing. The organization considered several suggestions, and reported that "Henderson-Brown State College for Teachers" was the most preferred.[73] The suggestion was received, but the general assembly styled the institution, Henderson State Teachers College. The status of the nomenclature was not a novelty, for it represented the recurring theme of name changes: Arkadelphia Methodist College, Henderson College, Henderson-Brown College, and Henderson State Teachers College.

In this state of limbo, the college held its thirty-ninth commencement, conferring thirty-four degrees. At that ceremony, as in previous ones, there were those graduated who would perform lasting service to the nation. One was Oren Harris, the class representative, who has distinguished himself in the United States House of Representatives and as a respected federal judge. The senior class presented a twenty-volume *Oxford Dictionary of the English Language* as its memorial, and the trustees made cash gifts totaling $1,000 to the faculty. Trustee Couch and Trustee Ribenack gave a $500-gift to be distributed among campus employees and assured their continued interest in and assistance to the college.[74] The conferring of the aforementioned honorary degree upon distinguished alumnus Charles W. Pipkin concluded the ceremony.

But commencement was not the last function of Henderson-Brown College. The trustees had earlier authorized the operation of a summer session; and under the direction of Professor Olin E. McKnight, it began on the first day of June and extended to August 13, 1929.[75] Although it was explicitly stated that the classes were in no way connected with Henderson State Teachers College,[76] the exact legal condition of the institution was subject to doubt.

While the statute creating the state college provided that the governor appoint a board of trustees within sixty days following its passage, such was not done. Therefore, throughout the remainder of the session and until late June confusion existed concerning sovereignty over the institution. The Henderson-Brown College trustees, which the united board had earlier authorized to dispose of properties, exclusive of records and endowment, was compelled to assume administration until the state formally accepted transfer and named its trustees. A committee consisting of Chairman H. C. Couch, Secretary Leslie Goodloe, Trustee W. E. Barkman, and Trustee W. C. Ribenack was appointed to formally convey the properties to the city of Arkadelphia for subsequent transfer to the state of Arkansas.[77] Trustee Barkman was then designated a committee of one to "sell any and all securities" belonging to the college for the purpose of liquidating the mortgage indebtedness of $90,000 and all other debts, including an operational deficit for the year of nearly $30,000, as quickly as possible. Thereupon Barkman named Trustee Ribenack as his agent to dispose of the school's securities held by Bankers Trust Company of Little Rock, which also held the mortgage on the institution, and to proceed with payments.[78]

On May 7, 1929, the lien on the property held by the Little Rock bank was released and the deed given to the Henderson-Brown College trustees.[79] On June 25, they conveyed the real estate and personal property of Henderson-Brown College, exclusive of records, accounts, and bills receivable, to J. H. McMillan, F. S. DeLamar, and J. L. Newberry, serving as trustees for the Arkadelphia Chamber of Commerce. The deed, made by Henderson-Brown College and its name signed by Trustee Couch, Trustee Barkman, and Trustee Ribenack, reiterated that Henderson-Brown College was the corporation and that its board of trustees was the body politic (not the Methodist Episcopal Church, South, nor the conferences) and as such was owner and holder of the titles to the real estate and personal property. The instrument of transfer also directed that the college "Shall not revert to the Methodist Episcopal Church, South, or its representatives." [80]

The issue of disposition of the endowment contained uncertain elements. The final statement concerning the fund in the minutes of the trustees (March 6, 1928) listed the endowment as $355,-330.89. The principal amounts were in stocks ($187,623.00), gifts from Chairman Couch and other trustees, and in individual pledges ($124,208.97) in interest bearing notes payable to the endowment.[81] The stated value of the endowment, therefore, did not represent the monies in reserve. The trustees used all available cash and converted those stocks necessary to liquidate the college's indebtedness so that the institution could be transferred unencumbered to the state of Arkansas.[82] In their final hour the trustees once again exerted complete authority as granted them in the charter and retained jurisdiction over the remaining stock securities of the unrestricted endowment—their own contributions to the school that they had honorably served—giving them, if there were any, neither to the consolidated Methodist college nor to the state successor.

On June 28, 1929, legal conveyance to the state of Arkansas occurred, with Trustee Robert W. Huie, Jr., heading the receiving board for the state; and on July 8, formal transfer was made to the state of Arkansas.[83] Two days later the state board of trustees was appointed, and Henderson-Brown College Trustee Joseph Pitts Womack, by virtue of his position as state superintendent of public instruction, was named chairman. Chairman Womack called the board's first session on July 20 for the purpose of electing a president. That day they elected him to that position and empowered him to select a faculty.[84] On August 8, President Womack informed all seven members of the conservatory faculty that they would be retained; and one week later he made known that all members of the literary faculty would, if they so desired, be retained.[85] Only five of the Henderson-Brown College faculty did not return. Of all the involved situations during these trying times, that of President Workman was perhaps the most awkward. Without authority to administer or remain in office, he spent the summer of 1929 teaching at Emory University. Although he was considered the most likely to serve as the state president and the position was offered to him, Workman rejected the proposal, for it was his belief that as an ordained minister he should not serve as the president of a state supported institution.[86]

But he did perform one final deed of lasting merit, an expression of his love and faith in the institution from which he was graduated and of which he had served as president in its trying final year as a Methodist college. In June, 1929, before his departure, he composed the words and with the help of others, the melody for the alma mater song, "Alma Mater, Henderson." In four stanzas, the hymn symbolically portrays the story of the college, noting memories of personalities, joys of friendship, beauties of the campus; the crisis of change through which the college passed; its educational comprehensiveness; and a pledge of spiritual immortality.[87]

The change of status for the college had its curious ingredients. In the official eyes of the church the institution had been merged with Hendrix College in Conway. But in the hearts and minds of loyal alumni and friends the college had in no way been consolidated with its rival on alien soil. Henderson State Teachers College was the direct successor—the same school with only a new name and a new patron. Feelings of ill will and hostility over the concepts were frequent and open. The following letter written by a loyal alumnus summarizes the aura of contempt that shrouded the Methodist Church's withdrawal and the "so-called merger":

Russellville, Arkansas,
October 16, 1929.

Rev. Paul W. Quillian
Winfield Memorial Church,
Little Rock, Arkansas.
Dear Sir:

I have your letter of October 14, 1929 requesting me to sign as [sic] order to Mr. W. E. Barkman to turn over certain Henderson-Brown papers. I decline to do anything of the sort. If you "felt that this gift was made to our Methodist program" you were feeling something that was not true.

I resent the scheming and chicanery which resulted in the rape of Henderson-Brown and I have utterly lost faith in the leadership of the church which was responsible. I suppose you are too close to this heirarchy to know what people outside this charmed circle are thinking and feeling. I know that the cause of Methodism is hurt and that there is a schism which neither you nor I will live to see closed.

I am ready to admit the legality of the proceedings. The letter of the law was observed but the entire affair was immoral. It may be the naked legal right of the elect to take the name of Henderson—they were certainly not welcome to it. The name Henderson belongs to the thousands who have fought, bled and died for it. Unless they want to give it up, no one else has a moral right to assume it. I consider Henderson State the successor of Henderson-Brown, the successor of Henderson, the successor of Arkadelphia Methodist College. Any effort to pretend that the legal merger was a spiritual union is bunk. The personnel of the student bodies at Conway and at Arkadelphia is evidence that there was no merger except on paper.

I suggest that since you seem near to the administration of the "merged" institution—your letter was mailed in Conway—that since they have run out on the Reddies and escaped a drubbing —you recommend that they call themselves the Yellow Warriors.

Very truly,

G. R. Turrentine [88]

The Henderson-Brown College clubs throughout the state and individual alumni expressed in appropriate resolutions pledges of loyalty and continued support to the college under its new name.[89] The Arkadelphia club determined that the organizations should take the new name of the college and amended their charter and constitution to read Henderson State College Club.[90] To demonstrate their rejection of the concept of merger, the club voted to sponsor the Reddie Blanket fund and to host a luncheon for former Henderson-Brown College students at the annual meeting of the state teachers association scheduled to meet in Little Rock.[91] The club also conducted a project to write letters of appreciation to all those who had campaigned to "save the college" and guarantee its survival.[92] To exemplify their support of the state successor they voted to give $1,000 to the Henderson State Teachers College Library,[93] and made plans to "beautify the college parlors and landscape the grounds." Likewise, members of the group spoke publicly to school groups and sent letters to prospective students urging them to attend "Henderson." [94] Two years later, the Methodist Church eased the controversy by tacitly recognizing that the new state college was apparently the successor of Henderson-Brown College when in March, 1931, it removed the name "Henderson" from that of the Conway institution, returning it to the traditional name Hendrix College.

Despite anxieties, as the Methodist era ended, signs of the future college were on every hand. In thirty-nine years the institution had grown from an incomplete building and heavy indebtedness to a $350,000 physical plant with an equal amount in endowment. The student body had increased from 110 to 240; and the faculty from ten to twenty-five, with seven holding the doctor's degree. In its time the Methodist institution had been party to more history than any annalist could ever hope to relate; and at this turning point in its life, looking toward the state, the college embarked upon its future with greater confidence than at any time in its past.

CHAPTER X

Epilogue

H ENDERSON State Teachers College began operation
September 10, 1929, with a faculty of twenty-seven and
an enrollment of 175. With the stock market crash of October, 1929, economic prosperity, a factor in the state's willingness
to assume the college, was temporarily abated. Therefore, in less
than two months following opening under new auspices, the institution was faced with its predecessor's chronic plight, severely
limited resources. Nevertheless, the college made great progress. In
1931 it received first class recognition from the American Association of Teachers Colleges; and in April, 1934, it attained full membership in the North Central Association of Colleges and Secondary Schools.

Although there were adverse effects of the depression felt by
faculty and students, the physical plant benefited from Franklin D.
Roosevelt's New Deal; six major structures—three dormitories, the
science hall, a gymnasium, and an armory—were constructed and
major improvements were made on existing facilities. But as the
nation was recovering from the depression and the college was
completing its first decade under state control, Henderson's future
was again darkened by war clouds from Europe. Faced with the
new crisis, the college became a war community, from all outward
appearances a military post. With victory in 1945, the school stag-
gered under the influx of returning veterans, and the enrollment
grew to more than 500, double that of the previous session.

To meet increasing demands, the college organized a division of

176

extension and correspondence work in 1945, and in 1950 completely reorganized its curriculum into two divisions, General College and Senior College. The next year, Henderson State Teachers College, along with fourteen other schools in the state, accepted the Ford Foundation's offer to finance an experimental program based on the theory that a general education with one year of intensive training would improve teacher education. And the school, in addition to offering its regular teacher training curriculum, participated in a fifth-year program known as the "Arkansas Experiment in Teacher Education."

Beginning in 1951, the college also served as a graduate studies center for the University of Arkansas, and in 1955 instituted its own graduate program leading to the Master of Science in Education degree. In 1967, this program was expanded to offer the Master of Music Education degree, and in 1973 the Master of Science in Social Agency Counseling degree was begun.

Although the purpose of the college was teacher education, degrees in the arts, sciences, and music were continued. In 1964 the Bachelor of Science in Business Administration degree was added, and by 1967 the students enrolled in that school accounted for some twenty per cent of the total enrollment. That the college was becoming a multipurpose institution was reflected in the most recent name change. Act 4 of the 1967 General Assembly made the name Henderson State College.

If Charles Christopher Henderson could return to Arkadelphia today, more than seventy years since the college came to bear his name, he would note little change in the appearance of his mansion, but he would be awed by the college's transformation. In his most vivid imagination, it would have been difficult for him to have perceived the existing institution valued at more than eighteen million dollars with a faculty of 176 and an annual enrollment of over 3,000. No doubt, the early patron would take pride in the present status of the college bearing his name.

Notes

CHAPTER I

INTRODUCTION

1. William Ritchie, "Henderson, Today and Yesterday: The Story of the First Fifty Years," in *Essays on Southern Life and Culture: A Henderson Symposium*, A. B. Bonds, ed. (Arkadelphia: Henderson State Teachers College, 1941), 237.

CHAPTER II

THE SETTING

1. Pipkin was born November 4, 1899. After graduation from Henderson, he received the M.A. from Vanderbilt in 1919, studied 3 years at Harvard, received the D. Phil. from Oxford in 1925; in 1934 Hendrix College conferred upon him the LL.D. From 1920 to 1922 he taught history and English at M.I.T.; from 1925 to 1931 he was professor of government at L.S.U.; and from 1931 until his death August 4, 1941, he was dean of the Graduate School of L.S.U. He served as president of the Conference of Deans of Southern Graduate Schools, was a member of the Gulf District Rhodes Scholar Selection Committee, and participated in the National Conference on Graduate Study and Research. Internationally, he was a member of the American Commission to Geneva and served on the Executive Board of the American Society of International Law. Author of a number of books, including *The Idea of Social Justice, Social Legislation in the South,* and *The Duty of the Educated Mind,* he was also editor of *Southern Review* and *Southwest Review. Who's Who in America,* XX (Chicago: A. N. Marquis Co., 1938), 1996; Alberta Lawrence, ed., *Who's Who Among North American Authors* (Los Angeles: Golden Syndicate Publishing Co., 1939), 775; A. B. Bonds, ed., *Essays on Southern Life and Culture: A Henderson Symposium* (Little Rock: Democrat Printing & Lithographing Co., 1941), 98; and Arkadelphia *Siftings Herald,* June 3, 1929. This newspaper will hereinafter be cited thus: *Siftings Herald,* followed by the date of the issue.

2. Proposal to award the degree was presented to members of the board by letters from Trustee R. W. Huie, Jr., on May 27, 1929, as the trustees had earlier held their final meeting. The letters requested that approval be granted to confer the LL.D. and that the secretary be permitted to enter said action in the minutes of the last meeting. The vote was unanimous in favor of the requests, but two trustees expressed concern for the legality of their doing so, for it was their understanding that the college was then under control of the state. The decision was never incorporated into the minutes, but the letters authorizing it are attached. Manuscript Minutes of the Board of Trustees of Henderson-Brown College under the date of March 1, 1929.

3. The Ouachita River originates in the Ouachita Mountains (Polk County, Arkansas). From its source the river traverses southwest Arkansas, meandering in an easterly direction past the hot springs before turning in a southerly direction for an approximate total of 610 river miles to a confluence with the Red River in Catahoula Parish, Louisiana. The word *Ouachita*, spelled "Washita" in early accounts of the area, is likely of poetic origin. There is no authentic explanation for the name, but there is an interesting theory advanced by the late Hardy L. Winburn, a scholarly minister who presided at the First Baptist Church in Arkadelphia for more than 30 years. Winburn became interested in the name and did much research in Indian lore on the subject. According to him, the Caddo Indians, who inhabited the area, were a commercial people who carried on an extensive trade as far south as the Gulf of Mexico. This necessitated their use of the Mobhilian tongue, employed by the tribes for which Mobile Bay was named. "In the Mobhilian tongue there are found two words, *owa*, meaning east or sunrise, and *cita*, meaning little or small." In the Mobhilian tongue, "each syllable was accented alike, thus O-wa-ci-ta." Winburn concludes that *Owa-cita* was given by the Caddoés in very early times to the beautiful river that bounded their territory on the north and east for more than 200 miles. W. H. Halliburton, "The Nation's Rivers Inspire the Nation's Poets," Little Rock *Arkansas Gazette*, Nov. 8, 1964. Another plausible explanation is that the word means "Good Hunting Grounds." In Choctaw and Quapaw, *owa* means hunt, and *cita* means big. According to French explorers, the Choctaws traveled west to the Ouachita River on their "Owa-cita" for buffalo. Later, the English immigrants used the French name, spelling it "Washita." Frederick W. Allsopp, *Folklore of Romantic Arkansas* (New York: Grolier Society, 1931), 53. Pronunciation and spelling of Ouachita continues to offer its problems. On September 27, 1970, during a nationally televised professional football game between the Dallas Cowboys and the New York Giants, the spectacular performance of Cliff Harris, a rookie for the Cowboys and former Ouachita Baptist

University athlete, prompted a lengthy discussion between the sportscasters concerning the pronunciation, spelling, and location of the institution. It was later reported that while Harris had led the Cowboys in their surprise victory over the Giants, "he was also responsible for blowing two computers that were aiding the network in attempting to pronounce, spell, and locate the Baptist institution," Little Rock *Arkansas Gazette*, Sept. 28, 1970. This newspaper will hereinafter be cited thus: *Arkansas Gazette*, followed by the date of the issue. In 1843 Ouachita appears in the court records under this spelling for the first time. Manuscript Clark County Records, 1840–44. Clark County Courthouse, Arkadelphia, Ark., 174. Clark County is one of the few Arkansas counties to have complete records dating from establishment to present.

4. The first official reference to the town by the name Arkadelphia appears in the court proceedings of Jan. 11, 1842. Manuscript County Court Records, 1840–44, 91. And Fay Hempstead, *Historical Review of Arkansas: Its Commerce, Industry, and Modern Affairs*, I (Chicago: Lewis Publishing Co., 1911), 80. Also see *Biographical and Historical Memoirs of Southern Arkansas* (Chicago: Goodspeed Publishing Co., 1890), 29–30.

5. Clarence E. Carter, ed., *The Territorial Papers of the United States*, XIX, *Arkansas Territory, 1819–1825* (Washington: Government Printing Office, 1953), 245. Clark County, when created, contained all of present Clark, Garland, Hot Spring, Pike, and Dallas counties. William Clark, who was then serving as governor of Missouri Territory, was a younger brother of General George Rogers Clark. He was born in Caroline County, Virginia, August 1, 1770. When he was fourteen years of age, his parents moved to Kentucky and settled where the city of Louisville now stands. In 1788 he entered the army. He served under General Anthony Wayne in his campaigns against the Indians in Ohio and Indiana. In 1803, at the request of Captain Meriwether Lewis, he was appointed joint commander of the exploring expedition to the Pacific coast. President Jefferson appointed him brigadier general of the Missouri militia in 1806, and the following year he was appointed Indian agent. Early in 1813 he was appointed governor of Missouri Territory and held that office until the state was admitted into the Union. In 1822 he was again appointed Indian agent. In 1828 he founded the city of Paducah, Ky. He died in St. Louis, September 1, 1838. Hempstead, *Historical Review*, I, 53–54. Also see Dallas T. Herndon, *Centennial History of Arkansas*, I (Chicago: S. J. Clark Publishing Co., 1922), 140–141.

6. The route of De Soto in his wanderings east of the Mississippi has been traced with tolerable accuracy, but his course west of the great river has been the subject of much speculation, and there are conflicting accounts of his travels in Arkansas. The United States De Soto Expedition Commis-

sion's report in 1939 indicated that he crossed the Mississippi 20 miles below
Helena. For a complete account of the report see U.S., Congress, House
Committee on the U.S. De Soto Expedition, *Final Report of the United
States De Soto Expedition Commission, House Document*, 71, 76th Cong.,
1st Sess. (Washington: Government Printing Office, 1939), 254. This document will hereinafter be cited thus: *House Document* 71. The principal
sources concerning De Soto's travels and discoveries are the reports of
Luis Hernandez de Biedma, factor of the Spanish crown; the narrative of
a mysterious Portuguese adventurer in the expedition, who signs himself,
"A Gentleman of Elvas"; De Soto's personal secretary, Rodrigo Ranjel;
the account of Garcilaso de la Vega el Inca; and the writings of the Spanish
historian, Antonio de Herrea. Another account of the expedition in Arkansas is an article written by Ada Mixon, "What Was Hernando De Soto's
Route Through Arkansas?" *Publications of the Arkansas Historical Association*, IV (Conway: Arkansas Historical Association, 1917), 292–311.
Also see Herndon, *Centennial History*, I, 73–85. Also see *House Document*,
71, 226–257.

7. For an account of the Caddo Indians in the area consult V. L. Huddleston, "Indians in Clark County," *Arkansas Historical Quarterly*, II
(March, 1943), 105–115. This journal will hereinafter be cited thus: *AHQ*,
followed by the volume number of the issue.

8. Josiah H. Shinn, *Pioneers and Makers of Arkansas* (Baltimore: Genealogical Publishing Co., 1967), 101.

9. President Jefferson was anxious to learn about the new lands and to
find out just what lay beyond the Miss. River. He therefore obtained
money from Congress for exploratory expeditions into the newly-acquired
lands. The first endeavor was the famous Lewis and Clark Expedition; the
second was the exploration of the Ouachita River Valley. Jefferson's friend,
distinguished scientist William Dunbar suggested that exploration of the
Ouachita should be made, for it would provide an opportunity to observe
that "curiosity" (the hot springs) found in the mountainous region along
the upper reaches of the Ouachita. Jefferson appointed Dunbar to lead
such an expedition. Accompanied by George Hunter, Dunbar and his
small party left Natchez, Miss., Oct. 16, 1804, and arrived Nov. 30 at the
confluence of the Fourche de Cadaux [Caddo]. They recorded it to be
"one hundred yards wide at its entrance into the Washita [Ouachita]."
Their thorough report of the exploration of the river was included in
Jefferson's message to Congress on Feb. 9, 1806, when he informed that
body of the findings of Meriwether Lewis and William Clark: ". . . it
was thought best to employ the autumn of that year [1804] in procuring
a knowledge of an interesting branch of the Red River called the Washita.
This was undertaken under the direction of Mr. Dunbar of Natchez, a

citizen of distinguished science, who had aided and continues to aid us with his disinterested and valuable service in the prosecution of these enterprises. He ascended the river of the remarkable hot springs near it. . . . Extracts from his observations and copies of his map of the river from its mouth to the hot springs make part of the present communications." Letter, William Dunbar to Thomas Jefferson, June 9, 1804; *Ibid.*, Aug. 18, 1804, in *Life, Letters, and Papers of William Dunbar, 1749–1810*, Dunbar Roland (Evon Roland), ed. (Jackson: Press of the Mississippi Historical Society, 1930), 133–137, 139–140, 161; *Travels in The Interior Parts of America: Communicating Discoveries Made in Exploring The Missouri, Red River and Washita, By Captains Lewis and Clark, Dr. Sibley and Mr. Dunbar As Laid Before The Senate by The President of The United States in February 1806.* (London: Richard Phillips, 1807), 91; Walter Lowrie and Mathew St. Clair Clarke, eds., *American State Papers, Indian Affairs: Documents, Legislative and Executive of the Congress Of The United States, From The First Session Of The First To The Third Session Of The Thirteenth Congress, Inclusive: Commencing March 3, 1789 and Ending March 3, 1815*, IV (Washington: Gales & Seaton, 1832), 731–743; Isaac Joshin Cox, *The Exploration of the Louisiana Frontier, 1803–1806*, VIII (n.p., 1904), 151–174; James D. Richardson, ed., *A Compilation of the Messages and Papers of the Presidents, 1789–1817*, I (Washington: Government Printing Office, 1896), 399; and Fred L. Israel, ed., *The State of the Union Messages of the Presidents*, I (New York: R. R. Bowker Co., 1967), 86. Noted historian of the American frontier, Ray Allen Billington, was, therefore, in error when he wrote that "they [Dunbar and Hunter] did not pass beyond present-day Louisiana." Ray Allen Billington, *Westward Expansion: A History of the American Frontier* (New York: Macmillan Co., 1967), 450. Billington is also in error when he refers to Hunter as John Hunter. The Philadelphia chemist who accompanied Dunbar was George Hunter. *Ibid.* John Hunter did publish a journal in 1823 which included a description of rivers in Arkansas, but the Ouachita is not cited. See John D. Hunter, *Memoirs of A Captivity Among The Indians of North America, From Childhood to the Age of Nineteen: with [sic] Anecdotes Descriptive of Their Manners and Custom: To Which Is Added, Some Account of the Soil, Climate, and Vegetable Productions of the Territory Westward of the Mississippi* (London: Longman, Hurst, Rees, Orme, Brown & Green, 1823), 154–163.

10. Hempstead, *Historical Review*, I, 80. Little is known concerning Blakely, but he did die before 1830: his name does not appear in the census for that year. "Tradition has it that he was killed by one of his slaves." Farrar Newberry, "Historical Spot in Arkadelphia's History Brings Memories to Many," Arkadelphia *Southern Standard*, July 15, 1959. This news-

paper will hereinafter be cited thus: *Southern Standard*, followed by the
date of the issue. In 1961 the Arkadelphia Chamber of Commerce placed a
marker near the site of the blacksmith shop. For the inscription see Appendix A:1.

11. U.S., Congress, "An Act Making Further Provision for the Sale of
Public Lands," *Annals of The Congress of The United States*, 16th Cong.,
1st Sess., II (Washington: Gales & Seaton, 1855), 1898–1901.

12. Hemphill was born in South Carolina (near Augusta, Ga.). Herndon,
Centennial History, 871. Barkman was born December 20, 1784, in the
"Kentucky Country" and spent the first 27 years of his life there. It is
believed that his immediate ancestors were Virginians, and that his father
emigrated from there to Kentucky, either with or about the same time as
Daniel Boone. Farrar Newberry, "Jacob Barkman," *AHQ*, XIX, 315. Hemphill's family consisted of his wife, Nancy, their eight children, and his
mother-in-law, Mary Dixon. "It is apparent from the number of slaves and
cattle he brought along that he was a man of some financial resources."
Farrar Newberry, "John Hemphill and the Old Salt Works Near Here,"
Southern Standard, Feb. 6, 1964. The Barkman party included Jacob and
his wife, Rebecca, his brother John and his wife, and two slaves. Newberry,
AHQ, XIX, 315.

13. David Y. Thomas, ed., *Arkansas and Its People: A History, 1541–1930*,
II (New York: American Historical Society Inc., 1930), 405. See also
Dallas T. Herndon, ed., *Annals of Arkansas*, I (Little Rock: Historical
Record Association, 1947), 339. In observation of Arkansas' Centennial in
1936, the Arkansas History Commission placed a marker near the site. For
the inscription see Appendix A:2. Exactly when the Indians began extracting salt from this location is unknown, but it is certain that the first
white men to find them doing it were members of De Soto's expedition.
The De Soto Commission Report states that, "the expedition spent several
days extracting salt above Arkadelphia." *House Document* 71, 254. "The
Gentleman of Elvas" gives the following description of the Indians' crude
method. He wrote "The river [no doubt the Ouachita into which the
bayou flows] when it goes down, leaves it upon the sand. As they cannot
gather the salt without a large mixture of sand, it is thrown together into
certain baskets they have for the purpose, and large at the mouth and small
at the bottom. These are set in the air on a ridge-pole; and water being
thrown on, vessels are placed under them wherein it may fall; then, being
strained and placed on the fire, it is boiled away, leaving salt at the bottom." Theodore H. Lewis, ed., "The Narrative of the Expedition of
Hernando De Soto by the Gentleman of Elvas," *Spanish Explorers in the
Southern United States, 1528–1543*, Frederick W. Hodge and Theodore H.
Lewis, eds. (New York: Barnes & Noble, Inc., 1965), 218. For additional

information see Farrar Newberry, "John Hemphill and the Old Salt Works Near Here," Arkadelphia *Southern Standard*, Feb. 6, 1964; Virginia Buxton, "Salt Springs and Salt Works in Arkansas," *AHQ*, XVI, 383–397. Also see Mixon, *Arkansas Historical Association*, IV, 305.

14. The kettle is located near Arkansas Hall, formerly the library and museum of Henderson. For the inscription on the plaque of the kettle see Appendix A:3. For an interesting story about Hemphill's salt works, see W. H. Halliburton, "When Salt Was a Sweet Discovery," Little Rock *Arkansas Democrat Magazine*, Oct. 14, 1962, 11. This newspaper will hereinafter be cited thus: *Democrat Magazine*, followed by the date of the issue.

15. Hemphill's will is dated September 27, 1814. Manuscript Deed Record Book A-C, Clark County Courthouse, Arkadelphia, Ark., 40.

16. Barkman did not acquire legal title from the government until the land office was opened at Washington, Ark. in 1823. His first purchase is validated by Certificate No. 7, dated December 5, 1823. This original certificate, under the hand of President James Monroe, is property of the Henderson Museum.

17. Austin was convinced that developing lands in the public domain was a road to wealth. After a careful study of maps, transportation routes, and population movements, he selected three sites for proposed cities in Arkansas country. The other two were the "Little Rock" on the Arkansas River, and the confluence of the Red and Little Red rivers. Letter, Stephen F. Austin to William M. O'Hara, March 10, 1819, in Eugene C. Barker, ed., *The Austin Papers*, Part I, *Annual Report of the American Historical Association For the Year 1919*, II (Washington: Government Printing Office, 1924), 339. For an account of Austin in Arkansas see Robert L. and Pauline H. Jones, "Stephen F. Austin in Arkansas," *AHQ*, XXV, 336–353.

18. Letter, Stephen F. Austin to William M. O'Hara, June 16, 1819, in Barker, *The Austin Papers*, Part I, 344.

19. Hempstead, *Historical Review*, I, 80, and *Memoirs of Southern Arkansas*, 105.

20. Orville W. Taylor, *Negro Slavery in Arkansas* (Durham: Duke University Press, 1958), 116; and *Southern Standard*, June 21, 1895.

21. Herndon, *Centennial History*, I, 516. Acquiring a secondhand boiler and some old engine parts, Barkman put together the first steamboat to ever grace the Ouachita. When it was about finished, one of the slaves laughingly said, "Dat boat ain't no bigger than a dime." Newberry, *AHQ*, XIX, 322. The first steamboat on western waters was the *New Orleans* which left Pittsburgh in October, 1812, and arrived in New Orleans the following January. For an excellent account see Louis C. Hunter, *Steamboats on the*

Western Rivers: An Economic and Technological History (Cambridge: Harvard University Press, 1949). In 1964 the Arkadelphia Chamber of Commerce placed a marker to honor Jacob Barkman. For the inscription see Appendix A:4.

22. Of Georgian design, the house consisted of two rooms on each side of a central hall, both upstairs and down; a large wing for dining; and a kitchen at the rear. The plastered rooms, each served by a fireplace, were 20 feet square. Newberry, "Jacob Barkman," *AHQ*, XIX, 317.

23. One Missouri traveler, William Switzler, wrote "The place at which we were entertained the previous night is the first cotton farm that can be called extensive . . . on the route to the South . . . and at once presents a beautiful and picturesque aspect to the forest-familiar-vision of the tourist on his arrival. . . . A beautiful garden of numerous roses and lilies, with a row of Quinci and clusters of Katolps add to the fantastical and decorated mansion of the proprietor . . . and surrounding all, is the elegantly fitted and graceful featured farm. . . . After an excursion through a country . . . the approach of a plantation like this, opening its diversified expanse in the midst of a wilderness, is attended with a strictness of curiosity and sublimity of sensation totally unknown to those who spend a life in densely populated country." Entry of October 10, 1836, William F. Switzler MS Diary, "My Second Tour in the South or Multum in parvo, tempore mores prateres," Western Historical Manuscripts Collection, University of Missouri Library. Transcribed copy in the Arkansas History Commission, Old State House, Little Rock, Ark. Switzler (3-16-1819—5-24-1906) was a noted Missouri journalist, historian, and politician. In 1885 he was appointed chief of the Bureau of Statistics in the Treasury Department. One of the best informed men of his time on the history of Missouri, he spent his last years writing a history of the University of Missouri. Account taken from a biographical essay by Irving Dilliard. This paper is on file at the Arkansas History Commission, Old State House, Little Rock, Ark. Another traveler in 1836, wrote: "This is one of the finest farms we have seen and it is handsomely improved with a large brick dwelling and a fine chance of rich Caddo bottom land." William N. Wyatt, *Wyatt's Travel Diary 1836: With Comment by Mrs. Addie Evans Wynn and W. A. Evans (Grandchildren of W. N. Wyatt)* (Chicago: n.p., 1930), 13. Also see Newberry, "Jacob Barkman," *AHQ*, XIX, 317-318.

24. James Cummins and Stephen Clanton were commissioned as magistrates. Carter, *Territorial Papers*, XIX, *Arkansas Territory, 1819-1825* (1953), 814.

25. Herndon, *Centennial History*, I, 508; Little Rock *Arkansas Gazette*, Dec. 16, 1820; July 29, 1829. This newspaper will hereinafter be cited thus: *Arkansas Gazette*, followed by the date of the issue. For a somewhat un-

even account of early communications see Anna N. Yarbrough, "Arkansas' Struggle For Communication," *AHQ*, XVIII, 44–49.

26. This one-time buffalo trail was from Jackson's administration on the major thoroughfare across the state and later served as a gateway to the gold fields of California. Charlean M. Williams, *The Old Town Speaks* (Houston: Anson Jones Press, 1951), 4; George W. Featherstonhaugh, *Excursion Through the Slave States, From Washington on The Patomac to The Frontier of Mexico; With Sketches of Popular Manners and Geological Notices*, II (New York: Harper & Brothers, 1844), 1; Jack B. Scroggs, "Arkansas Statehood," *AHQ*, XX, 228; and Newberry, "Jacob Barkman," *AHQ*, XIX, 321.

27. U.S., Bureau of the Census, *Ninth Census of the United States: 1870*, I, *Statistics of Population* (Washington: Government Printing Office, 1872), 13–14.

28. Carter, *Territorial Papers*, XX, *Arkansas Territory*, 582. Ray Allen Billington discusses the "Blakeytown" settlement on the Ouachita as one of attraction in the expanding Miss. Valley frontier. He is in error, however, when he refers to it as "Blakeytown." The settlement was called "Blakelytown" before adoption of the name Arkadelphia. Ray Allen Billington, *Westward Expansion: A History of the American Frontier* (New York: The Macmillan Co., 1967), 467, 469.

29. Carter, *Territorial Papers*, XX, *Arkansas Territory*, 582.

30. Richard G. Biedleman, ed., "The 1818–20 Arkansas Journey of Thomas Nuttall," *AHQ*, XV, 254. The complete account of Nuttall's journey was published by Thomas H. Palmer of Philadelphia in 1821 and later reprinted as vol. 13 of Reuben Thwaites' *Early Western Travels*. Also see Ira D. Richards, *Story of a Rivertown, Little Rock in the Nineteenth Century* (n.p., 1969), 22–23.

31. Though Featherstonhaugh was complimentary of the Barkman estate and the hospitality he received, his account of the mistress is somewhat classic: "Mr. Barkman we did not see, but I shall certainly not forget his lady soon, as I have never seen anyone, as far as manners and exterior went, with less pretensions to be classed with the feminine gender. . . . She chewed tobacco, she smoked a pipe, she drank whiskey, and cursed and swore as heartily as any backwoodsman, all at the same time. . . . She must have been a person of surprising power in her youth, for I was informed that she was now comparatively refined to what she had been before her marriage; at that period, so full of interest to a lover, she was commonly known by the name of 'She Bar.' Mrs. Barkman, notwithstanding her habits, was not deficient in good nature to us. . . ." Featherstonhaugh, *Excursion Through The Slave States*, II, 114–115. Also see Richards, *Rivertown*, 24.

32. Farrar Newberry, "Clark County's Plantation Prince," *Democrat Magazine*, Dec. 13, 1959, 6–7.

33. "Let no one destroy this memorandum of plantation affairs," wrote Henry I. Bozeman on the fly-leaf of his 88-page journal covering the management of the farms of his Uncle Michael for the year 1857. Farrar Newberry, ed., "A Clark County Plantation Journal For 1857," *AHQ*, XVIII, 401–409.

34. Bozeman paid $1500 and one slave for the cost of the labor to build the handsome story-and-a-half frame house. Farrar Newberry, "Clark County's Plantation Prince," *Democrat Magazine*, Dec. 13, 1959, 6–7; and Newberry, "Plantation Journal," *AHQ*, XVIII, 401. The academy building is described as "having painted weatherboarding and glass in the windows." *Ibid.*, 407. There is recent evidence that the Nathan Strong house was built in 1843, and therefore could be a few years older than the Bozeman house. Interview, Amy Jean Greene, executive secretary, Clark County Historical Association, April 28, 1974.

35. Carter, *Territorial Papers*, XXI, *Arkansas Territory*, 1024–1025. Randolph, a son of Thomas Mann and Martha Jefferson Randolph, was a clerk in the State Department at the time of his appointment on February 23. Endorsement to letter of Randolph to Secretary of State, March 7, 1835, *Ibid.*, 1030.

36. *Southern Standard*, May 5, 1883. The information is taken from an article in a series by the late Dr. W. S. Smith. It is possible that Randolph was also associated with Samuel Swartwouth, perhaps the most notorious civil servant of the Jacksonian Era.

37. Known as "pretty Betty Martin of the White House," her marriage to Lewis Randolph had been performed at the home of her parents in Clifton (Davidson County) Tenn. in 1835. Grace Benton Nelson, *Arkansas Gazette*, Feb. 15, 1956. John Hallum gives much misinformation about the Randolphs, including a glowing account of their marriage which he describes as having been performed in the White House. John Hallum, *Biographical and Pictorial History of Arkansas*, I (Albany: Weed, Parson & Co., Printers, 1887), 211. According to research conducted by Grace Benton Nelson and librarians at both the Library of Congress and the Alderman Library of the University of Virginia, Hallum is in error about the setting for the marriage. Interview, Grace Benton Nelson, retired teacher, August 26, 1973. Randolph's wife later married Andrew Jackson's adopted son and accompanied him on his foreign missions. No doubt she was the only woman in Clark County history to adorn with equal grace the White House, a cabin in the wilderness, and the palaces of Europe.

38. In township 10 South, Range 19 West, Randolph owned all of Sections 4, 5, 6, 7, 8, 13, 14, and 15; the West half of 12; the South half of 3.

Land entries and patents are recorded in Manuscript Clark County Records, Book V, throughout. When I was researching Randolph's estate, the veteran clerk remarked to me, "There's something mighty strange 'bout all this." No doubt, there was.

39. His obituary read: "Death struck him from the stage of active life and by that death the citizens of his adopted county of Clark have lost a useful man and a good neighbor and the state a citizen of high promise." *Arkansas Gazette*, Oct. 3, 1837. The grave of Jefferson's grandson remained unmarked for more than 120 years until the Daughters of the American Colonists adopted the project, and now a handsome marker graces the place. For the inscription see Appendix A:5.

40. Randolph died intestate. Ex-President Jackson assisted the widow Randolph in attempting to maintain possession of the estate. Letter, Andrew Jackson to The Hon. William S. Fulton, Jan. 29, 1838, in Hallum, *History of Arkansas*, I, 214.

41. In 1825 the county seat was removed to the house of Henry Biscoe; in 1827 it was relocated at Adam Stroud's home on the Old Military Road; and in 1830 it was changed to Greenville (Hollywood). Herndon, *Centennial History*, I, 741; Thomas, *Arkansas and Its People*, II, 678. Manuscript Clark County Records, 1840–44, 91.

42. "An Act to Incorporate the Town of Arkadelphia," *Acts of Arkansas, November 2–December 23, 1846;* and "An Act to Incorporate the City of Arkadelphia," *Acts of Arkansas, November 3, 1856—January 15, 1857.*

43. W. H. Halliburton, "Arkadelphia, Rainbow City, Finds Pot of Gold," *Democrat Magazine*, March 22, 1953, 3; James R. Green, "Old Trunk Surrenders Some Interesting Documents Regarding Early History of School City, Clark's County Seat," *Democrat Magazine*, March 16, 1947, 6–7; and Allsopp, *Folklore*, I, 74.

44. Herndon, *Centennial History*, I, 871.

45. The story of the construction of the courthouse can be found in the Manuscript Clark County Court Records, 1840–44, 91, 218–219, and 268–271. Also see *Arkansas Gazette*, Nov. 23, 1842; Feb. 8, 1843; and Farrar Newberry, "Old Courthouse Saw Much History," *Southern Standard*, Feb. 23, 1961.

46. The house was originally a store, and the family lived in the rear of the building. Farrar Newberry, "Oldest Brick House in City Stands on Main Street Today," *Siftings Herald*, Dec. 13, 1962. Until razed in 1972, another of the antebellum business houses stood at 315 Main. That historic structure, built in 1857, had housed the Freedman's Bureau during Reconstruction days. Farrar Newberry, "Old Building Here Holds Historical Interest," *Siftings Herald*, Nov. 29, 1962. In 1963 the Chamber of Commerce placed a plaque on the structure. For the inscription see Appendix A:6.

47. Farrar Newberry, "Some Hotels of The Long Ago," *Southern Standard*, Oct. 1, 1959; and Farrar Newberry, "Some Hotels of The Long Ago," (A typescript in File Box 3, Farrar Newberry Papers, Division of Social Sciences, Henderson State College). Callaway's grandmother was Gemima Boone, daughter of Daniel Boone. Laura Scott Butler states that the Callaway Hotel was built in 1824. Laura Scott Butler, "History of Clark County," *Publications of the Arkansas Historical Association*, II (Fayetteville: Arkansas Historical Association, 1908), 568.

48. *Southern Standard*, July 31, 1969.

49. Act 127, *Acts of Arkansas, December, 1874—March, 1875*.

50. Born in Tuscaloosa, Ala., on November 19, 1824, he was a graduate of Union University in New York and a kinsman of John Witherspoon, a signer of the Declaration of Independence. In 1852 he was elected representative to the state legislature and in 1867 mayor of Arkadelphia. Governor Augustus Garland appointed him special Associate Justice of the Arkansas Supreme Court. Farrar Newberry, "Witherspoon Builds Law Offices 105 Years Ago." *Siftings Herald*, April 16, 1963. A plaque was placed on the building by the Woodmen of the World. For the inscription see Appendix A:7.

51. Flanagin, seventh governor of Arkansas, was born in Roadstown, New Jersey, November 3, 1817. He was educated in a Quaker school in that state and studied law in Illinois. In 1861 he was the Clark County delegate to the secession convention, and on November 15, 1862, was installed as governor. He died on October 23, 1874, and was buried in Arkadelphia. Allen Johnson and Dumas Malone, eds., *Dictionary of American Biography*, III (New York: Charles Scribner's Sons, 1959), 454.

52. Mattie C. Maxted, "Services for the Blind in Arkansas," *AHQ*, VIII (Spring, 1949), 82; Orval T. Griggs, Jr., "The Issues of the Powell Clayton Regime, 1868–1871," *AHQ*, VIII, 38; and Newberry, "Witherspoon."

53. Herndon, *Centennial History*, I, 284–285.

54. Lonnie J. White, *Politics on the Southwestern Frontier: Arkansas Territory, 1819–1836* (Memphis: Memphis State University Press, 1964), 23.

55. Hempstead, *Historical Review of Arkansas*, I, 131; and Herndon, *Centennial History*, I, 239. On Dec. 4, 1837, during the extra session of the state legislature an argument developed between Speaker John Wilson and Representative Maj. Joseph J. Anthony. Although accounts of the affair are confusing, Speaker Wilson killed Anthony in the House chamber. The tragedy, "truly a bloody baptism for the new capitol building," destroyed Wilson's political career. Herndon, *Centennial History*, I, 242.

56. Frank Vinsonhaler, "Early Doctors in Arkansas," in *The Scrapbook of Arkansas Literature: An Anthology for the General Reader*, Octavius Coke, ed. (Little Rock: American Caxton Society Press, 1939), 59.

57. Paul Hardage, *A Brief History of Dentistry* (n.p., n.d.), taken from a paper read before the Arkadelphia Rotary Club in 1955. This paper is on file in the Henderson Museum.

58. The *Arkansas Gazette,* founded in 1819, is the oldest newspaper in publication west of the Mississippi. For the early history of the paper see Margaret Ross, *Arkansas Gazette: The Early Years, 1819–1866* (Little Rock: Arkansas Gazette Foundation, 1969).

59. Hempstead, *Pictorial History,* 856; and *Southern Standard,* May 20, 1965.

60. Farrar Newberry, "Adam Clark: Faithful Recorder," *Southern Standard,* March 29, 1962.

61. *The Signal* was begun in 1881 and changed its name to *The Clipper* and became *The Herald* under George M. Beck. *The Siftings* was started by Ed and Claud McCorkle in 1886 and shortly afterward consolidated with *The Herald* to become the *Siftings Herald. The Arkadelphia Story* (n.p., n.d.), 5. A pamphlet published by the Arkadelphia Chamber of Commerce.

62. Manuscript Minutes of the First Baptist Church of Arkadelphia, Arkansas, under the date of July 15, 1851.

63. *Ibid.,* Dec. 10, 1852.

64. Interview with Royce L. Eaves, Past Master, Ancient, Free and Accepted Masons, Lodge 381, March 25, 1971.

65. Horace Jewell, *History of Methodism in Arkansas* (Little Rock: Press Printing Co., 1892), 344–345; and Farrar Newberry, "Arkadelphia Methodists' Early Churches," *Southern Standard,* April 12, 1962.

66. The noted minister was Dr. A. R. Winfield. See James A. Anderson, *Centennial History of Arkansas Methodism* (Benton, Arkansas: L. B. White Printing Co., 1935), 135; *Southern Standard,* June 15, 1872; and Newberry, "Arkadelphia Methodists' Early Churches," April 12, 1962.

67. A Brief History of the First Presbyterian Church, Arkadelphia, Arkansas (n.p., n.d.), 2–5. A book published by the local church. Sessional records date only from April 11, 1877. A plaque was placed on the building in 1959 by the Woodmen of the World. For the inscription see Appendix A:8.

68. Farrar Newberry, "Some Arkadelphia Church Bells of Other Days," *Southern Standard,* Oct. 19, 1961.

69. Boyd W. Johnson, *The Arkansas Frontier* (n.p., 1957), 102; and W. H. Halliburton, "Oaklawn Not Site of First Pony Race Course in State," Hot Springs *Sentinel-Record,* March 2, 1969.

70. *Siftings Herald,* June 9, 1960; and *Arkansas Gazette,* June 26, 1966.

71. Under the dates of January 23, 1857, and September 3, 1857, Newberry, ed., *AHQ,* XVIII, 402, 408.

72. Farrar Newberry, "The Yankee Schoolmarm Who 'Captured' Post-War Arkadelphia," *AHQ*, XVII (Autumn, 1958), 268; and *Southern Standard*, Aug. 24, 1961.

73. Arkadelphia *Arkansas Traveler*, Sept. 7, 1854; and *Southern Standard*, Aug. 7, 1969.

74. Herndon, *Centennial History*, I, 871–872; Farrar Newberry, "The Old Mooney Tannery," *Southern Standard*, Jan. 31, 1963; and Halliburton, *Democrat Magazine*, March 22, 1953, 3.

75. Elsie M. Lewis, "Economic Conditions in Ante-Bellum Arkansas: 1850–1861," *AHQ*, VI (Autumn, 1947), 261; Little Rock *Arkansas True Democrat*, July 19, 1854; and Newberry, *AHQ*, XIX, 323.

76. On January 13, 1863, William H. Pierre informed Major-General Samuel R. Curtis, commander of the Department of the Missouri, that Arkadelphia was the great depot for the trans-Mississippi Confederate States Army. Margaret Ross, "Chronicles of Arkansas, the Years of the Civil War: Scout of Federals Urges Attack on Arkadelphia," *Arkansas Gazette*, Feb. 13, 1963; Feb. 14, 1963. And Robert L. Kerby, *Kirby Smith's Confederacy: The Trans-Mississippi South, 1863–1865* (New York: Columbia University Press, 1972), 68–70, 74, 379.

77. Margaret Ross, "Chronicles of Arkansas, the Years of the Civil War: Need of Army Spurred Arkadelphia's Industry," *Arkansas Gazette*, Feb. 14, 1963; Halliburton, *Democrat Magazine*, March 22, 1953, 12; and Kerby, *Kirby Smith's Confederacy*, 68–70, 74.

78. U.S., Bureau of the Census, *Compendium of the Sixth Census of the United States: 1840* (Washington: Blair & Rives, 1841), 321.

79. Jacob Barkman owned 65. U.S., Bureau of the Census, *Seventh Census of the United States: 1850, Slave Inhabitants*, Table 1, Schedule No. 2, 548. Microfilm copy in the Arkansas History Commission, Old State House, Little Rock, Arkansas, Also see Robert B. Waly, "Arkansas Slaveholdings and Slaveholders in 1850," *AHQ*, XII, 52–73.

80. U.S., Bureau of the Census, *Eighth Census of the United States: 1860*, I, *Statistics of Population* (Washington: Government Printing Co., 1864), 13.

81. *Ibid.*, 19.

82. The occupation of Arkadelphia (March 29 to April 2) was part of the expedition of the Union forces into southern Arkansas in the spring of 1864. Led by General Frederick Steele, the Red River Campaign resulted in battles at Prairie De Ann, Poison Spring, Marks' Mill, and Jenkins' Ferry. For an excellent account see Ludwell H. Johnson, *Red River Campaign: Politics and Cotton in the Civil War* (Baltimore: Johns Hopkins Press, 1958); and Robert N. Scott, ed., *The War of the Rebellion: A Compilation of the Official Records of the Union and Confederate Armies*, XXXIV,

Series I, Part I (Washington: Government Printing Office, 1891), 177–849; and Kerby, *Kirby Smith's Confederacy*, 236.

83. Entries of March 29 and 30, 1864, John P. Wright MS Diary, in Ralph R. Rea, ed., "Diary of Private John P. Wright, U.S.A., 1864–1865," *AHQ*, XVI (Autumn, 1957), 313–314.

84. Report, Lieutenant-Colonel Adolph Dengler, June, 1864, in Scott, ed., *The War of the Rebellion*, 731.

85. Of note is Magnolia Manor, built for John B. McDaniel. For informative articles see W. H. Halliburton, "Historic Arkansas Homes," *Gazette Magazine*, June 8, 1941, 8–9; W. H. Halliburton, "D.A.R. Sponsors Pilgrimage to Residences of Special Note in Arkadelphia," *Democrat Magazine*, May 3, 1953, 6–7; W. H. Halliburton, "Historic House in Arkadelphia," *Ibid.*, Sept. 24, 1967, 3; Farrar Newberry, "A Fine Old Home and the Cook Family," *Southern Standard*, Feb. 4, 1965; Farrar Newberry, "A Real 'Forty-Niner' and His Palatial Arkadelphia Home," *Ibid.*, Oct. 8, 1964; and Farrar Newberry, "J. C. Saunders—Public Spirited Merchant," *Ibid.*, Sept. 10, 1964.

86. The purchase price was $65,000. Manuscript Minutes of the Board of Trustees of Henderson State College under the date of April 24, 1968. Also see W. H. Halliburton, "New Belles in Old House," *Democrat Magazine*, Nov. 17, 1968, 1.

87. Report, Lieutenant-Colonel Adolph Dengler, June, 1864, in Scott, ed., *The War of the Rebellion*, 732.

88. Farrar Newberry, "The Arkadelphia of 90 Years Ago," *Southern Standard*, Aug. 24, 1961.

89. *Ibid.*

90. Manuscript Minutes of the City Council of Arkadelphia, Arkansas, under the date of June 6, 1866, City Hall, Arkadelphia, Ark.

91. Farrar Newberry, "The Old Market Place," *Southern Standard*, March 1, 1962. The City Council Minutes from 1866 to 1873 tell much of the story of this interesting enterprise.

92. The *Southern Standard*, Nov. 8, 1882, announced arrival of the *Niroba*, the first steamboat to arrive since 1877; and Herndon, *Centennial History*, I, 516.

93. Halliburton, "Rainbow City," *Democrat Magazine*, March 12, 1953, 12; and Herndon, *Centennial History*, I, 522–523. The railroad is now a part of the Missouri Pacific system.

94. *Southern Standard*, Aug. 24, 1961.

95. Farrar Newberry, "The Old Opera House," *Ibid.*, April 25, 1958.

96. *The Arkadelphia Story*, 2–3.

97. *Southern Standard*, Feb. 22, 1879.

98. *Ibid.*

99. Farrar Newberry, "Proud Heritage of The Callaways," *Southern Standard*, Aug. 28, 1969. A marker was placed by the Chamber of Commerce in 1966 at the site of the first tuition school. For the inscription containing a list of teachers see Appendix A:9.

100. *Compendium of the Sixth Census*, 91; and U.S., Bureau of the Census, *Seventh Census of the United States: 1850*, I, *Statistics of Population* (Washington: Robert Armstrong, Public Printer, 1853), 550.

101. Newberry, *AHQ*, XVII, 265–266. The Chamber of Commerce placed a marker at the site in 1968. For the inscription see Appendix A:10.

102. *Ibid.*, 265–271.

103. *Southern Standard*, Sept. 7, 1961.

104. "We understand the Arkadelphia High School opened on Monday last with three teachers and one scholar." *Southern Standard*, Jan. 15, 1870. The Chamber of Commerce placed a marker at the location in 1962. For the inscription see Appendix A:11.

105. *Minutes of the Ouachita Annual Conference of the Methodist Episcopal Church, South*, under the dates of Dec. 3–6, 1859, 85. Rare Books Collection, Bailey Library, Hendrix College, Conway, Arkansas.

106. Act 72, *Acts of Arkansas, December, 1860–1861.*

107. For a somewhat complete account of the institution, see Appendix E. This account was prepared by the late William Oscar Wilson. At the time of his death, he was writing a history of education in Arkansas. This material is in the Rare Books Collection, Bailey Library, Hendrix College, Conway, Arkansas. Also see Willis Brewer Alderson, "A History of Methodist Higher Education in Arkansas, 1836–1933," unpublished dissertation (University of Arkansas, 1971), 103–111.

108. Margaret Ross, "Chronicles of Arkansas, the Years of the Civil War: General Frederick Steele and the Camden Expedition," *Arkansas Gazette*, Dec. 8, 1958.

109. The short life of the college can be followed through a series of articles appearing in the *Southern Standard;* among them are issues of Aug. 3, 1872; April 26, 1873; June 14, 1873; and Aug. 16, 1873. See also Newberry, *AHQ*, XVII, 265–271.

110. Griggs, *AHQ*, VIII, 38–39; and Maxted, *AHQ*, VIII, 82.

111. *Ibid.; Arkansas Gazette*, July 11, 1868; July 17, 1868.

112. Private Act I, *Acts of Arkansas*, 1879. This property had been sold on May 1, 1877, by the Commissioner of State Lands for the sum of $1,050. *Ibid.*, Section 1, released the Association from the balance of the debt of $350.

113. The announcement stated that the "press" had been delayed await-

ing the news of the location of the state Baptist college. *Southern Standard*, April 10, 1886. Editorials in the *Southern Standard* of Feb. 13, 20, and 27, 1886, cited the advantages for Arkadelphia in securing the college.

114. Herndon, *Centennial History*, I, 571. For preparation of this chapter on Arkadelphia, the author wishes to express his indebtedness to the late Farrar Newberry for use of a series of articles on Arkadelphia and its personages, to Ira Don Richards for helpful suggestions and use of his publication, *Story of a Rivertown, Little Rock in the Nineteenth Century*, and to Eugene Taylor Jackman for his generous aid. Richards and Jackman are, respectively, professor and associate professor of history at Henderson State College.

CHAPTER III

THE FOUNDING OF THE COLLEGE

1. Manuscript Minutes of the Board of Trustees of the Arkadelphia College of the Methodist Episcopal Church, South, under the dates of April 16 and June 4, 1890. These minutes will hereinafter be cited thus: Board Minutes, followed by the date of the meeting. For information concerning the Manuscript Minutes, see Appendix C. Horace Jewell in *History of Methodism in Arkansas* (Little Rock: Press Printing Co., 1892), 365, states "Arkadelphia Female College, located at Arkadelphia, was organized in 1891." In this statement the author is in error. Apparently he confused the college with the earlier Methodist institution of that name; how he arrived at the incorrect date of founding is a complete mystery. This is an example of an early writer stating data incorrectly and that information being repeated as fact by subsequent historians. This error has been repeated by numerous writers, including Dallas T. Herndon, Director of State Archives and History, in his *Centennial History of Arkansas*, I (Chicago: S. J. Clarke Publishing Co., 1922), 569.

2. Interview, Amy Jean Greene, associate professor, Sept. 11, 1970. Miss Greene was graduated from Henderson-Brown in 1928, and from 1945 until retirement in 1972 was a member of the faculty of Henderson State.

3. William Ritchie, "Henderson, Today and Yesterday: The Story of the First Fifty Years," in *Essays on Southern Life and Culture: A Henderson Symposium*, A. B. Bonds, ed. (Arkadelphia: Henderson State Teachers College, 1941), 238.

4. Arkadelphia *Southern Standard*, Nov. 8, 1889. This newspaper will hereinafter be cited thus: *Southern Standard*, followed by the date of the issue.

5. U.S., Dept. of the Interior, Bureau of Education *Bulletin* No. 27

(Washington: Government Printing Office, 1912), 29. The optimistic view
of the editor of the *Arkansas Gazette* concerning the future of the institution was evidenced when he wrote "we understand all the lands are first
class and if judiciously disposed of, the proceed arising from their sale or
lease may constitute a fund to establish an institution for the education of
the youth of the present day, and of future generations, which may resound
to the credit of our territory, and to the imperishable honor of the future
state of Arkansas." Little Rock *Arkansas Gazette*, Feb. 2, 1831. Also see
Herndon, *Centennial History*, I, 551; and Robert A. Leflar, *The First 100
Years: Centennial History of the University of Arkansas* (Fayetteville:
University of Arkansas Foundation, Inc., 1972), 1.

6. For the history of the University of Arkansas see Leflar, *Centennial
History of the University of Arkansas;* and Harrison Hale, *University of
Arkansas* (Fayetteville: The University of Arkansas Alumni Association,
1948). Although the University of Florida uses 1851 as its founding date,
Donald G. Tewksbury in *The Founding of American Colleges and Uni-
versities Before the Civil War* (New York: Columbia University, 1932),
28, 31, states that no institution of higher learning in that state survived the
Civil War. The three states are Arkansas, Florida, and Texas.

7. When created in 1836, Arkansas Conference embraced all of Arkansas
and the northern portion of Louisiana. In 1854 the General Conference divided Arkansas Conference, forming its southern territory into Ouachita
Conference. In 1866 Ouachita Conference was renamed and henceforth
known as Little Rock Conference. An additional division of Arkansas Conference was made in 1870 when the eastern section was designated White
River Conference. This arrangement stood until 1914 when reorganization
abolished the White River, and renamed the Arkansas the North Arkansas
Conference. James A. Anderson, *Centennial History of Arkansas Methodism: A History of the Methodist Episcopal Church, South, in the State
of Arkansas, 1815–1935* (Benton, Ark.: L. B. White Printing Co., 1935),
221.

8. Manuscript Minutes of the Arkansas Annual Conference of the Methodist Episcopal Church, under the date of November, 1836. These first
minutes of the conference do not give the specific dates, nor are the pages
numbered; they are on file in the Arkansas History Commission, Old State
House, Little Rock, Ark.

9. The academy under the direction of a Mr. and Mrs. Mecklin, opened
Feb. 2, 1836. Emily M. Penton, "Typical Women's Schools in Arkansas
Before the War of 1861–65," *Arkansas Historical Quarterly*, IV (Winter,
1945), 325. This journal will hereinafter be cited thus: *AHQ*, followed by
the volume number of the issue.

10. *Minutes of the Arkansas Annual Conference of the Methodist Epis-*

copal Church, South, under the dates of November 20–25, 1844, 6; also see Anderson, *History of Arkansas Methodism,* 71–72.

11. For an account of Washington Male and Female Seminary, see Penton, "Typical Women's Schools in Arkansas," *AHQ,* IV, 325–339.

12. This Methodist institution, chartered in 1850 was the first Arkansas school to be chartered by the name "college." The name was changed to Soulesbury Institute in 1852. U.S., Dept. of the Interior, Bureau of Education *Bulletin* No. 27, 19. Also see Emily M. Penton, "Higher Education for Women in Arkansas Prior to the Civil War," unpublished thesis (University of Chicago, 1930), 65; and *Minutes of the White River Annual Conference of the Methodist Episcopal Church, South,* under the dates of December 12–17, 1883, 50. The minutes of this conference will hereinafter be cited thus: *Minutes, White River Conference,* followed by the dates of the session.

13. Act 51, *Acts of Arkansas, December, 1856—January, 1857;* also see Penton, "Typical Women's Schools in Arkansas," *AHQ,* IV, 334–335.

14. Act 37, *Acts of Arkansas, December, 1860—January, 1861;* also see Penton, "Typical Women's Schools in Arkansas," *AHQ,* IV, 334–335.

15. *Minutes of the Little Rock Annual Conference of the Methodist Episcopal Church, South,* under the dates of November 20–25, 1868, 14. The minutes of this conference will hereinafter be cited thus: *Minutes, Little Rock Conference,* followed by the dates of the session.

16. *Minutes, Little Rock Conference,* November 21–26, 1869, 12; and Little Rock *Daily Arkansas Gazette,* Feb. 27, 1870.

17. *Minutes, Little Rock Conference,* November 25–30, 1873, 10; Jewell, *Methodism in Arkansas,* 232; *Minutes of the Arkansas Annual Conference of the Methodist Episcopal Church, South,* under the dates of November 14–19, 1873, 12. The minutes of this conference will hereinafter be cited thus: *Minutes, Arkansas Conference,* followed by the dates of the session. And *Minutes, White River Conference,* Oct. 30–Nov. 3, 1872, 15.

18. Little Rock *Daily Arkansas Gazette,* Aug. 23, 1874.

19. *Biographical and Historical Memoirs of Central Arkansas* (Chicago: Goodspeed Publishing Co., 1890), 406, 514; and Little Rock *Arkansas Democrat,* Nov. 8, 1931.

20. Anderson, *History of Arkansas Methodism,* 399.

21. Guy A. Simmons, "Hendrix College: A Brief Historical Sketch, 1884–1944" (A typescript in Bailey Library, Hendrix College, Conway, Arkansas, 1944), 9.

22. *Minutes, Arkansas Conference,* Nov. 15–20, 1882, 7; Nov. 14–19, 1883, 6; *Minutes, White River Conference,* Dec. 12–17, 1883, 50; and *Minutes, Little Rock Conference,* Nov. 22–27, 1882, 19.

23. Anderson, *History of Arkansas Methodism,* 399.

24. *Minutes, Arkansas Conference,* Nov. 14–19, 1883, 10; *Minutes, Little Rock Conference,* Nov. 28–Dec. 3, 1883, 12; and *Minutes, White River Conference,* Dec. 12–17, 1883, 6, 21. It appears that the Central Centenary Committee meeting in Nashville, Tennessee, 1883, named a Centenary Committee for the Little Rock Conference. *Minutes, Little Rock Conference,* Nov. 28–Dec. 3, 1883, 12.

25. In 1874 the Arkansas Conference proposed the establishing of a state male college by the three conferences, and in 1875 the three proposed establishment of both a male and female college in Little Rock. In 1822 proposal was made to accept Quitman as the state male college; none of the proposals, however, were enacted. The Commission on Education in its report to the conference in 1883 stated "We deeply deplore the want of educational facilities in this Conference." *Minutes, White River Conference,* Dec. 12–17, 1883, 50.

26. C.C.I. was founded in 1876 by its owner, Isham L. Burrow, who related it sympathetically to the Methodist Church. *Minutes, Arkansas Conference,* Nov. 14–19, 1883, 7.

27. The meeting was held June 10–11, 1884. *Ibid.,* Nov. 19–24, 1884, 7.

28. *Minutes, Little Rock Conference,* Nov. 22–27, 1882, 19.

29. The purchase price was $12,500. *Minutes, Arkansas Conference,* Nov. 19–24, 1884, 8; and *Minutes, Little Rock Conference,* Nov. 26–Dec. 1, 1884, 20.

30. *Minutes, White River Conference,* Dec. 18, 1886, 7, 13–14; and *Minutes, Arkansas Conference,* Nov. 16–21, 1887, 8.

31. At that time Bishop Hendrix was Presiding Bishop over Arkansas; he had formerly been President of Central College, Fayette, Missouri, when Dr. A. C. Millar, the new president of Hendrix, was a student in the Missouri institution. *Hendrix College Catalogue,* 1891–1892, 7.

32. *Minutes, Arkansas Conference,* Nov. 16–21, 1887, 8. That same year in Mississippi Bishop Galloway was involved with former Confederate President Jefferson Davis in a painful controversy over prohibition. See Frances Allen Cabaniss and James Allen Cabaniss, "Religion in Mississippi Since 1860," *Journal of Mississippi History,* IX (Oct., 1947), 212. Also see Allen Cabaniss, *The University of Mississippi: Its First Hundred Years* (Hattiesburg: University & College Press of Mississippi, 1971), 95–96.

33. *Minutes, White River Conference,* Dec. 10, 1888, 23.

34. *Ibid.,* Dec. 11–16, 1889, 28.

35. *Minutes, Arkansas Conference,* Nov. 20–25, 1889, 7, 13.

36. Simmons, "Hendrix College," 19.

37. Anderson, *History of Arkansas Methodism,* 401.

38. *Southern Standard,* March 14, 1890.

39. *Ibid.*

40. *Ibid.*, March 21, 1890. Ritchie in "Henderson, Today and Yesterday," 240, states that the meeting was held March 21, but he apparently confused the meeting date with the publication date of the weekly *Southern Standard*.

41. *Southern Standard*, March 21, 1890.

42. Anderson, *History of Arkansas Methodism*, 401; and Simmons, "Hendrix College," 19–20.

43. *Ibid.*

44. *Ibid.*

45. *Southern Standard*, March 28, 1890.

46. *Ibid.*

47. *Ibid.*

48. *Ibid.*, June 13, 1890.

49. *Ibid.*, April 18, 1890.

50. Board Minutes, April 16, 1890; and *Catalogue of The Arkadelphia Methodist College*, 1890–1891, 4. This bulletin will hereinafter be cited thus: *Catalogue*, followed by the date.

51. *Minutes, Little Rock Conference*, Dec. 3–8, 1890, 24; and *Southern Standard*, April 18, 1890.

52. *Ibid.*

53. Board Minutes, April 16, 1890; and *Catalogue*, 1890–1891, 4.

54. *Minutes, Little Rock Conference*, Dec. 13–17, 1890, 25; Simmons, "Hendrix College," 16; and J. H. Riggin, *Lest We Forget or Character Gems Gleaned From South Arkansas* (Pine Bluff, Ark.: Norton-Vail Printing Co., n.d.), 11.

55. Board Minutes, April 16, 1890; and *Minutes, Little Rock Conference*, Dec. 3–8, 1890, 23.

56. For an account of the development of the trustee system see Morris Bishop, *A History of Cornell* (Ithaca, N.Y.: Cornell University Press, 1962), 69.

57. Board Minutes, April 16, 1890.

58. *Southern Standard*, Nov. 28, 1890.

59. *Minutes, Little Rock Conference*, Dec. 3–7, 1896, 23–24; and Farrar Newberry, "John McLaughlin: Founder of Old Henderson," *Southern Standard*, Dec. 26, 1963. There are a number of discrepancies in the spellings of *McLauchlan*, i.e., the above title; your historian has chosen to use that found in the manuscript Board Minutes.

60. Board Minutes, April 16, 1890; and Riggin, *Lest We Forget*, 162.

61. *Ibid.*

62. Farrar Newberry, "Captain Huie, Arkadelphia Enterpriser," *Southern Standard*, Aug. 3, 1961.

63. *Ibid.*; and Clifton E. Hull, *Shortline Railroads of Arkansas* (Norman: University of Oklahoma Press, 1969), 282.

64. Newberry, "Captain Huie," *Southern Standard*, Aug. 3, 1961; *Biographical and Historical Memoirs of Southern Arkansas* (Chicago: Goodspeed Publishing Co., 1890), 144-45; Riggin, *Lest We Forget*, 164-66; and Arkadelphia *Siftings Herald*, July 1, 1929.

65. *Memoirs of Southern Arkansas*, 135-36; and Farrar Newberry, "John R. Dale—Noted Doctor of Former Days," *Southern Standard*, July 6, 1961.

66. *Ibid.*, Sept. 14, 1894.

67. *Memoirs of Southern Arkansas*, 136; and Newberry, "John R. Dale," *Southern Standard*, July 6, 1961.

68. *First Annual Report of the Railroad Commission of the State of Arkansas, 1899–1900* (Little Rock: Thompson Lithograph & Printing Co., 1901), 441.

69. Newberry, "John R. Dale," *Southern Standard*, July 6, 1961.

70. Board Minutes, April 16, 1890.

71. Riggin, *Lest We Forget*, 163-64.

72. Board Minutes, April 16, 1890.

73. *Ibid.*, June 4, 1890.

74. *Ibid.* For a complete copy of the constitution see Appendix D.

75. Board Minutes, June 4, 1890.

76. *Ibid.*

77. *Ibid.*

78. *Ibid.*

79. This document is on display in the Henderson State College Museum. For the complete content of the charter see Appendix D.

CHAPTER IV

THE LAUNCHING OF THE COLLEGE

1. *Oracle*, May 17, 1910. The *Oracle*, student newspaper of the college, was first published October 6, 1908.

2. *Ibid.*

3. The manuscript minutes of the Arkadelphia Public School Board reveal the story of the rental of the public school facilities. The trustees' original proposition was to rent the building until Sept. 29, 1890, for $15.00. An extension to Oct. 13 was later granted, and the public school term delayed until that time. The total fee paid for the one and one-half months rent was $22.50. Manuscript Minutes of the Arkadelphia Public School Board, under the dates of June 16, 1890; Sept. 17, 1890; Dec. 16, 1890. Also

see Arkadelphia *Southern Standard,* Sept. 5, 1890. This newspaper will hereinafter be cited thus: *Southern Standard,* followed by the date of the issue. And Little Rock *Arkansas Methodist,* June 9, 1892. The *Arkansas Methodist* is the official newspaper of Arkansas Methodism. This newspaper will hereinafter be cited thus: *Arkansas Methodist,* followed by the date of the issue.

4. *Catalogue of The Arkadelphia Methodist College,* 1890–1891, 7–10. This bulletin will hereinafter be cited thus: *Catalogue,* followed by the date.

5. *Ibid.*

6. Manuscript Minutes of the Board of Trustees of The Arkadelphia College of the Methodist Episcopal Church, South, under the date of June 4, 1890. These minutes will hereinafter be cited thus: Board Minutes, followed by the date of the meeting.

7. Weston A. Goodspeed, ed., *The Provinces and the States: A History of the Province of Louisiana Under France and Spain, and of the Territories and States of the United States Formed Therefrom,* VII (Madison: Western Historical Association, 1904), 326.

8. Farrar Newberry, "George C. Jones, First President of Old Henderson," *Southern Standard,* April 16, 1964.

9. *Methodist College Magazine,* I (Oct., 1891), 12.

10. *Arkansas Methodist,* July 9, 1902.

11. *Ibid.,* Aug. 10, 1893; and *Methodist College Magazine,* I, 12.

12. H. W. Brooks, "Stuttgart Institute and Its New President, Prof. G. C. Jones," *Arkansas Methodist,* Aug. 28, 1889.

13. Jones attended Drew Theological Seminary, Madison, New Jersey. *The Arkansas Technic,* II (Feb., 1896), ii.

14. *Arkansas Methodist,* Nov. 27, 1901.

15. *Methodist College Magazine,* I (Oct., 1891), 10.

16. Letter, Mary Dale Jones Nelms to Farrar Newberry, May 4, 1964. Mary Nelms is the daughter of the late President Jones, File Box 3, Farrar Newberry Papers, Division of Social Sciences, Henderson State College.

17. *Arkansas Methodist,* Aug. 10, 1893.

18. Letter, Mary Dale Jones Nelms to Farrar Newberry, March 28, 1964, Newberry Papers.

19. Martha R. Stuart, "H S T C Diary: 1891," *The Pines,* I (Spring, 1941), 14. A literary magazine of original material published by the students of Henderson State Teachers College for the encouragement of creative writing.

20. *Catalogue,* 1890–1891, 12, 14–17.

21. *Ibid.,* 5–6.

22. *Methodist College Magazine*, I (Oct., 1891), 11; Letter, Registrar, Randolph-Macon College, to John G. Hall, July 31, 1973, in my possession; and *Oracle*, Oct. 5, 1909.
23. *Ibid.*, May 17, 1910.
24. *Catalogue*, 1890–1891, 5; and *Southern Standard*, Aug. 2, 1917.
25. *Catalogue*, 1890–1891, 6.
26. *Oracle*, May 17, 1910.
27. *Catalogue*, 1890–1891, 6.
28. *Ibid.*, 5, 11.
29. *Ibid.*, 6; and *Oracle*, May 17, 1910.
30. *Catalogue*, 1890–1891, 21–22.
31. The New England Association of Colleges and Secondary Schools was founded in 1885. The Middle States Association of Colleges and Secondary Schools was founded in 1887. Lloyd E. Blauch, ed., *Accreditation in Higher Education* (Washington: Government Printing Office, 1959), 10.
32. Letter, Maurice R. Horton, Principal, Dollarway School District, Pine Bluff, Ark., to John G. Hall, April 4, 1974, in my possession; and Interview, Maurice R. Horton, April 20, 1974.
33. *Catalogue*, 1890–1891, 14, 12.
34. *Ibid.*, 13.
35. *Ibid.*, 1893–1894, 12.
36. *Ibid.*, 1890–1891, 12–13.
37. *Ibid.*, 14–17.
38. Morris Bishop, *A History of Cornell* (Ithaca, N.Y.: Cornell University Press, 1962), 163.
39. *Catalogue*, 1890–1891, 15.
40. *Ibid.*, 1970–1971, 52, 139–142.
41. *Ibid.*, 1890–1891, 14–17.
42. *Ibid.*, 17, 7–10.
43. Board Minutes, May 26, 1903.
44. *Catalogue*, 1890–1891, 21.
45. *Ibid.*, 24.
46. *Ibid.*, 17–18, 23.
47. *Ibid.*, 21.
48. *Ibid.*, 19–20.
49. *Ibid.* One scholar who wrote on college life in the 19th century stated students had no rights worthy of respect, were not intended to be important enough to have rights, and that fear on the one side and suspicion on the other marked the relationship between professor and student. A professor popular with his minions was likely to be looked upon as a failure. E. Merton Coulter, *College Life in the Old South* (New York: Macmillan

Co., 1928), 63, as cited in Eugene Taylor Jackman, "The New Mexico Military Institute 1891–1966: A Critical History," unpublished dissertation (University of Mississippi, 1967), 38.

50. *Catalogue*, 1891–1892, 23.

51. *Ibid.*, 1890–1891, 20, 22.

52. *Ibid.*, 19–20.

53. *Ibid.*, 18.

54. *Southern Standard*, May 8, 1891.

55. *Catalogue*, 1890–1891, 18–19.

56. *Ibid.*

57. *Ibid.*, 23.

58. *Southern Standard*, June 6, 1890; June 27, 1890.

59. *Ibid.*, June 27, 1890.

60. *Ibid.*, Sept. 5, 1890.

61. *Minutes of the Little Rock Annual Conference of the Methodist Episcopal Church, South*, under the dates of December 3–8, 1890, 24. These minutes will hereinafter be cited thus: *Minutes, Little Rock Conference*, followed by the dates of the session.

62. *Ibid.*

63. *Ibid.*

64. *Southern Standard*, Dec. 12, 1890.

65. *Minutes of the Arkansas Annual Conference of the Methodist Episcopal Church, South*, under the dates of November 19–24, 1890, 13.

66. *Southern Standard*, Dec. 12, 1890; and *Arkansas Methodist*, Jan. 28, 1891.

67. *Southern Standard*, Feb. 6, 1891.

68. Interview, Mrs. R. B. Thomas, July 23, 1970. Also see *Oracle*, April 30, 1971. At the time of the interview, the late Mrs. Thomas was Henderson's oldest living graduate.

69. *Catalogue*, 1890–1891, 21.

70. Interview, Mrs. R. B. Thomas.

71. *Ibid.*

72. *Catalogue*, 1891–1892, 23.

73. *Southern Standard*, Jan. 2, 1891; Jan. 30, 1891. For an account of the theater see Farrar Newberry, "The Old Opera House," *Ibid.*, April 25, 1958.

74. *Ibid.*, May 15, 1891.

75. *Oracle*, May 17, 1910.

76. Stuart, "H S T C Diary," *The Pines*, I, 14. For an account of the Arkadelphia artist see Farrar Newberry, "Charles Richardson—Noted Arkadelphia Artist," *Southern Standard*, July 12, 1962.

77. *Ibid.*, June 12, 1891.

78. *Ibid.*, Sept. 5, 1891.
79. *Ibid.*, Oct. 23, 1891.
80. *Ibid.*, May 8, 1891.
81. Farrar Newberry, "Arkadelphia in the Gay Nineties," *Southern Standard*, Oct. 29, 1964; and Farrar Newberry, "City's First Telephone Exchange," *Ibid.*, April 25, 1959.
82. *Ibid.*, May 8, 1891.
83. *Ibid.*
84. U.S., Bureau of the Census, *Compendium of the Eleventh Census of the United States: 1890* (Washington: Government Printing Office, 1892), 365.
85. *Southern Standard*, Aug. 22, 1890; Sept. 11, 1891.
86. *Ibid.*, Jan. 2, 1891; Sept. 25, 1891. The Institute was founded in Little Rock in 1886 as Bethel University; the name was changed to Bethel Institute in 1888, and to Shorter University in 1892. In 1898 the school was removed to North Little Rock where it operates today as Shorter College. *Shorter College Catalogue*, 1970–1971, 10–11.
87. *Southern Standard*, Dec. 5, 1890; May 8, 1891. The article asserted that students from 11 states were attending.
88. *Ibid.*, April 3, 1892; April 29, 1892; and Roy L. Davis, *Centennial History of Presbyterianism (U.S.) in Arkansas* (Little Rock: Arkansas Book House, 1954), 49. The College of the Ozarks is operated by the Presbyterian Church, USA, in Arkansas. In 1951 the two church groups made an unsuccessful attempt to merge the colleges.
89. *Southern Standard*, April 8, 1898; and Dallas T. Herndon, *Centennial History of Arkansas*, I (Chicago: S. J. Clarke Publishing Co., 1922), 576.
90. *Southern Standard*, May 8, 1891.
91. *Ibid.*, Sept. 18, 1891.
92. *Ibid.*, Aug. 22, 1890; Atlanta [Texas] *Herald*, as reprinted in *Southern Standard*, May 8, 1891.
93. *Southern Standard*, Sept. 4, 1891.
94. *Minutes, Little Rock Conference*, Dec. 2–7, 1891, 19.
95. *Catalogue*, 1891–1892, 8–12.
96. *Ibid.*, 5–6.
97. *Southern Standard*, April 24, 1891; May 1, 1891; and *Catalogue*, 1890–1891, 21.
98. *Southern Standard*, April 24, 1891.
99. *Catalogue*, 1890–1891, 22.
100. *Ibid.*, 1891–1892, 21.
101. *Henderson State College Student Guide*, 1973–1974, 47.
102. *Methodist College Magazine*, I (Oct., 1891), 26.
103. *Ibid.*, III (May, 1894), cover page.

104. *Ibid.*, I (Nov., 1891), 37.
105. *Catalogue*, 1890–1891, 14; and *Ibid.*, 1891–1892, 15.
106. *Southern Standard*, May 1, 1896.
107. *Methodist College Magazine*, I (Nov., 1891), 22.
108. *Southern Standard*, May 1, 1896; May 7, 1897.
109. *Ibid.*, Oct. 23, 1891.
110. *Methodist College Magazine*, I (Nov., 1891), 23.
111. *Minutes, Little Rock Conference*, Dec. 2–7, 1891, 20.
112. Farrar Newberry, "Capt. Henderson—Savior of the College," *Southern Standard*, May 31, 1962.
113. Interview, Roma Garrett Meier, June 22, 1971. Mrs. Meier is a second cousin of the late C. C. Henderson.
114. J. H. Riggin, *Lest We Forget or Character Gems Gleaned From South Arkansas* (Pine Bluff, Ark.: Norton-Vail Printing Co., n.d.), 168.
115. *Ibid.;* and Newberry, "Capt. Henderson," *Southern Standard*, May 31, 1962.
116. *Ibid.*, Feb. 28, 1880; Sept. 9, 1880.
117. Interview, Roma Garrett Meier. Miss Hall was a cousin of Mrs. Walter E. Barkman, also a native of New Orleans.
118. James A. Anderson, *Centennial History of Arkansas Methodism* (Benton, Ark.: L. B. White Printing Co., 1935), 365, 475.
119. Interview, Roma Garrett Meier.
120. Newberry, "Capt. Henderson," *Southern Standard*, May 31, 1962.
121. Clifton E. Hull, *Shortline Railroads of Arkansas* (Norman: University of Oklahoma Press, 1969), 258.
122. *Ibid.*
123. For a complete account of Henderson's railroad interests see Hull, *Shortline Railroads*, 257–305.
124. Newberry, "Capt. Henderson," *Southern Standard*, May 31, 1962.
125. *Ibid.*, March 19, 1897.
126. Henderson and Key sold the 27 acres to the town for the sum of $2,205.30, provided that the city of Arkadelphia used and maintained said property as a public park. Manuscript Deed Record Book 73, Clark County Courthouse, Arkadelphia, Arkansas, 246.
127. *Catalogue*, 1890–1891, 9.
128. *Southern Standard*, June 10, 1892; and *Catalogue*, 1891–1892, 8.

CHAPTER V

THE TROUBLED YEARS

1. *Minutes of the Little Rock Annual Conference of the Methodist Episcopal Church, South*, under the dates of December 7–11, 1892, 14. These

minutes will hereinafter be cited thus: *Minutes, Little Rock Conference,* followed by the dates of the session.

2. Arkadelphia *Southern Standard,* Aug. 1, 1890. This newspaper will hereinafter be cited thus: *Southern Standard,* followed by the date of the issue.

3. *Catalogue of The Arkadelphia Methodist College,* 1892–1893, 27–28. This bulletin will hereinafter be cited thus: *Catalogue,* followed by the date.

4. *Ibid.,* 1893–1894, 2.

5. *Ibid.,* 1904–1905, 27.

6. *Ibid.,* 1893–1894, 3.

7. *Southern Standard,* Feb. 26, 1897.

8. *Catalogue,* 1894–1895, 3.

9. *Southern Standard,* Feb. 26, 1897, as reprinted from *St. Louis Republic.*

10. *Minutes, Little Rock Conference,* Dec. 7–11, 1892, 14.

11. *Ibid.,* Dec. 6–11, 1893, 12.

12. *Ibid.,* Dec. 7–11, 1892, 14; and Little Rock *Arkansas Methodist,* June 16, 1892. The Methodist newspaper will hereinafter be cited thus: *Arkansas Methodist,* followed by the date of the issue.

13. *Minutes, Little Rock Conference,* Dec. 7–11, 1892, 14.

14. *Ibid.,* Dec. 13–17, 1894; and Manuscript Deed Record Book 47, Clark County Courthouse, Arkadelphia, Ark., 87.

15. *Catalogue,* 1894–1895, 9–10.

16. *Southern Standard,* Dec. 21, 1894.

17. *Minutes, Little Rock Conference,* Dec. 13–17, 1894, 12; and *Arkansas Methodist,* Dec. 20, 1894.

18. *Minutes, Little Rock Conference,* Dec. 13–17, 1894, 12.

19. *Ibid.,* 25; and *Ibid.,* Dec. 5–10, 1895, 24.

20. *Southern Standard,* Dec. 21, 1894.

21. *Catalogue,* 1893–1894, 8–10; and *Ibid.,* 1895–1896, 9–11.

22. *Ibid.,* 1895–1896, 30–31.

23. Proceedings of the Board of Trustees of Arkadelphia Methodist College on June 6, 1892, as reported in *Southern Standard,* June 10, 1892.

24. *Arkansas Methodist,* May 4, 1911.

25. *Ibid.;* Letter, Fred P. Entler, Alumni Association Executive Secretary, Emory & Henry College, to John G. Hall, July 31, 1973, in my possession; Letter, William O. Batts, Jr., University Registrar, Vanderbilt University, to John G. Hall, October 12, 1973, in my possession; *Alumni Directory: "Who's Who" Among Vanderbilt Men and Women,* I (Nashville: Vanderbilt University, 1923), 588; Letter, Herbert Hucks, Jr., Archivist, Wofford College, to John G. Hall, September 14, 1973, in my possession; David Duncan Wallace, *History of Wofford College* (Nashville:

Vanderbilt University Press, 1951), 112, 272; Charleston, S.C. *News and Courier*, July 28, 1890; and Charleston, S.C. *Southern Christian Advocate*, Sept. 30, 1886.

26. *Arkansas Methodist*, May 4, 1911.

27. *Ibid.;* and *Oracle*, April 4, 1911. The *Oracle* is the student newspaper of the college and was first published Oct. 6, 1908.

28. *Catalogue*, 1894–1895, 7.

29. *Ibid.*, 1894–1895, 7.

30. *Ibid.*, 28–29.

31. Little Rock *Arkansas Gazette*, Dec. 26, 1895, as reprinted in Little Rock *Arkansas Gazette*, Dec. 26, 1970.

32. *Southern Standard*, Jan. 10, 1896; Jan. 24, 1896.

33. *Catalogue*, 1894–1895, 7.

34. *The Arkansas Technic*, I (Nov., 1895), 49.

35. *Ibid.*

36. *Catalogue*, 1895–1896 (Announcements for 1896–1897), 7.

37. Drummond, Chairman of the Division of Social Sciences since 1957, has also served as Dean of the School of Liberal Arts since 1969.

38. The other two are James S. Chase, Chairman, Department of History, and Gordon H. McNeil, professor of history, University of Arkansas, Fayetteville.

39. *Southern Standard*, Aug. 21, 1896.

40. *Ibid.*

41. Arlington J. Stone, "The Dawn of a New Science," *The American Mercury*, Aug., 1928, 446, as cited in George E. Mowry, ed., *The Twenties: Fords, Flappers & Fanatics* (Englewood Cliffs, N.J.: Prentice-Hall, Inc., 1963), 10.

42. *Southern Standard*, April 3, 1896.

43. *Catalogue*, 1895–1896 (Announcements for 1896–1897), 30.

44. *Southern Standard*, Feb. 28, 1896.

45. *Catalogue*, 1895–1896, 30. Of the students completing the business course, perhaps none achieved higher recognition than Frank O. Garrett who received a certificate at the last commencement of Arkadelphia Methodist College. Son of a college employee and cousin to Charles C. Henderson, he attained an international reputation. He enjoyed a distinguished career in railroading, wrote several books on railroad safety, and in 1956, under the auspices of Westinghouse Air Brake Company, supervised modernization of the Turkish National Railways and trained their personnel in use of those innovations. Interview, Roma Garrett Meier, sister of the late Frank O. Garrett, June 22, 1971; and Letter, Frank O. Garrett to Farrar Newberry, July 10, 1965, File Box 3, Farrar Newberry Papers, Division of Social Sciences, Henderson State College. Also see Arkadelphia *Daily Siftings Herald*, June 3, 1958.

46. *Catalogue*, 1894–1895, 5.

47. For the story concerning return of the diploma see *Southern Standard*, July 12, 1962. A Mistress of English Literature diploma, awarded to Georgia Ann Crawford in 1896, is also property of the Henderson museum.

48. *Catalogue*, 1894–1895, 5; and *Ibid.*, 1903–1904, 3.

49. Thirty M.S.E. degrees were granted on that date. The other graduate degrees are the Master of Music Education (M.M.E.), and Master of Science in Social Agency Counseling (M.S.S.A.C.). Interview, Waldo A. Dahlstedt, Dean of Graduate Studies, Henderson State College, July 28, 1970; and February 1, 1974.

50. *Catalogue*, 1895–1896, 5.

51. *Ibid.*, 1893–1894, 13.

52. *Methodist College Magazine*, IV (Dec., 1894), 17.

53. *Catalogue*, 1893–1894, 13.

54. Fannie B. Wright, "H S T C Diary: 1896," *The Pines*, I (Spring, 1941), 14.

55. *Methodist College Magazine*, IV (Dec., 1894), 16.

56. Farrar Newberry, "The College Lake," *Southern Standard*, Sept. 22, 1960; and *Oracle*, Oct. 6, 1908.

57. *Ibid.*, Oct. 6, 1908.

58. Wright, "H S T C Diary," 14.

59. *Catalogue*, 1896–1897, 9.

60. *Arkansas Methodist*, Aug. 22, 1895.

61. *Southern Standard*, Jan. 24, 1896.

62. *Arkansas Methodist*, June 16, 1897.

63. *Minutes, Little Rock Conference*, Dec. 1–6, 1897, 15; *Arkansas Methodist*, June 16, 1897; *Southern Standard*, July 16, 1897; Aug. 20, 1897; and *Catalogue*, 1896–1897 (Announcements for 1897–1898), 3.

64. Bishop Warren A. Candler, "Dr. Cadesman Pope," in James A. Anderson, *Centennial History of Arkansas Methodism: A History of the Methodist Episcopal Church, South, in the State of Arkansas, 1815–1935* (Benton, Ark.: L. B. White Printing Co., 1935), 310–311; Letter, G. C. Jones to Board of Trustees, May 20, 1898; *Arkansas Methodist*, July 7, 1897; July 30, 1908; *Southern Standard*, July 16, 1897; June 11, 1897. Pope served a one-year appointment to First Church in 1868 and a two-year one in 1876 and 1877.

65. *Catalogue*, 1896–1897 (Announcements for 1897–1898), 6.

66. *Ibid.*

67. *Ibid.*, 8.

68. *Ibid.*, 10.

69. *Oracle*, April 5, 1910.

70. *Ibid.*

71. *The Arkadelphian*, I, No. 4 (June, 1898), 28–29.

72. *Ibid.*, 29.
73. *Ibid.*, 15, 18.
74. *Arkansas Methodist*, June 14, 1899.
75. *Ibid.*
76. *Minutes, Little Rock Conference*, Nov. 25–30, 1903, 35.
77. *Catalogue*, 1903–1904, 12–17, 20.
78. *Oracle*, May 17, 1910.
79. *Methodist College Magazine*, Dec., 1894, 16.
80. *Southern Standard*, Nov. 13, 1902.
81. *Ibid.*
82. *Ibid.*, Dec. 13, 1900.
83. *Ibid.*, Feb. 7, 1901.
84. *Ibid.*, March 4, 1901.
85. *Ibid.*, March 28, 1901.
86. *Catalogue*, 1903–1904, 3–5, 7; and *Ibid.*, 1904–1905, 28, 31–32.
87. *Ibid.*, 27.
88. *Ibid.*
89. Interview, Nila Embree Turner, Sept. 9, 1970. Mrs. Turner, a former student, is Associate Professor Emeritus of English.
90. *Catalogue*, 1894–1895, 3.
91. Miss Blackeney died suddenly on May 4, 1895. *Southern Standard*, May 10, 1895.
92. McLauchlan died in Arkadelphia on May 1, 1896, and is buried in the town cemetery. *Ibid.*, May 8, 1896.
93. John Amos, 6-day-old son, died March 24, 1902; James Pope died June 2, 1900; and Lelia Adell died Dec. 18, 1893. All three are buried in Arkadelphia.
94. Granville Goodloe, "The Royal Succession," *Southern Standard*, Feb. 7, 1901.
95. *Ibid.*, Oct. 16, 1902.
96. *Ibid.*, Oct. 23, 1902.
97. *Catalogue*, 1904–1905, 6.
98. *Southern Standard*, Oct. 16, 1902.
99. *Catalogue*, 1904–1905, 25.
100. *Biennial Report of the State Superintendent of Public Instruction, 1899–1900* (Little Rock: Arkansas Democrat Co., Printers, 1900), 131.
101. *Catalogue*, 1904–1905, 6.
102. *Ibid.*, 26; and Letter, G. C. Jones to Board of Trustees, May 20, 1898, in *The Arkadelphian*, June, 1898, 41.
103. *Catalogue*, 1903–1904, 26; *Oracle*, May 3, 1922; and *Star*, 1922.
104. *The Arkadelphian*, June, 1898, 41.
105. *Minutes, Little Rock Conference*, Dec. 3–7, 1896, 14.

106. *Ibid.*, Nov. 23–28, 1898, 15.

107. *Ibid.*

108. *Ibid.*, Dec. 3–7, 1896, 13.

109. *Southern Standard*, April 12, 1900.

110. *Minutes, Little Rock Conference*, Nov. 21–26, 1900, 25; and *Southern Standard*, Dec. 6, 1900.

111. *Minutes, Little Rock Conference*, Nov. 20–25, 1901, 27; and *Arkansas Methodist*, Nov. 27, 1901.

112. *Ibid.*

113. Manuscript Minutes of the Board of Trustees of Arkadelphia Methodist College under the date of May 29, 1902. These minutes will hereinafter be cited thus: Board Minutes, followed by the date. *Arkansas Methodist*, Aug. 6, 1902; Granville Goodloe, "Capt. Henderson's Gift," *Ibid.*, Aug. 27, 1902; and *Ibid.*, Sept. 3, 1902.

114. *Ibid.*, July 9, 1902. The dedication was postponed and apparently never held. *Ibid.*, July 23, 1902; but complete transfer was made before July 30. *Ibid.*, July 30, 1902. The minutes of the trustees under the date of May 27, 1902 state that a copy of the agreement, transfer and lease is recorded as a supplement; however, the reserved pages remain blank.

115. *Arkansas Methodist*, July 9, 1902; July 23, 1902; July 30, 1902; Aug. 6, 1902; Aug. 27, 1902; Sept. 3, 1902; Sept. 24, 1902.

116. Board Minutes, May 26, 1902; and *Arkansas Methodist*, Sept. 24, 1902.

117. *Catalogue*, 1903–1904, 9.

118. Board Minutes, May 27, 1902.

119. *Ibid.*, April 15, 1904.

120. *Ibid.*, April 23, 1904; and *Southern Standard*, April 28, 1904.

121. Board Minutes, May 23, 1904; *Minutes, Little Rock Conference*, Dec. 7–12, 1904, 33; and *Southern Standard*, May 26, 1904. The conference had authorized the name change in 1903, if the trustees so desired. *Minutes, Little Rock Conference*, Nov. 25–30, 1903, 36.

CHAPTER VI

THE PROGRESSIVE YEARS

1. Manuscript Minutes of the Board of Trustees of Arkadelphia Methodist College under the date of April 23, 1904. These minutes will hereinafter be cited thus: Board Minutes, followed by the date.

2. H. E. Brill, *Story of Oklahoma City University and Its Predecessors: Texas Wesleyan College, Fort Worth University, Epworth University, Methodist University, Oklahoma City College* (Oklahoma City: University Press, 1938), 39. Jones left that position and founded the Oklahoma College

for Young Ladies and remained its head until it burned in 1910. He then held the chair of physics at the University of Oklahoma before going into the oil business with his sons. He died of a heart attack August 18, 1938 and was buried in Oklahoma City and not with his children in his family plot in Arkadelphia. Farrar Newberry, "G. C. Jones First President of Old Henderson," Arkadelphia *Southern Standard*, April 16, 1964. This newspaper will hereinafter be cited thus: *Southern Standard*, followed by the date of the issue.

3. Board Minutes, April 23, 1904; *Southern Standard*, April 28, 1904; and *Minutes of the Little Rock Annual Conference of the Methodist Episcopal Church, South*, under the dates of December 7–12, 1904, 33. These minutes will hereinafter be cited thus: *Minutes, Little Rock Conference*, followed by the dates of the session.

4. David Y. Thomas, ed., *Arkansas and Its People: A History, 1541–1930*, IV (New York: American Historical Society, Inc., 1930), 504.

5. *Minutes, Little Rock Conference*, Nov. 25–30, 1903, 36.

6. Board Minutes, May 29, 1906.

7. *Southern Standard*, May 5, 1906.

8. Thomas, *Arkansas and Its People*, IV, 504.

9. Little Rock *Arkansas Democrat* editorial, as reprinted in *Southern Standard*, Feb. 7, 1907; *Ibid.*, Oct. 31, 1907; Nov. 25, 1909; and *Oracle*, Dec. 21, 1909. The *Oracle* is the student newspaper of the college and was first published Oct. 6, 1908.

10. Carl F. Price, ed., *Who's Who in American Methodism* (New York: E. B. Treat & Co., 1916), 97.

11. *Oracle*, Dec. 21, 1909; Feb. 21, 1911. For a complete biographical sketch of Hinemon see Thomas, *Arkansas and Its People*, IV, 504.

12. *Southern Standard*, April 28, 1904; and *Catalogue of Henderson College*, 1904–1905, 4. This bulletin will hereinafter be cited thus: *Catalogue*, followed by the date.

13. *Ibid.*, 1904–1905, 10.

14. *Ibid.*

15. *Ibid.*, 5.

16. Board Minutes, May 23, 1904; and *Catalogue*, 1904–1905, 11.

17. For a complete statement see *Ibid.*, 1909–1910, 40.

18. *Ibid.*, 1904–1905, 12.

19. *Minutes, Little Rock Conference*, Dec. 7–12, 1904, 33.

20. *Catalogue*, 1904–1905, 12.

21. *Ibid.*, 9–10, 23–25.

22. *Ibid.*, 1906–1907, 11.

23. *Ibid.*, 1905–1906, 13; and *Ibid.*, 1906–1907, 11.

24. *Ibid.*, 1904–1905, 12.

25. *Ibid.*, 1908–1909, 11.

26. Board Minutes, May 26, 1909.

27. Final report of John H. Hinemon, President, to Board of Trustees, May 22, 1911, attached to Board Minutes, May 23, 1911.

28. *Catalogue*, 1909–1910, 27–29; and *Ibid.*, 1910–1911, 37.

29. *Ibid.*, 1910–1911, 37.

30. *Ibid.*, 1905–1906, 13.

31. Board Minutes, May 25, 1909; and *Catalogue*, 1909–1910, 25–29.

32. Daniel Walker Hollis, *University of South Carolina: College to University*, II (Columbia: University of South Carolina Press, 1956), 267.

33. *Catalogue*, 1910–1911, 23.

34. *Ibid.*, 22–23.

35. *Minutes, Little Rock Conference*, Dec. 7–12, 1904, 33; *Ibid.*, Nov. 25–30, 1908, 37; *Ibid.*, Nov. 16–21, 1910, 33; and Board Minutes, May 25, 1909.

36. *Catalogue*, 1904–1905, 4; Guy A. Simmons, "Hendrix College: A Brief Historical Sketch, 1884–1944" (A typescript in Bailey Library, Hendrix College, Conway, Arkansas, 1944), 25; and James A. Anderson, *Centennial History of Arkansas Methodism: A History of the Methodist Episcopal Church, South, in the State of Arkansas, 1815–1935* (Benton, Ark.: L. B. White Printing Co., 1935), 534. Before joining the Henderson faculty, Williams had taught in the Harrell International Institute, Muskogee, Okla. (1898–1900); and Clay Training School, Fordyce, Ark. (1900–1901); and had been superintendent of public schools, Magnolia, Ark.

37. *Catalogue*, 1909–1910, 4.

38. *Ibid.*, 1910–1911, 4.

39. Fay Williams, *Arkansans of the Years*, III (Little Rock: C. C. Allard & Associates, 1953), 250; and *St. Louis Post-Dispatch*, Feb. 13, 1915.

40. Williams, *Arkansans*, III, 246, 252. Active in cultural and civic affairs, he was a Mason, a Methodist, and a regent of the University of Omaha. In 1960 the Newberrys donated the land for the present Wesley Foundation Building serving Henderson State College.

41. Ann S. McDaniel, "Farrar Newberrys Restore Family Home," Little Rock *Arkansas Gazette*, Dec. 4, 1955; Omaha *World-Herald Sunday Magazine*, Oct. 16, 1955, 23; and *Vanderbilt Alumnus*, Feb., 1956.

42. *Catalogue*, 1907–1908, 3; Letter, Ruth Halloran, Assistant Director, The University of Chicago Alumni Association, to John G. Hall, July 30, 1973, in my possession; Letter, Nancy C. Fox, Registrar Records Division, Duke University, to John G. Hall, Oct. 30, 1973, in my possession; and *Oracle*, Nov. 20, 1941. His degrees were awarded in 1910 and 1924. Letter, Albert M. Hayes, Registrar, The University of Chicago, to John G. Hall, Aug. 16, 1973, in my possession.

43. For the various assignments see the catalogues from 1907–1949. Also see Little Rock *Arkansas Gazette*, Feb. 13, 1949; *Oracle*, Nov. 20, 1941; May 29, 1923. Proctor died Oct. 13, 1952.

44. J. J. Galloway, ed., *Doctor Benjamin S. Foster, A Great Teacher* (Little Rock: Epworth League Press, n.d.), 4.

45. Farrar Newberry, "Grand Old Man of Henderson-Brown," *Southern Standard*, Dec. 10, 1964.

46. For the various assignments see the catalogues from 1908–1925. In 1918 and 1919 the title Secretary of the Faculty was used in lieu of Dean of the Faculty.

47. Newberry, "Grand Old Man."

48. Galloway, *Doctor Foster*, 7.

49. *Ibid.*, 6.

50. Newberry, "Grand Old Man."

51. Board Minutes, Dec. 26, 1904.

52. *Ibid.*, May 25, 1905.

53. Manuscript Records Book 51, Clark County Courthouse, Arkadelphia, Ark., 434.

54. Board Minutes, Feb. 14, 1906.

55. *Southern Standard*, March 1, 1906; and Oklahoma City *Western Christian Advocate*, March 14, 1906.

56. Chairman Henderson granted authority Feb. 14, 1906. Board Minutes, May 29, 1906.

57. *Ibid.*, May 28, 1907.

58. *Minutes, Little Rock Conference*, Nov. 27–Dec. 2, 1907, 49.

59. *Ibid.*, 50.

60. *Ibid.*, 51.

61. *Ibid.*, Nov. 24–29, 1909, 36.

62. *Ibid.*, 29.

63. *Southern Standard*, Dec. 2, 1909.

64. *Ibid.*

65. Board Minutes, May 24, 1910; and *Southern Standard*, Dec. 2, 1909. For some reason, the Little Rock Conference minutes do not record this extraordinary action.

66. These trustees pledged the following amounts: Henderson, $10,000; Brown, $10,000; W. K. Ramsey, $2,500; President Hinemon, $1,500; R. W. Huie, $1,200; R. B. F. Key, $1,000; and W. E. Barkman, $1,000. Board Minutes, May 24, 1910; *Oracle*, Dec. 21, 1909; and *Southern Standard*, Dec. 2, 1909.

67. Walter W. Brown was not a trustee when he made his pledge, but was elected to take the place of W. K. Ramsey who died in spring, 1910. Board Minutes, May 24, 1910.

68. These trustees pledged the following amounts: Henderson, $5,000; President Hinemon, $2,500; Key, $2,500; Barkman, $2,500; Ramsey, $2,500; and Huie, $1,000. Board Minutes, May 24, 1910; and *Oracle*, Dec. 21, 1909.

69. Board Minutes, May 23, 1911.

70. *Catalogue*, 1909–1910, 51.

71. Board Minutes, May 23, 1904.

72. *Ibid.*

73. *Ibid.*, May 28, 1907.

74. *Ibid.*, May 26, 1909.

75. A picture of this ceremony is found in the *Catalogue*, 1906–1907, 29. Also see *Oracle*, March 16, 1909.

76. *Minutes, Little Rock Conference*, Dec. 7–12, 1904, 33.

77. *Southern Standard*, Sept. 8, 1904.

78. Billy Orr, "Dormitory Life: Boys," *The Pines*, I (Winter, 1940), 24.

79. *Catalogue*, 1909–1910, 10.

80. Letter, Albert Brown Key to Farrar Newberry, March 22, 1965; Letter, Marcus Key to Farrar Newberry, April, 1965; Letter, Annie Lydia Key to Farrar Newberry, n.d. The letters are from two sons and a daughter-in-law of the late R. B. F. Key, and are in File Box 3, Farrar Newberry Papers, Division of Social Sciences, Henderson State College. Also see Farrar Newberry, "R. B. F. Key Christian Benefactor," *Southern Standard*, April 8, 1965; and J. H. Riggin, *Lest We Forget or Character Gems Gleaned From South Arkansas* (Pine Bluff, Ark.: Norton-Vail Printing Co., n.d.), 170–171.

81. *Oracle*, May 13, 1936.

82. *Catalogue*, 1910–1911, 8.

83. Riggin, *Lest We Forget*, 175–176.

84. *Alumni Bulletin of Henderson-Brown College*, IV, No. 6 (May, 1916), n.p.; and *Catalogue*, 1912–1913, 58.

85. *Ibid.*; and *Oracle*, Nov. 20, 1941.

86. *Ibid.*, May 17, 1910; Nov. 20, 1941; and *Catalogue*, 1910–1911, 8–9.

87. *Oracle*, Nov. 20, 1941.

88. *Ibid.*

89. The contract was in the amount of $35,000, excluding the windows and furnishings. *Southern Standard*, March 7, 1907. The windows were fashioned by Jacoby Company, St. Louis, Mo., *Ibid.*, April 5, 1907.

90. Beginning in 1906, the catalogues carry this statement.

91. *Catalogue*, 1895–1896, 24.

92. *Ibid.*, 1903–1904, 8.

93. *Ibid.*, 23.

94. Letter, G. R. Turrentine to Farrar Newberry, May 16, 1966, File Box 3, Farrar Newberry Papers, Division of Social Sciences, Henderson

State College; and Farrar Newberry, "The Military Department of Old Henderson," *Southern Standard,* June 9, 1966; and *Oracle,* Nov. 13, 1941.

95. *Catalogue,* 1905–1906, 6.

96. Letter, G. R. Turrentine to Farrar Newberry; and Newberry, "Military Department."

97. *Southern Standard,* Sept. 14, 1905; Oct. 19, 1905; and *Catalogue,* 1906–1907, 3.

98. Newberry, "Military Department;" and *Oracle,* Nov. 13, 1941.

99. Trustee H. L. Remmel announced that he had arranged with the White House for the president to stop in Arkadelphia. *Southern Standard,* Oct. 21, 1909. President Taft's train traveled through Arkansas on Oct. 24, 1909, and he made three short speeches in the state: Arkadelphia, Benton, and Little Rock. *Ibid.,* Oct. 28, 1909.

100. Board Minutes, May 27, 1908.

101. *Ibid.,* May 25, 1909; and *Ibid.,* May 29, 1912.

102. *Star,* 1905, 4; and *Oracle,* Feb. 15, 1910. The *Star* is the college yearbook.

103. *Oracle,* Oct. 6, 1908. The paper has been published weekly, bimonthly, and monthly, under the names *The Henderson Oracle, The Oracle,* and *Oracle.*

104. *Star,* 1905, 63–64.

105. *Catalogue,* 1907–1908, 37.

106. *Oracle,* Nov. 23, 1909.

107. *Ibid.,* Oct. 20, 1908.

108. *Star,* 1905, 20.

109. "Henderson in Song," *The Pines,* I (Winter, 1940), 32.

110. *Oracle,* Feb. 15, 1910.

111. *Catalogue,* 1904–1905, 27; and *Oracle,* Feb. 1, 1910; Oct. 25, 1910; Nov. 22, 1910.

112. *Catalogue,* 1904–1905, 9.

113. *Ibid.,* 1905–1906, 10.

114. *Oracle,* Oct. 6, 1908.

115. Pauline Rucks, "Dormitory Life: Girls," *The Pines,* I (Winter, 1940), 23; and *Oracle,* Oct. 4, 1910; Nov. 25, 1910.

116. *Catalogue,* 1909–1910, 14.

117. *Oracle,* Oct. 20, 1908; April 5, 1910.

118. *Catalogue,* 1910–1911, 22.

119. *Star,* 1906.

120. The score was Arkansas 51, Henderson 48. *Southern Standard,* May 4, 1911.

121. *Arkansas Gazette,* Nov. 19, 1905; *Southern Standard,* Nov. 23, 1905; Oct. 9, 1896; and *Star,* 1906. The *Southern Standard,* Nov. 1, 1973, carries a partial reprint of the 1905 story.

122. *Star*, 1907; and *The Troubadour*, 1907, 93 (*The Troubadour* is the yearbook of Hendrix College, Conway, Ark.).

123. *Vanderbilt Alumni*, I, 1923, 240–241.

124. *Oracle*, Dec. 8, 1919. Haygood officially resigned as Athletic Director, June 18, 1925. Board Minutes, June 18, 1925.

125. *Southern Standard*, Oct. 17, 1907; Oct. 31, 1907. During these years a touchdown was five points.

126. *Oracle*, Nov. 3, 1908.

127. *Ibid.*

128. *Ibid.*, Dec. 15, 1908.

129. *Ibid.*, Oct. 2, 1909.

130. *Ibid.*, Nov. 23, 1909; and *Southern Standard*, Nov. 18, 1909.

131. Sunny Wilkerson, "Why Reddies Are Reddies," *Oracle*, Oct. 6, 1950.

132. *Ibid.*, Oct. 6, 1908.

133. Rapp, holding the M.A. from Kentucky Wesleyan and the B.D. from Vanderbilt, joined the faculty in 1907. For a complete statement concerning the European tours, see *Catalogue*, 1909–1910, 19.

134. This was the trustees' opinion as expressed in a lengthy memorial to Hinemon and his wife. The grateful board presented them a silver service in appreciation. Board Minutes, May 23, 1911; and also see *Southern Standard*, May 23, 1911.

135. Board Minutes, April 4, 1911; *Ibid.*, April 15, 1911; *Ibid.*, April 17, 1911; *Ibid.*, May 23, 1911; Thomas, *Arkansas and Its People*, IV, 504. Also see *Southern Standard*, May 25, 1911. Hinemon served the School for the Blind for six years, retiring to Rector, Arkansas. He died Dec. 22, 1946.

136. Letter, John H. Hinemon to Board of Trustees, May 23, 1911, in Board Minutes, May 23, 1911.

137. Board Minutes, April 4, 1911.

138. *Ibid.*, May 25, 1910.

139. Letter, Mrs. G. C. Harrison, only child of the late W. W. Brown, to Mrs. D. W. Harrell, Oct., 1973, in my possession; Letter, Mrs. D. W. Harrell, cousin of the late W. W. Brown, to John G. Hall, Oct. 22, 1973, in my possession; Interview, Mrs. D. W. Harrell, Oct. 31, 1973; and Letter, W. C. Washburn, executive secretary, Washington and Lee University Alumni, Inc., to John G. Hall, Nov. 14, 1973, in my possession.

CHAPTER VII

THE RISE OF THE PHOENIX

1. Manuscript Minutes of the Board of Trustees of Henderson-Brown College under the date of May 23, 1911. These minutes will hereinafter be cited thus: Board Minutes, followed by the date.

2. His honors included Senior Speaker at his graduation; The Representative Medal, given jointly by the Dialectic and Philanthropic Literary Societies; the Willie P. Mangum Medal, given for the best commencement oration. Letter, Clarence E. Whitefield, Alumni Secretary, The University of North Carolina, to John G. Hall, Feb. 4, 1972, in my possession; Letter, William S. Powell, Curator, North Carolina Collection, University of North Carolina Library, to John G. Hall, Feb. 4, 1972, in my possession; Diane Sasson, Reference Assistant, Humanities Division, University of North Carolina Library, to John G. Hall, Feb. 28, 1972, in my possession; Dolphus Whitten, Jr., President, Oklahoma City University, to John G. Hall, Feb. 7, 1972, in my possession; Loretta S. Glaze, Research Analyst, State of Indiana Commission for Higher Education, to John G. Hall, Feb. 28, 1972, in my possession; and Gene E. Sease, President, Indiana Central College, Feb. 11, 1972, in my possession. Information concerning Crowell's Ph.D. has led to conflicting reports. Sources disagree as to location and the very existence of the school, the granting of the degree, and the date of its conferment. There were at least three Central Universities in existence in the first decade of this century; Indiana Central University, Indianapolis, was among them, but that institution, now Indiana Central College, has no record of ever granting the degree, but did not exclude the possibility. This, along with the early date, suggests that perhaps the degree was honorary, although the extensive North Carolina records show that he attended Central University, Indiana, for three years. *Who's Who in American Methodism* (New York: E. B. Treat & Co., 1916), 51, states that Crowell received the degree in 1904 rather than in 1907 as recorded in the North Carolina Collection files. Neither the records of Henderson State College nor those of Oklahoma City University give the date of the degree. *The Campus*, a student publication at Epworth University (OCU), carries the information that Crowell "took his doctor's degree at Central College, Indianapolis." *The Campus*, III (Nov., 1908), 8.

3. Little Rock *Arkansas Methodist*, May 11, 1911; *Minutes of the Little Rock Annual Conference of the Methodist Episcopal Church, South*, under the dates of November 15–20, 1911, 16; and James A. Anderson, *Centennial History of Arkansas Methodism: A History of the Methodist Episcopal Church, South, in the State of Arkansas, 1815–1935* (Benton, Ark.: L. B. White Printing Co., 1935), 226. The Methodist newspaper will hereinafter be cited thus: *Arkansas Methodist*, followed by the date of the issue. The minutes of the Little Rock Conference will hereinafter be cited thus: *Minutes, Little Rock Conference*, followed by the dates of the session.

4. Board Minutes, May 23, 1911; and *Arkansas Methodist*, May 11, 1911.

5. *Oracle*, Oct. 31, 1911. The *Oracle* is the student newspaper of the college and was first published Oct. 6, 1908.

6. *Minutes, Little Rock Conference,* Dec. 4–9, 1912, 43.

7. *Ibid.;* and Board Minutes, May 29, 1912.

8. *Minutes, Little Rock Conference,* Dec. 4–9, 1912, 44; Nov. 18–24, 1913, 13.

9. Rhodes joined the faculty in 1912. *Catalogue of Henderson-Brown College,* 1912–1913, 3. This bulletin will hereinafter be cited thus: *Catalogue,* followed by the date.

10. Letter, David A. Warren, Director of Registration and Records, Johns Hopkins University, to John G. Hall, August 1, 1973, in my possession; *Who's Who in America,* XII (Chicago: A. N. Marquis & Co., 1922); and *Catalogue,* 1913–1914, 3. Wise was on the faculty from 1913 until 1916. He died Dec. 16, 1964.

11. Board Minutes, May 28, 1912.

12. *Ibid.*

13. *Ibid.,* April 2, 1913.

14. *Ibid.,* May 27, 1913.

15. *Ibid.*

16. *Minutes, Little Rock Conference,* Nov. 18–24, 1913, 51.

17. The first by-law reads: "No college shall be eligible to membership in this Association which furnishes preparatory instruction in any subject as part of its college organization." This regulation carries out fully the last of the three purposes outlined in the call issued for the organizational meeting. *Proceedings of the First Meeting, Association of College and Preparatory Schools of the Southern States,* Nov. 6, 1895, 6. Also see Guy E. Snavely, "A Short History of the Southern Association of Colleges and Secondary Schools," as reprinted from *Southern Association Quarterly,* IX (Nov. 1945), 125, 6.

18. John Samuel Ezell, *The South Since 1865* (New York: Macmillan Co., 1964), 266.

19. *Minutes, Little Rock Conference,* Dec. 4–9, 1912, 43.

20. *Ibid.,* Nov. 18–24, 1913, 51.

21. Little Rock *Arkansas Gazette,* Feb. 4, 1914; *Southern Standard,* Feb. 5, 1914; and *Arkansas Methodist,* Feb. 5, 1914. The Little Rock *Arkansas Gazette* will hereinafter be cited thus: *Arkansas Gazette,* followed by the date of the issue.

22. *Ibid.*

23. *Ibid.*

24. *Ibid.*

25. Interview, Nila Embree Turner, associate professor emeritus, Henderson State College, Sept. 9, 1970. Mrs. Turner was a student at Henderson-Brown living in the women's dormitory when the fire occurred.

26. *Arkansas Gazette,* Feb. 5, 1914.

27. *Southern Standard*, Feb. 5, 1914.

28. Interview, Nila Embree Turner; and *Catalogue*, 1914–1915, 11.

29. Farrar Newberry, "Henderson Won Victory from Disaster," *Southern Standard*, July 25, 1964.

30. *Ibid.*, Feb. 12, 1914; *Catalogue*, 1914–1915, 11; *Arkansas Methodist*, Feb. 12, 1914; and *Minutes, Little Rock Conference*, Nov. 25–30, 1914, 45.

31. Interview, Nila Embree Turner.

32. Board Minutes, Feb. 17, 1914.

33. *Ibid.*, Feb. 18, 1914.

34. *Ibid.*

35. *Ibid.*, April 7, 1914.

36. Biographical data on George Henry Crowell, File Box 3, Farrar Newberry Papers, Division of Social Sciences, Henderson State College.

37. *Southern Standard*, March 5, 1914. The firm was Walker Bros. and Company, Ltd. The letter, dated Feb. 21, 1914, was reprinted in the paper.

38. *Arkansas Gazette*, Feb. 26, 1914, as reprinted in *Southern Standard*, March 5, 1914.

39. The plans were approved June 4, 1914, Board Minutes, June 4, 1914; and *Southern Standard*, June 4, 1914. The bids were received June 10, 1914, Board Minutes, June 10, 1914; and *Southern Standard*, June 11, 1914. The contract was let June 13, 1914, Board Minutes, June 13, 1914; *Southern Standard*, June 18, 1914; and *Arkansas Methodist* (*Western Methodist*) June 18, 1914.

40. Guy A. Simmons, "Hendrix College: A Brief Historical Sketch, 1884–1944" (A typescript in Bailey Library, Hendrix College, Conway, Arkansas, 1944), 41–43.

41. *Minutes, Little Rock Conference*, Nov. 25–30, 1914, 46.

42. *Ibid.*, 32.

43. *Ibid.*, 46.

44. *Ibid.*, 47.

45. *Southern Standard*, Dec. 31, 1914; Jan. 21, 1915.

46. Interview, Roma Garrett Meier, daughter of the late J. B. Garrett, Aug. 1, 1971; and Farrar Newberry, "J. B. Garrett 'Dad' to Hendersonians," *Southern Standard*, June 10, 1965.

47. *Ibid.*, Nov. 12, 1914; and *Arkansas Methodist*, Nov. 26, 1914.

48. *Southern Standard*, Feb. 11, 1915; and *Arkansas Methodist*, Feb. 18, 1915.

49. Simmons, "Hendrix College," 28.

50. *Southern Standard*, Feb. 11, 1915; *Catalogue*, 1914–1915, 18; and *Arkansas Methodist*, Jan. 21, 1915; Feb. 18, 1915.

51. *Ibid.*; and *Catalogue*, 1914–1915, 19.

52. *Oracle*, Oct. 21, 1926.

53. *Southern Standard*, Nov. 26, 1914.

54. Edith Zinn, "The Story of Laura Lee Henson," *The Pines*, I (Winter, 1940), 19; and *Oracle*, March 9, 1951.

55. *Southern Standard*, March 18, 1915.

56. *Ibid.*, May 6, 1915; June 3, 1915. The total enrollment for the 1914–1915 session was only 135. See *Minutes, Little Rock Conference*, Dec. 1–6, 1915, 52.

57. Interview, Nila Embree Turner.

58. Board Minutes, May 28, 1912; April 2, 1913; April 7, 1914; May 11, 1915. At its second meeting the Henderson-Brown Club formally recognized Crowell's leadership and paid high tribute to him, and informed him of their action. Manuscript Minutes of the Henderson-Brown Club, under the date of Oct. 24, 1927.

59. Biographical data on George Henry Crowell, File Box 3, Farrar Newberry Papers, Division of Social Sciences, Henderson State College.

60. *Ibid.*

61. Board Minutes, May 11, 1915; and *Southern Standard*, May 13, 1915.

62. *Ibid.*

63. Board Minutes, June 15, 1915; and *Southern Standard*, June 17, 1915.

64. Letter, William S. Powell.

CHAPTER VIII

THE SCHOOL WITH A HEART

1. Manuscript Minutes of the Board of Trustees of Henderson-Brown College under the date of June 15, 1915. These minutes will hereinafter be cited thus: Board Minutes, followed by the date.

2. *Who's Who in America*, XII (Chicago: A. N. Marquis & Co., 1922), 3394; and Interview, the Reverend James Warthen Workman, March 19, 1974. The Reverend Workman is a son of the late Reverend James Mims Workman and the last president of Henderson-Brown College.

3. Board Minutes, June 15, 1915; and *Ibid.*, March 1, 1921.

4. *Ibid.*, June 15, 1915; and Guy A. Simmons, "Hendrix College: A Brief Historical Sketch, 1884–1944" (A typescript in Bailey Library, Hendrix College, Conway, Arkansas, 1944), 28.

5. Interview, James W. Workman.

6. *Ibid.*; *Catalogue of Henderson-Brown College*, 1924–1925, 6; and *Ibid.*, 1926–1927, 10. This bulletin will hereinafter be cited thus: *Catalogue*, followed by the date.

7. Interview, James W. Workman.

8. Little Rock *Arkansas Methodist*, July 13, 1916; Simmons, "Hendrix

College," 14; and William Ritchie, "Henderson, Today and Yesterday: The Story of the First Fifty Years," in *Essays on Southern Life and Culture: A Henderson Symposium*, A. B. Bonds, ed. (Arkadelphia: Henderson State Teachers College, 1941), 249. The Methodist newspaper will hereinafter be cited thus: *Arkansas Methodist*, followed by the date of the issue.

9. *Minutes of the Little Rock Annual Conference of the Methodist Episcopal Church, South*, under the dates of December 5–9, 1917, 67–68; and *Catalogue*, 1920–1921, 17. The minutes of the Little Rock Conference will hereinafter be cited thus: *Minutes, Little Rock Conference*, followed by the dates of the session.

10. *Catalogue*, 1920–1921, 17; and Ritchie, "Henderson, Today and Yesterday," 248.

11. Interview, H. Grady Smith, Trustee, July 13, 1971; and Board Minutes, March 1, 1921. Upon his retirement from the board, the trustees passed a resolution of appreciation for his service to the institution. Board Minutes, April 4, 1974; and Little Rock *Arkansas Gazette*, April 12, 1974. This newspaper will hereinafter be cited thus: *Arkansas Gazette*, followed by the date of the issue.

12. *Minutes, Little Rock Conference*, Dec. 5–9, 1917, 44–45; and *Arkansas Methodist*, Feb. 21, 1918.

13. *Minutes, Little Rock Conference*, Dec. 5–9, 1917, 45; and Ritchie, "Henderson, Today and Yesterday," 250; and Simmons, "Hendrix College," 29.

14. *Ibid.*

15. *Arkansas Methodist*, April 4, 1918; and Ritchie, "Henderson, Today and Yesterday," 250.

16. Board Minutes, March 2, 1920.

17. *Ibid.*, March 1, 1921.

18. *Minutes, Little Rock Conference*, Nov. 25, 1914, 45; *Ibid.*, Dec. 1–6, 1915, 52; and *Ibid.*, Nov. 29–Dec. 3, 1916, 48–49.

19. *Ibid.*, Nov. 18–24, 1913, 47. The merger became effective in May, 1914, and the first annual conference under the new name convened Nov. 18–24, 1914, at Batesville. *Minutes of the North Arkansas Annual Conference of the Methodist Episcopal Church, South*, under the dates of November 18–23, 1914, 1. These minutes will hereinafter be cited thus: *Minutes, North Arkansas Conference*, followed by the dates of the session.

20. *Minutes, Little Rock Conference*, Nov. 26–30, 1919, 67.

21. Board Minutes, March 2, 1920.

22. *Minutes, Little Rock Conference*, Nov. 17, 1920, 67; and *Minutes, North Arkansas Conference*, Nov. 24–28, 1920, 50.

23. *Minutes, Little Rock Conference*, Dec. 1, 1921, 51; *Ibid.*, Nov. 29–

Dec. 4, 1922, 56; and *Minutes, North Arkansas Conference,* Nov. 21–25, 1923, 75.

24. Board Minutes, March 1, 1921; *Minutes, North Arkansas Conference,* Nov. 24–28, 1920, 50; *Oracle,* March 1, 1921; March 8, 1921. The *Oracle* is the student newspaper of the college and was first published October 6, 1908.

25. *Minutes, Little Rock Conference,* Dec. 1, 1921, 51.

26. Board Minutes, March 4, 1924. He died in San Diego, California, while visiting in his daughter's home. For the resolution see Appendix B.

27. Board Minutes, March 4, 1924.

28. Bessie Newsom Allard, ed., *Who Is Who in Arkansas,* I (Little Rock: Pioneer Press, 1959), 72; and David Y. Thomas, ed., *Arkansas and Its People: A History, 1541–1930,* III (New York: American Historical Society, Inc., 1930), 310–312.

29. *Ibid.,* 35–37; and *Who's Who in America,* VIII.

30. *Ibid.;* and Board Minutes, March 1, 1927.

31. *Oracle,* Jan. 9, 1924. On March 12, the college was host to 150 bankers. *Ibid.,* March 19, 1924.

32. Board Minutes, March 2, 1926.

33. *Catalogue,* 1912–1913, 33.

34. *Ibid.,* 32; and *Ibid.,* 1915–1916, 31.

35. *Ibid.,* 1912–1913, 41.

36. *Ibid.,* 1913–1914, 44, 46–47.

37. Board Minutes, March 6, 1923; and *Oracle,* March 14, 1923.

38. *Catalogue,* 1918–1919, 32.

39. *Ibid.,* 1920–1921, 49.

40. *Ibid.,* 1923–1924, 51, 53.

41. *Ibid.,* 1921–1922, 87, 94.

42. *Ibid.,* 1905–1906, 13; and *Ibid.,* 1906–1907, 11.

43. Membership was obtained in May, 1923. *Oracle,* May 30, 1923; Sept. 19, 1923; Oct. 27, 1923.

44. *Ibid.,* Nov. 23, 1920, 1.

45. *Catalogue,* 1924–1925, 62.

46. *Oracle,* May 17, 1921.

47. Board Minutes, June 2, 1926.

48. *Oracle,* Sept. 17, 1925; Sept. 24, 1925; and *Arkansas Gazette,* Oct. 3, 1925.

49. Board Minutes, June 2, 1926. The first year of state control, four courses in Bible were listed; in the catalogue these decreased to three in 1931–1932 and to two in 1934–1935. Bible does not appear as a course in the catalogues from 1935–1936 on. *Catalogues,* inclusive years.

50. Interview, Bola Martin Ohls, retired Henderson professor, Feb. 18,

1972; Bola Martin Ohls, "Tribute to a Noble Spirit," *Arkansas Gazette Magazine*, May 28, 1944; Bonds, *A Henderson Symposium,* v; and Letter, Elizabeth Kannard, Alumni Office Secretary, to John G. Hall, July 23, 1973, in my possession. The trustees' resolution read: "Recognizing in Miss Mary Sue Mooney a valuable asset to this college and in her Christian example and influence a strong factor in building up the character of its young women students, be it resolved that: This board expresses to her by a vote of thanks its entire approval of and hearty co-operation with her, in her capacity as Lady Principal." Board Minutes, April 1, 1919.

51. *Oracle,* Sept. 27, 1920; *Catalogue,* 1920–1921, 6; and David W. Bailey, ed., *Harvard Alumni Directory* (Cambridge: Harvard University, 1929), 944.

52. Interview, Bola Martin Ohls; and *Catalogue,* 1925–1926, 7.

53. Board Minutes, March 2, 1920; *Catalogue,* 1920–1921, 6; and *Ibid.,* 1949–1950, 10.

54. *Ibid.,* 1959–1960.

55. Interview, Mildred Sherrod, professor emeritus, Henderson State College, Feb. 18, 1972; Letter, Mildred Sherrod to John G. Hall, Feb. 23, 1972, in my possession; Board Minutes, March 3, 1924; and *Catalogue,* 1923–1924, 10. The American universities included Chicago, Wisconsin, Minnesota, Colorado, and Louisiana State.

56. Interview, Dora Sellard Harwood, wife of the late Professor Harwood, Aug. 23, 1971; W. H. Halliburton, "Dr. Frederick Harwood," *Arkansas Gazette,* Sept. 15, 1946; and *Oracle,* Nov. 8, 1928; Nov. 15, 1928; May 13, 1936.

57. *Ibid.; Oracle,* April 3, 1959; May 22, 1959; and Arkadelphia *Southern Standard,* May 28, 1959. This newspaper will hereinafter be cited thus: *Southern Standard,* followed by the date of the issue.

58. *Ibid.;* and *Catalogue,* 1933–1934, 12.

59. Board Minutes, May 27, 1913; *Ibid.,* March 25, 1921; and *Ibid.,* March 3, 1924.

60. Interview, Lois McNabb Smith, professor emeritus, Sept. 16, 1972; and Board Minutes, April 3, 1923.

61. Interview, Mae Whipple, professor of music, Henderson State College, May 4, 1971; and Board Minutes, June 30, 1928.

62. Board Minutes, March 3, 1925; *Catalogue,* 1924–1925, 7; *Oracle,* April 30, 1924; and *Arkansas Gazette,* Jan. 7, 1955.

63. *Ibid.,* Jan. 7, 1955.

64. Board Minutes, March 1, 1921; *Catalogue,* 1920–1921, 5; and *Ibid.,* 1922–1923, 10.

65. *Ibid.,* 1922–1923, 69–73; and *Alumni Directory: "Who's Who" among*

Vanderbilt Men and Women, I (Nashville: Vanderbilt University, 1923), 177.

66. Interview, Matt Locke Ellis, former president of Henderson State, April 13, 1974; Jacques Cattell, ed., *Dictionary of American Scholars: A Biographical Directory* (Lancaster, Pa.: Science Press 1951), 264; *Dictionary of American Scholars*, IV (New York: R. R. Bowker Co., 1964), 55; Jacques Cattell and E. E. Ross, eds., *Leaders in Education: A Biographical Directory* (Lancaster, Pa.: Science Press, 1948), 319; Board Minutes, May 31, 1921; June 20, 1921.

67. *Oracle*, Oct. 27, 1950.

68. Interview, Diane Huie Balay, granddaughter of the late Mrs. Robert W. Huie, Jr., Feb. 4, 1971; *Ibid.*, March 1, 1972; *Oracle*, Sept. 21, 1921; *Catalogue*, 1921–1922, 11; and *Ibid.*, 1922–1923, 11.

69. Manuscript Accession Book, I, Huie Library, Henderson State College, Arkadelphia, Ark.; and *Oracle*, Sept. 27, 1950.

70. *Oracle*, Nov. 23, 1909; Oct. 19, 1921; Nov. 7, 1923.

71. *Ibid.*, Jan. 14, 1925.

72. *Ibid.*, March 18, 1925.

73. Board Minutes, March 2, 1926.

74. Information released in 1920 concerning statistics for 1920 was based on studies made during the 1917–1918 academic year. U.S. Dept. of the Interior, Bureau of Education *Bulletin*, 1920, No. 34, 180, 32; and *Oracle*, Feb. 16, 1933.

75. George F. Zook, *Accredited Higher Institutions*, U.S. Dept. of the Interior, Bureau of Education *Bulletin* No. 30 (Washington: U.S. Government Printing Office, 1922), 5, 40–41; and *Catalogue*, 1923–1924, 113.

76. Zook, *Accredited Higher Institutions*, 40–41, 5.

77. *Bulletin of Henderson-Brown College: Endow the College* (Endowment campaign brochure, Oct., 1923), 2.

78. Board Minutes, March 6, 1923.

79. *Ibid.*, Aug. 3, 1923.

80. Board Minutes, June 12, 1924; *Bulletin of Henderson-Brown College: Team Work* (Endowment campaign brochure, 1924); *Arkansas Gazette*, Sept. 25, 1924; *Bulletin of Henderson-Brown College: Serve and Save Henderson-Brown College* (Endowment campaign brochure, 1924); *Arkansas Gazette*, Oct. 27, 1924; Arkadelphia *Siftings Herald*, Oct. 29, 1924; *Arkansas Gazette*, Oct. 31, 1924; and *Camden (Arkansas) News*, Nov. 5, 1924. The Arkadelphia newspaper will hereinafter be cited thus: *Siftings Herald*, followed by the date of the issue.

81. *Bulletin of Henderson-Brown College: To Be Or Not To Be*, 3; and *Arkansas Democrat*, Dec. 15, 1924; Dec. 17, 1924.

82. *Arkansas Democrat,* Dec. 16, 1924; Dec. 17, 1924; Dec. 15, 1924; and *Siftings Herald,* Dec. 15, 1924; Dec. 14, 1924.

83. Board Minutes, Dec. 22, 1924; and *Arkansas Gazette,* Jan. 4, 1925; Jan. 11, 1925.

84. Letter, J. J. Galloway, Executive Secretary, to Mrs. E. H. Johnson, Jan. 17, 1925, property of Henderson State College Museum.

85. *Oracle,* Feb. 4, 1925; and *Southern Standard,* Feb. 5, 1925.

86. Board Minutes, March 3, 1925. The vote to discontinue the academy was taken Dec. 22, 1924.

87. *North Central Association Quarterly,* IX (July, 1934), 51; and *Oracle,* Oct. 18, 1928; Nov. 15, 1928; May 3, 1934.

88. *Ibid.,* May 31, 1917.

89. *Ibid.,* Nov. 13, 1941. This article, entitled "Military History," covered the years 1905–1941.

90. *Ibid.; Southern Standard,* Dec. 19, 1918; Sept. 27, 1973; and Daniel Walker Hollis, *University of South Carolina: College to University,* II (Columbia: University of South Carolina Press, 1956), 288.

91. Pursuing his academic interests in economics and sociology, for six years he studied at Vanderbilt, Harvard, and the University of North Carolina from which he received the Ph.D. degree in 1928. From then until 1934 he taught at Alabama College when the Roosevelt Administration called him to Washington, where he soon came to head the U.S. Conciliation Service. From this successful career he advanced to the position of special presidential advisor to Truman, earning recognition as "the link between the New and Fair Deals." For the complete story of Steelman see William O. Wagnon, Jr., "John Roy Steelman: Native Son to Presidential Advisor," *Arkansas Historical Quarterly,* XXVII (Autumn, 1968), 205–225.

92. *Oracle,* Nov. 13, 1941; *Southern Standard,* Dec. 19, 1918; Sept. 27, 1973; and *Catalogue,* 1919–1920, 67.

93. *Oracle,* Oct. 17, 1917; Dec. 17, 1917; and *Star,* 1919, n.p. The *Star* is the college yearbook. During these years the *Oracle* was published as a monthly literary magazine.

94. *Oracle,* Feb. 10, 1920.

95. *Ibid.* The tradition of planting holly trees to honor the college's war dead has been continued and on April 20, 1974, a memorial service for the nine men who lost their lives in the Vietnam conflict was held. The following tribute was composed and read by Associate Professor Emeritus Amy Jean Greene:

Dedication of Holly Trees   April 20, 1974

We remember . . .

We remember when the world was young

and they walked this campus,
   young, happy, full of sprizerinktum,
     the joy of living . . .
We remember them with tender love,
And because we remember
  we dedicate these holly trees
    to their memory and honor and glory.
Grow, little hollies,
Grow toward the heavens and the blue skies . . .
Keep our memories ever green . . .
Let your red berries remind us
  of the blood which they shed
    so willingly . . .
Keep our memories young, and fresh, and loving.
So we assemble here today . . . for a joyous occasion . . .
To dedicate these holly trees
  planted on the hills and in the ravines
    of our beautiful campus.
We hereby dedicate these hollies
  to the memory of Henderson's sons
    who have given their lives in past wars.
May we keep this institution *strong—strong—*
  to prove that we—and it—
    are worthy of the sacrifice of these young lives.
                    —Amen

96. *Oracle*, Feb. 17, 1920.

97. *Ibid.*, Jan. 20, 1920.

98. *Ibid.*, Nov. 11, 1919; April 20, 1920.

99. *Catalogue*, 1918–1919, 76; and *Minutes, North Arkansas Conference,* Nov. 5–9, 1924, 71.

100. Board Minutes, Dec. 19, 1919.

101. *Ibid.*, March 1, 1921.

102. *Oracle*, Nov. 30, 1921; May 3, 1922; Feb. 23, 1928; and *Southern Standard*, Sept. 27, 1973.

103. Board Minutes, Aug. 3, 1923.

104. *Catalogue*, 1921–1922, 34.

105. Board Minutes, March 6, 1923; and *Oracle*, Oct. 4, 1922.

106. Board Minutes, May 31, 1921.

107. *Oracle*, Nov. 21, 1923; Jan. 30, 1924.

108. *Minutes, North Arkansas Conference,* Nov. 21–25, 1923, 73.

109. Board Minutes, March 2, 1926; and *Oracle*, Jan. 17, 1923.

110. Board Minutes, March 2, 1926.

111. *Southern Standard*, July 22, 1915.
112. *Ibid.*
113. Board Minutes, March 6, 1923.
114. *Ibid.*, March 4, 1924; James A. Anderson, *Centennial History of Arkansas Methodism: A History of the Methodist Episcopal Church, South, in the State of Arkansas, 1815–1935* (Benton, Ark.: L. B. White Printing Co., 1935), 270–271; and J. H. Riggin, *Lest We Forget or Character Gems Gleaned From South Arkansas* (Pine Bluff, Ark.: Norton-Vail Printing Co., n.d.), 43–45.
115. Board Minutes, March 3, 1925.
116. *Catalogue*, 1918–1919, 59.
117. Board Minutes, March 2, 1920; *Ibid.*, Sept. 7, 1925; *Catalogue*, 1921–1922, 122–123; and *Ibid.*, 1925–1926, 86–87.
118. *Catalogue*, 1912–1913, 67; and *Ibid.*, 1918–1919, 56.
119. *Ibid.*, 1912–1913, 67; and *Ibid.*, 1914–1915, 74.
120. Board Minutes, March 1, 1921; and *Ibid.*, March 2, 1926.
121. The initial gift was $5,000, and the fund increased to the total amount in 1924. Board Minutes, March 6, 1923; and *Minutes, North Arkansas Conference*, Nov. 5–9, 1924, 71.
122. *Catalogue*, 1908–1909, 1.
123. *Ibid.*, 1919–1920, 3; and *Oracle*, Feb. 8, 1934.
124. *Catalogue*, 1913–1914, 26.
125. *Ibid.*, 1914–1915, 25.
126. *Oracle*, Jan. 12, 1920, 3.
127. *Ibid.*, April 20, 1920; Dec. 16, 1919.
128. *Ibid.*, Dec. 16, 1919.
129. *Ibid.*, Nov. 18, 1919.
130. *Ibid.*
131. *Ibid.*, April 23, 1924.
132. *Southern Standard*, March 19, 1914.
133. *Oracle*, May 24, 1920.
134. *Star*, 1920, n.p.; and *Ibid.*, 1926, n.p.
135. *The Reddie*, March 1, 1915. *The Reddie* was a newspaper published bi-monthly by the Athletic Association for several years.
136. *Ibid.*
137. *Oracle*, Feb. 24, 1920; March 2, 1920.
138. *Ibid.*, Nov. 22, 1922.
139. *Ibid.*, May 24, 1920.
140. *Minutes, Little Rock Conference*, Nov. 18–24, 1913, 40.
141. Letter, James W. Workman, to John G. Hall, March 2, 1972, in my possession.
142. *Southern Standard*, Oct. 9, 1913; Oct. 23, 1913; Oct. 30, 1913.

143. *Ibid.*, Nov. 6, 1913.

144. *Ibid.*, Nov. 12, 1914; Nov. 11, 1915.

145. *Ibid.*, Nov. 18, 1915.

146. Board Minutes, March 2, 1926.

147. *Oracle*, Nov. 11, 1919; Dec. 8, 1919.

148. Board Minutes, March 2, 1920; and *Oracle*, Nov. 11, 1919.

149. The purchase price was $11,000; $1,000 cash, $10,000 payable in 5 years in Liberty Bonds. Board Minutes, March 2, 1920; and Manuscript Deed Record Book 85, Clark County Courthouse, Arkadelphia, Ark., 622.

150. *Oracle*, March 8, 1921.

151. Interview, Anna Lee Chidister Harrell, member of the class of 1924, Oct. 31, 1973 and Jan. 6, 1974. Mrs. Harrell was the roommate of Frederica Mintern when Miss Mintern was named the first football sponsor. And *Oracle*, Nov. 11, 1919; April 13, 1920; Nov. 22, 1922; Nov. 27, 1941.

152. Buford Thomas, "The Reddie Blankets," *The Pines*, 20; and *Oracle*, Nov. 27, 1933.

153. Conflicting versions of the legend exist, varying from one student generation to the next. Another popular account credits an Ouachita College freshman girl with having won the love of the Henderson boy, but offers no explanation as to why the "Black Lady" seeks revenge among Henderson freshmen women. Interview, Amy Jean Greene, January 7, 1974. Also see "The Black Woman," *The Pines*, I (Winter, 1941), 21.

154. Interview, Anna Lee Chidister Harrell; and *Oracle*, Nov. 27, 1941.

155. Letter, Paul Vernon Galloway to John G. Hall, Aug. 23, 1971, in my possession. Bishop Galloway was born April 5, 1904, at Mountain Home, Ark. He also studied at S.M.U. and later did graduate work at the University of Chicago. He holds honorary degrees from five schools, the most recent, the LL.D. from S.M.U. in 1964.

156. Board Minutes, March 3, 1925; *Ibid.*, June 18, 1925; *Star*, 1921; *Ibid.*, 1922; *Ibid.*, 1923; *Ibid.*, 1924; *Ibid.*, 1925; and *Oracle*, Oct. 10, 1923; Nov. 28, 1923, Oct. 1, 1924; Nov. 11, 1924; Nov. 19, 1924; Dec. 10, 1924. The season records are: 1920—won 2, lost 3; 1921—won 2, lost 4, tied 1; 1922—won 2, lost 6; 1923—won 3, lost 5, tied 1; and 1924—won 3, lost 4, tied 1. Because of ill health, during his last year at Arkadelphia Haygood spent several months in Florida. Upon his departure, he became head coach at Southern College, Lakeland, Florida and two years later was named freshman football coach and head track coach at the University of Alabama. Although not a graduate of Henderson, he was truly a "son of the school and many of the traditions of the college have been woven around Coach Jimmy Haygood and his golden smile." *Oracle*, Feb. 2, 1928.

157. In the 1919 *Star* there is a composite picture of the student body in the shape of a heart.

158. Board Minutes, March 2, 1926.

159. *Ibid.*, May 21, 1926.

CHAPTER IX

THE END OF AN ERA

1. Manuscript Minutes of the Board of Trustees of Henderson-Brown College under the date of May 21, 1926; and *Oracle*, June 3, 1926. The board minutes will hereinafter be cited thus: Board Minutes, followed by the date. The *Oracle* is the student newspaper of the college and was first published Oct. 6, 1908.

2. Letter, Office of the Registrar, Duke University, to John G. Hall, Feb. 2, 1972, in my possession; Letter, Director of Alumni, Duke University, to John G. Hall, Feb. 2, 1972, in my possession; and *Oracle*, Sept. 30, 1926.

3. Board of Minutes, May 21, 1926.

4. *Oracle*, Sept. 30, 1926.

5. Board Minutes, March 1, 1927; and *Oracle*, March 3, 1927. Reference to the donation as the largest single gift ever made to any cause in Arkansas is from Executive Secretary J. J. Galloway's original draft of a form letter sent to major contributors to the drive. The letter is dated 1/3/27.

6. *Oracle*, Oct. 21, 1926.

7. *Ibid.*, Dec. 2, 1926.

8. Richard Halliburton, Jr., "The Adoption of Arkansas' Anti-Evolution Law," *Arkansas Historical Quarterly*, XXIII (Fall, 1964), 273, 277, 282.

9. *Oracle*, Oct. 4, 1928.

10. The ceremony was held June 14, 1927. *Ibid.*, May 19, 1927.

11. *Henderson State Teachers College Alumni News and Notes*, VI, No. 3 (Dec., 1964), 2.

12. Manuscript Minutes, Henderson-Brown Club, Oct. 17, 1927. Formed by former women students, at the second meeting, friends, including males, were permitted membership. *Ibid.*, Oct. 24, 1927.

13. *Oracle*, Feb. 23, 1928; May 17, 1928. Arkadelphia *Southern Standard*, Feb. 23, 1928. This newspaper will hereinafter be cited thus: *Southern Standard*, followed by the date of the issue. Little Rock *Arkansas Methodist*, Feb. 23, 1928. This newspaper will hereinafter be cited thus: *Arkansas Methodist*, followed by the date of the issue.

14. *Oracle*, Nov. 18, 1919; Jan. 27, 1920.

15. *Ibid.*, Jan. 27, 1920.

16. Jackson, Miss., *Clarion-Ledger*, March 25, 1926.

17. *Oracle*, Feb. 14, 1923; Interview, Mildred Sherrod, professor emeritus,

Henderson State College, Feb. 18, 1972; Jan. 6, 1972; and Letter, Mildred Sherrod to John G. Hall, Feb. 23, 1972, in my possession.

18. Board Minutes, March 6, 1923; and Interview, Mildred Sherrod, Jan. 6, 1974.

19. *Oracle*, Feb. 9, 1928.

20. *Ibid.*, Feb. 23, 1928; March 1, 1928.

21. Interview, Amy Jean Greene, associate professor, Henderson State College, Feb. 18, 1972; Interview, Mildred Sherrod; and Letter, Mildred Sherrod. Miss Greene is a past president of the Arkansas Education Association and a former Arkansas Woman of the Year.

22. Interview, Amy Jean Greene.

23. *Ibid.* When seeking verification of the report, I confronted both Huie and Woodward. Both remarked that they did not recall that specific incident, but both stated also that "if Amy Jean said we did it, then we did." Both men recalled the conflicts with President Hornaday, and remarked "that they did so much and it was so long ago, that it was difficult to remember many details." Interview, C. Vann Woodward, Sterling Professor of History, Yale University, Nov. 8, 1973; and Interview, Cyrus Richard Huie, executive secretary, Arkansas Judicial Dept., April 19, 1974.

24. Interview, Diane Huie Balay, daughter of Cyrus Richard Huie, Feb. 18, 1972; and Interview, Cyrus Richard Huie.

25. Interview, C. Vann Woodward. Born Nov. 13, 1908, at Vandale, Ark., Woodward moved with his family to Arkadelphia where for a number of years his father was superintendent of schools. In 1926 he enrolled in the college as a freshman. Completing that year, he toured Europe, and returned to Henderson-Brown in the fall of 1927. During his two years at the school he was an active and popular student, a member of the *Oracle* staff and the Garland Literary Society; he also won a trophy in a state-wide oratorical contest. Though he liked history, he was much more interested in English and writing and became noted on campus for his humorous pieces. In a letter dated April 12, 1971, Professor Woodward remarked that he remembers with special gratitude his two English instructors, Boulware Martin Ohls and Mary Sue Mooney. The former instructor recalls that Woodward was an avid reader and probably read all the books in the library. After two years at Henderson, he entered Emory University and received the Ph.B. in 1930. In 1932 he received the M.A. from Columbia, and the Ph.D. in 1937 from North Carolina. That year he began what has become a distinguished career as teacher and author, holding positions at the universities of Florida and Virginia, Johns Hopkins, and Yale. A former president of the American and Southern Historical associations, he holds honorary degrees from North Carolina, Arkansas, Emory, and William and Mary. Among his notable publications are *The Burden of South-*

ern History; Tom Watson, Agrarian Rebel; Reunion and Reaction; Origins of The New South, 1877–1913; The Strange Career of Jim Crow; The Comparative Approach to American History. Woodward corresponds with former classmate Huie and from time to time returns to Arkadelphia and the college.

26. Board Minutes, June 20, 1928; *Southern Standard*, June 21, 1928; and Letter, Director of Alumni, Duke University, to John G. Hall, Feb. 2, 1972, in my possession. It is of significance that the press carried little coverage of the "student strike."

27. Board Minutes, June 20, 1928; and *Southern Standard*, June 28, 1928.

28. Interview, the Reverend James Warthen Workman, March 19, 1974; Letter, James W. Workman to John G. Hall, March 2, 1972, in my possession; and Board Minutes, June 20, 1928.

29. Interview, James W. Workman.

30. Board Minutes, March 6, 1928.

31. Interview, James W. Workman.

32. *Oracle*, Sept. 18, 1928; Sept. 27, 1928; Oct. 4, 1928; Jan. 10, 1929. Professor Leach joined the faculty in 1923, and returned in 1928 following additional graduate work and completion of the Ph.D. degree.

33. *Catalogue of Henderson-Brown College*, 1928–1929, 97–102. This bulletin will hereinafter be cited thus: *Catalogue*, followed by the date. And *Oracle*, Sept. 18, 1928.

34. *Southern Standard*, Sept. 27, 1928; and *Oracle*, Oct. 18, 1928.

35. Board Minutes, April 30, 1907.

36. *Minutes of the Little Rock Annual Conference of the Methodist Episcopal Church, South*, under the dates of November 27–December 2, 1907, 50. The minutes of the Little Rock Conference will hereinafter be cited thus: *Minutes, Little Rock Conference*, followed by the dates of the session.

37. *Ibid.*, Nov. 25–30, 1908, 35.

38. *Oracle*, Nov. 3, 1908.

39. Guy A. Simmons, "Hendrix College: A Brief Historical Sketch, 1884–1944" (A typescript in Bailey Library, Hendrix College, Conway, Arkansas, 1944), 43.

40. Board Minutes, February 15, 1927; and "Methodists Plan Unique Educational Plant," *The Dixie Magazine*, III, No. 3 (March, 1927), 7; J. M. Williams, "The Bishop's University Plan," *Ibid.*, III, No. 4 (April, 1927), 11; Clifford L. Hornaday, "An Educational Plan," *Ibid.*, III, No. 4 (April, 1927), 12; and *Arkansas Methodist*, Feb. 24, 1927; March 17, 1927; April 7, 1927; April 14, 1927.

41. *Ibid.*; J. J. Galloway, "The New Educational Plan of the Methodists," *The Dixie Magazine*, III, No. 6 (July, 1927), 31; G. N. Cannon, "Ob-

jections to the New University Plan," *Arkansas Methodist*, April 14; and
J. A. Sage, "Is the Little Rock Conference Under Either Legal or Moral
Obligation to Maintain Henderson-Brown College as a Senior College,"
Ibid.

42. *Minutes, Little Rock Conference*, Nov. 16–20, 1927, 49; and Printed
*Minutes of the North Arkansas Conference of the Methodist Episcopal
Church, South*, under the dates of November 23–27, 1927, 89–91. The minutes of the North Arkansas Conference will hereinafter be cited thus: *Minutes, North Arkansas Conference*, followed by the dates of the session. Also
see *Arkansas Methodist*, June 23, 1927.

43. *Ibid.; Arkansas Methodist*, Nov. 24, 1927; Dec. 15, 1927; Jan. 5, 1928.

44. Minutes of the Special Session, February 28, 1928, 1–6, in *Minutes,
North Arkansas Conference*, 1928. For the report of the Commission, see
3–6; for the report of the Consolidated Board, see 73–74; and for additional
information see *Minutes, Little Rock Conference*, 1928, 30–31; and 32–34.
Also see *Oracle*, March 1, 1928; and *Arkansas Methodist*, March 8, 1928.

45. *Ibid.;* Simmons, *"Hendrix College,"* 44–45; and *Arkansas Methodist*,
March 22, 1928.

46. Minutes of the Consolidated Board of Trustees, 74–77, in *Minutes,
North Arkansas Conference*, 1928. The minutes of this board shall hereinafter be cited thus: Consolidated Board Minutes. Also see *Southern Standard*, March 1, 1928; and *Arkansas Methodist*, March 22, 1928.

47. Board Minutes, March 6, 1928.

48. *Ibid.;* and *Southern Standard*, March 8, 1928.

49. The other members were J. J. Galloway, J. T. Robinson, W. C.
Ribenack, and R. W. Huie, Jr. Consolidated Board Minutes, *Minutes,
North Arkansas Conference*, 1928, 74; *Southern Standard*, April 19, 1928;
and *Arkansas Methodist*, March 22, 1928.

50. *Ibid.;* Simmons, "Hendrix College," 45; and *Arkansas Methodist*,
March 8, 1928.

51. Simmons, "Hendrix College," 45–46.

52. Consolidated Board Minutes, Oct. 22, 1928, as printed in *Oracle*,
Nov. 1, 1928.

53. *Ibid.; Oracle*, Nov. 15, 1928; and *Arkansas Methodist*, Nov. 29, 1928.

54. *Oracle*, Nov. 1, 1928.

55. *Ibid.*, Nov. 8, 1928.

56. *Minutes, Little Rock Conference*, 1928, 58. For the full report see
58–60; and *Minutes, North Arkansas Conference*, 1928, 89–93.

57. *Southern Standard*, Dec. 20, 1928.

58. *Arkansas Methodist*, Jan. 31, 1929; and *Southern Standard*, Dec. 27,
1928.

59. Manuscript Minutes of the Henderson-Brown Club, under the date

of Nov. 26, 1928. These minutes will hereinafter be cited thus: Henderson-Brown Club, followed by the date.

60. *Ibid.*, Dec. 10, 1929; Feb. 25, 1929.

61. Consolidated Board Minutes, Dec. 31, 1928, as reported in *Southern Standard*, Jan. 3, 1929; and *Arkansas Methodist*, Jan. 24, 1929.

62. *Southern Standard*, Jan. 17, 1929.

63. *Ibid.*; and Little Rock *Arkansas Democrat*, Nov. 18, 1928.

64. *Oracle*, Nov. 22, 1928.

65. Consolidated Board Minutes, Jan. 18, 1929, as reported in *Southern Standard*, Jan. 24, 1929.

66. Arkadelphia *Siftings Herald*, July 8, 1929. This newspaper will hereinafter be cited thus: *Siftings Herald*, followed by the date of the issue. And *Southern Standard*, Jan. 31, 1929. Adams was co-owner of Arkadelphia Milling Company and a past president (1920) of American Corn Millers' Association. He was the spearheader of the drive made by the local citizens' committee. Farrar Newberry, "Noel Adams, Man of Initiative and Courage," *Southern Standard*, March 26, 1963.

67. *Ibid.*, Feb. 14, 1929; Feb. 21, 1929.

68. *Ibid.*, Feb. 28, 1929.

69. *Oracle*, March 14, 1929.

70. Consolidated Board Minutes, March 14, 1929, as reported in *Arkansas Methodist*, March 14, 1929. Also see *Ibid.*, March 7, 1929; March 21, 1929; April 11, 1929; May 2, 1929.

71. *Siftings Herald*, Aug. 8, 1929; Aug. 15, 1929.

72. Henderson-Brown Club, May 13, 1929.

73. *Ibid.*, Feb. 25, 1929.

74. *Ibid.*; and *Siftings Herald*, June 3, 1929.

75. *Summer School Catalogue of Henderson-Brown College*, 1929, 1–2.

76. *Ibid.*

77. Manuscript Deed Record Book 134, Clark County Courthouse, Arkadelphia, Ark., 568–569.

78. Board Minutes, April 26, 1929; and Deed Record Book 134, 569.

79. Manuscript Miscellaneous Record Book 135, Clark County Courthouse, Arkadelphia, Ark., 572–575.

80. Deed Record Book 134, 566–568.

81. Board Minutes, March 6, 1928.

82. Interview, James W. Workman, March 19, 1974; and April 20, 1974.

83. Deed Record Book 134, 569, 572. The board was appointed on June 14; and *Siftings Herald*, July 8, 1929.

84. *Ibid.*, June 14, 1929; June 18, 1929; July 3, 1929; July 5, 1929; July 10, 1929; Board Minutes, July 20, 1920; and *Siftings Herald*, July 20, 1929; July 22, 1929; July 24, 1929; July 26, 1929.

85. *Ibid.*, Aug. 8, 1929; Aug. 15, 1929.

86. Interview, James W. Workman; and *Siftings Herald*, June 5, 1929.

87. Interview, James W. Workman; and Letter, James W. Workman to John G. Hall. According to Workman, he was assisted on the musical score and arrangement by Dr. and Mrs. Frederick Harwood, Paul Schultz, and Mrs. Eliza Harris Workman.

88. This letter was discovered in a box of discarded materials in Huie Library by Head Librarian Frank Turner who called it to my attention. A Xerox copy is in my possession.

89. Henderson-Brown Club, March 25, 1929; May 29, 1929.

90. *Ibid.*, Oct. 7, 1929.

91. *Ibid.*

92. *Ibid.*, Feb. 25, 1929.

93. *Ibid.*, The club borrowed the money from the Elk Horn Bank and the club minutes of Oct. 13, 1930, record that the note had been paid.

94. *Ibid.*, Feb. 25, 1929; March 25, 1929; April 22, 1929.

Appendix A

Marker 1. At or near this site Adam Blakely operated a blacksmith shop from 1810. The settlement was called Blakelytown until 1838 when the name Arkadelphia was adopted. It became the Clark County seat in 1842. Until the railroad came in 1873 river transportation to points as far as New Orleans flourished. The wharf was on the south bank between the present bridges. Prior to 1903 all vehicular river crossing was by ferry.

Marker 2. Clark County—First Manufactory in Arkansas—Indians in primeval times, De Soto in 1541, pioneers of the 1800's and Confederates during the Civil War obtained salt from the creek and old well here. John Hemphill in 1812 opened one of the first manufactories in Arkansas—A Salt Refinery. Recently removed from its obscure location, the marker now stands as a center of attention on Highway 7, some two miles east of Arkadelphia.

Marker 3. Salt kettle used in the production of salt from the waters of the Saline Bayou one mile east of Arkadelphia by John Hemphill, pioneer salt maker of Arkansas Territory, circa 1814. Given to the H.S.T.C. Museum by the family of Capt. Robert Huie, 1845–1929, friend and benefactor of the college.

Marker 4. To honor Jacob Barkman, pioneer settler, senator, magistrate, postmaster, promoter of river traffic, merchant, and frequently called the "Father of Clark County."

Marker 5. At or near this site was buried in 1837 Meriwether Lewis Randolph, Secretary of Arkansas Territory and grandson of Thomas Jefferson.

Marker 6. Here during Reconstruction years were the offices of the Freedman's Bureau. The building was at different times used as a harness shop, grocery store, barber shop, and a saloon.

Marker 7. Dedicated to the memory of Harris Flanagin, Governor of Arkansas, 1862–1865.

Marker 8. Here from 1859 to 1903 was the First Presbyterian Church. Its accommodations were frequently used for schoolroom classes, commencement exercises, and civic meetings. In the sanctuary were conducted the funeral services of Governor Harris Flanagin. To commemorate its religious, cultural, and historical significance, this marker was placed in 1959 by Camp 233 Woodmen of the World.

Marker 9. Near this site a log structure housed a private tuition school for many years before tax supported education was available in Arkadelphia.

The schoolhouse was used for community meetings and for religious services prior to the organization of the town's first churches.

Among those who conducted private schools were William Callaway, James Trigg, Thomas Heard, John Moseley, Thomas Malone, Samuel Stephenson, Elizabeth Webb, Mary Connelly, and Fannie Cook.

Marker 10. In this block the community's first frame school house, "a two-story with a cupola," served 40 years from 1850 as the elementary tuition school of Reverend Samuel Stephenson, then as Mary Connelly's Arkadelphia Female College, and later as a public school taught by Fannie Cook and others.

Marker 11. At this site the first Public or "Free" School in Arkadelphia was opened in 1870. Early teachers included R. D. Hearn, Elizabeth Webb, Harriet Crow, John Gordon, and Dutie Casey.

Appendix B

TO THE PRESIDENT AND MEMBERS OF THE BOARD OF TRUS-
TEES OF HENDERSON-BROWN COLLEGE—
Dear Brother:

We, your Committee appointed to prepare a tribute to the memory of
Capt. C. C. Henderson, respectfully submit the following:

Since our last annual meeting this Board of Trustees and the College
which we represent have suffered an irreparable loss in the death of Capt.
C. C. Henderson. The deceased had been an honored member of this
Board since 1891. For many years he served the Board as its President, a
position from which he was relieved by his brethren only when continued
ill health made it well nigh impossible for him to continue to perform the
duties of the office.

We are deeply conscious of our inability to frame a tribute which will
worthily express the measure of our obligation and the obligation of the
College which we represent, to the memory of this good man. He came
to the rescue of this College when the institution seemed hopeless, through
many years of struggle and uncertainty, when the fate of the college still
trembled in the balance, and the future seemed almost hopeless his loyalty
never wavered and his courage never failed. It is all together fitting that
the College should bear his honored name, and perpetuate his memory.

We gratefully place this tribute of love and appreciation on the permanent records of our Board, and beg to assure his bereaved family of our
fraternal regard, and sympathy. We further assure them that the College
which we represent will not cease to cherish the honored name which it is
proud to bear, and we devoutly trust that many generations yet unborn
shall bless the name of our honored benefactor, founder and friend.

J. A. Sage
Hugh D. Hart
W. E. Barkman

As recorded in Board Minutes under the date of March 4, 1924

Appendix C

The primary source for the history of the Methodist years of Henderson State College is the minutes of the Board of Trustees. Surprisingly, the institution maintains in its official records only those minutes dating from the first session of the state appointed trustees (July 20, 1929).

Present college officials had no knowledge of the whereabouts of the trustees' minutes covering the Methodist era and repeated the assumption that these documents had passed to Hendrix College before the state assumed control of the school. Investigation proved this declaration false and prompted this writer to begin an intense search for the missing manuscripts. Finally located in a store-room, formerly a kitchen, in the college museum, they and other valuable records for this study were found stacked among discarded materials, appropriately guarded by the skin of a rattlesnake.

These priceless manuscripts will be microfilmed and placed in Huie Library.

Appendix D

CHARTER
OFFICE OF
SECRETARY OF STATE,
LITTLE ROCK, ARK.

I, B. B. Chism, Secretary of State of Arkansas, do hereby certify that the annexed pages contain a true, complete and full copy of the Articles of Association of the "Arkadelphia Methodist College," as filed in this office on June 10, 1890, as appears by comparing the same with the original roll of said Articles now on file in this office.

IN TESTIMONY WHEREOF, I have hereunto set my hand and affixed my official seal at Little Rock, this 23rd day of May, A.D. Eighteen Hundred and Ninety-Two.

Ben B. Chism,
[SEAL]   Secretary of State.

(COPY)

WHEREAS, J. McLaughlin, R. H. Featherston, R. W. Huie, E. H. McDaniel, C. V. Murry, C. H. Cargile, J. R. Dale, H. A. Butler, W. R. White, J. R. Harvey, H. D. McKennon, J. H. Gold, J. R. Moore, C. D. McSwain and A. O. Evans have filed in the office of the Secretary of State their Articles of Association in compliance with the provisions of the law for the Incorporation of Institutions of Learning, with their petition for incorporation under the name and style of "Arkadelphia Methodist College," they and their successors are therefore hereby declared a body politic and corporate, by the name and style aforesaid, with all the powers, privileges and immunities granted in the law thereunto appertaining. And the said named persons and their successors are hereby constituted a Board of Trustees of said institution and invested with all the powers prescribed by their Articles of Association or by the law of the land.

238

Witness our hands this 10th day of June, 1890.
(Signed)

J. P. Eagle,
Governor.
B. B. Chism,
Secretary of State.
W. E. Thompson,
Supt. Public Instruction.

TO ALL WHOM IT MAY CONCERN:

Know Ye, That J. McLaughlin, R. H. Featherston, R. W. Huie, E. H. McDaniel, C. V. Murry, C. H. Cargile, J. R. Dale, H. A. Butler, W. R. White, J. R. Harvey, H. D. McKennon, J. H. Gold, J. R. Moore, C. D. McSwain and A. O. Evans, Trustees of the Little Rock Conference of the Methodist Episcopal Church, South, have associated themselves together under the name "Arkadelphia Methodist College," for the purpose of founding and incorporating under the laws of this State an institution of learning to be located at Arkadelphia, in the county of Clark, and State of Arkansas; and for the purpose of securing legal existence by Act of Incorporation, the above named persons, as the Trustees of said institution, have prepared the following charter and constitution for said college:

PREAMBLE.

The object of this institution shall be the promotion of Christian education in literature, science and art.

ARTICLE I.

SECTION 1. This institution shall be opened to students of both sexes.
SEC. 2. The name of the institution shall be "Arkadelphia Methodist College."

ARTICLE II.

SECTION 1. This college shall be under the direction and control of a Board of Trustees composed of the above named trustees and their successors in office, to be elected or appointed by the Little Rock Annual Conference of the Methodist Episcopal Church, South.
SEC. 2. The Board of Trustees shall consist of fifteen members, residents of the Little Rock Conference, who shall serve for a term of three years; provided, that one-third of the whole number of said trustees shall annually be retired from office, said number to be determined by lot, and others, or the same persons be elected to fill the vacancies, so that the official term of

one-third of the members of the board shall expire at the end of each conference year.

SEC. 3. If an appointment of trustees shall not take place at the Annual Conference, or if a vacancy shall occur from any cause, the same shall be filled by the board on nomination of the Board of Education of the Little Rock Annual Conference.

SEC. 4. The regular meeting of the board shall be held in the college building at 4 o'clock p.m. on Monday of Commencement week, unless the time and place be otherwise fixed by the board at a previous regular meeting.

ARTICLE III.

SECTION 1. The officers of the board shall be a President, a Vice President, a Secretary and a Treasurer, who shall be elected annually at the regular meeting from their own number.

SEC. 2. The President of the board shall be the presiding officer thereof, and perform such duties as may be required by the board.

SEC. 3. The President, when in his judgment shall think it necessary, may call a special meeting of the board.

SEC. 4. In case of a special meeting, ten days' notice in writing shall be given to each member of the board, and no business shall be transacted except that named in the call, unless the same be concurred in by two-thirds of the full board.

SEC. 5. The Vice President shall assist the President, and in the latter's absence shall act as President.

SEC. 6. The Secretary shall be the custodian of all records and other documents belonging to the board; he shall keep a correct record of all the proceedings of the board, conduct all correspondence thereof, and perform other duties required of him by the board.

SEC. 7. The Treasurer shall be the custodian of all moneys and other effects belonging to the board, and for the faithful performance of his duties shall be required to give bond in such sum as shall be fixed by the Executive Committee, with security to be approved by said committee.

ARTICLE IV.

SECTION 1. An Executive Committee, to consist of three members of the board, shall be elected annually by the board at its regular meeting, and the President and Secretary of the board shall be ex-officio members of the Executive Committee.

SEC. 2. The Executive Committee may organize under its own rules and may at will hold meetings for the transaction of its business.

SEC. 3. In the interim of the meetings of the Board, the Executive Committee shall have supervisory control of the business concerns of the college, and shall at the regular meetings of the board, and oftener if necessary, report its action to the Board for its approval.

ARTICLE V.

SECTION 1. On nomination of the President of the college, or if there be no President, of the Executive Committee, the board shall elect teachers to fill vacancies in the Faculty; provided, if a vacancy shall occur in the interim of the meeting of the board, the same shall be filled by the Executive Committee.

SEC. 2. The President shall be elected for one year on trial, but after one year's satisfactory service, he may be elected for a longer term, and all teachers shall hold their positions during the pleasure of the board, the President of the college concurring.

ARTICLE VI.

SECTION 1. The President of the college and the Faculty shall establish the curriculum and make all rules for the government of students, but these may be revised by the board, two-thirds of the members concurring.

SEC. 2. The President and faculty shall, at each regular meeting of the board, report any changes or improvements which they may deem necessary in the management of the institution and any others affecting its interests.

SEC. 3. The President of the college shall have all rights and privileges of a member of the board, except the right to vote and hold office.

SEC. 4. Degrees in course shall be conferred only on the recommendation of the President and Faculty.

SEC. 5. Honorary degrees shall be conferred only on the recommendation of the Executive Committee and said committee shall consider no application unless the same be made at least ten days previous to the regular meeting.

ARTICLE VII.

SECTION 1. At all meetings of the board eight members shall constitute a quorum.

SEC. 2. No member shall be represented at a meeting of the board by proxy.

ARTICLE VIII.

SECTION 1. Any contribution, endowment or trust fund given to the college shall be under the control of the Board, but must be applied as directed by the donor.

ARTICLE IX.

SECTION 1. The children of all ministers in the regular work, of super-annuated, supernumerary and deceased, traveling preachers of the Methodist Episcopal Church, South, and all young men preparing for the regular ministry in any orthodox Protestant denomination shall be admitted to all privileges of the college free of tuition in the Literary Department; provided, that all beneficiary students may at the discretion of the Faculty be charged contingent and expense fees; and all young men preparing for the regular ministry shall give their notes for tuition, payable only upon their failure to enter the regular ministry, and if any failure to enter the regular ministry be without fault of such beneficiary, he may be relieved of his obligation by the board.

ARTICLE X.

SECTION 1. The Board of Trustees shall have full power to take such steps and adopt such measures to advance the interest of the institution as may be deemed necessary and consistent with the provisions of this constitution.

ARTICLE XI.

SECTION 1. This constitution may be altered or amended by the concurrence of three-fourths of the members of the Board of Trustees at any regular meeting of the board, provided that notice in writing of any proposed alteration or amendment shall be given to each member of the board at least twenty days before the meeting at which such change may be made.

This constitution was read and adopted by the board in session at a meeting called by J. McLaughlin, R. H. Featherston, E. H. McDaniel, C. V. Murry, J. R. Dale, C. H. Cargile, W. R. White, J. R. Moore, to meet at Arkadelphia, Arkansas, on the 4th day of June, 1890, and each member of the above named Board of Trustees were notified in writing of the said meeting of the board more than ten days before the day for said meeting of the board.

In testimony of which we, the members of said board of trustees, have signed the same on this June 4th, 1890.

J. McLaughlin,
H. D. McKinnon,
R. H. Featherston,
Chas. H. Cargile,
W. R. White,
C. V. Murry,

E. H. McDaniel,
J. R. Moore,
R. W. Huie,
John H. Gold,
J. R. Harvey,
J. R. Dale.

Indorsement on back:
"Copy of Certificate and Articles of Association of the Arkadelphia
Methodist College.
"Filed in the office of Secretary of State, June 10, 1890.

"Ben B. Chism,
"Secretary of State."

Appendix E

History of Methodist Education in Arkansas
Minor Methodist Colleges

By William Oscar Wilson

ARKADELPHIA FEMALE COLLEGE

Organized, 1859 or 1860.—In 1859 a letter respecting the establishment of a female college at Arkadelphia was presented to the Ouachita Annual Conference by Rev. John M. Bradley, and referred to the committee on education.[1] The school was soon organized, as evidenced by the fact that a communication from the board of trustees of the Arkadelphia Female College was referred to the committee on education at the next session of the Ouachita Annual Conference in 1860.[2]

Incorporated, 1861.—The school was incorporated by an act of the State legislature, approved January 8, 1861.[3] Section one of the act stipulated that the institution should have "succession for ninety-nine years." Section two provided for the election of trustees by the Ouachita Conference at its regular annual sessions. Section seven gave the board of trustees power "to confer such literary and scientific degrees and honors as (were) usually conferred by institutions of learning of a like character, and to grant such diplomas or certificates, as (would) be necessary to attest said degrees and honors."

Presidents.—Rev. James E. Cobb served as president of the college for a period of two years, being appointed by the Ouachita Conference at its annual sessions held in 1860 and in 1861.[4] At the next annual session of the Conference, 1862, the committee on education recommended that L. J. Joyner be appointed president and Jas. E. Cobb agent, but the office of president was left "to be supplied."[5] The minutes of the Conference for 1862 show that the college was again left "to be supplied,"[6] but no reference to the institution is found in the minutes for either of the two following sessions.

Course of Instruction and Operation of the College.—Nothing is at hand

244

concerning the nature of the course of instruction or the operation of the actual work of the college. During the first year of his presidency, Rev. Cobb likely spent his entire time in the interest of the school, as he was financial agent as well as president.[7] The next year he was assigned to the pastorate of the Arkadelphia Church, in addition to his duties in connection with the college.[8] As already indicated, the Conference appointments for 1863 left the presidency "to be supplied." Rev. W. P. Whaley, in his History of the Ouachita Conference, states that the college did not persist throughout the Civil War.[9]

Final Disposition of the College.—At the annual session of the Little Rock Conference,[10] in October, 1865, the committee on education reported that the Arkadelphia Female College was under "considerable embarrassment in consequence of the debt hanging over the institution." Whereupon the Conference passed a resolution authorizing the board of trustees "to make any disposition of the property" in order to remove the embarrassment.[11] Two years later the Conference appointed a new board of trustees to legalize the transfer of whatever interest the Conference had in the college property.[12]

FOOTNOTES

1. Jour. Ouachita Annual Conf., 1859, p. 85.
2. Jour. Ouachita Annual Conf., 1860, pp. 106–7.
3. Act 73, Acts of Ark., 1860–61.
4. Jour. Ouachita Annual Conf., 1860, p. 116; Ibid., 1861, p. 132.
   Minutes Annual Conferences, M.E.C.S., Vol. II, 1858–65, pp. 287, 358.
5. Jour. Ouachita Annual Conf., 1862, pp. 146, 151.
   Minutes Annual Conferences, M.E.C.S., Vol. II, 1858–65, p. 419.
6. Jour. Ouachita Annual Conf., 1863, p. 165.
7. Minutes Annual Conferences, M.E.C.S., Vol. II, 1858–65, p. 287.
8. [Omitted]
9. Pub. Ark. Hist. Assoc., III, 236.
10. The name of the Ouachita Conference was changed to Little Rock Conference, beginning with the thirteenth annual session in 1866.
11. Jour. Little Rock Annual Conf., 1866, pp. 200–1.
12. Jour. Little Rock Annual Conf., 1868, p. 59.

Bibliography

Primary Sources

Manuscripts

Accession Book I. Huie Library, Henderson State College.
Deed Record Book A-C. Clark County Courthouse, Arkadelphia, Arkansas.
Deed Record Book 73, Clark County Courthouse, Arkadelphia, Arkansas.
Deed Record Book 85. Clark County Courthouse, Arkadelphia, Arkansas.
Deed Record Book 87. Clark County Courthouse, Arkadelphia, Arkansas.
Deed Record Book 134. Clark County Courthouse, Arkadelphia, Arkansas.
Minutes of the Arkadelphia Public School Board, June 16, 1890, to Dec. 16, 1890. Office of the Superintendent, Arkadelphia Public Schools, Arkadelphia, Arkansas.
Minutes of the Arkansas Annual Conference of the Methodist Episcopal Church, 1836. Arkansas History Commission, Old State House, Little Rock, Arkansas.
Minutes of the Board of Trustees of Arkadelphia Methodist College, 1890–1904. Museum, Henderson State College.
Minutes of the Board of Trustees of Henderson College, 1904–1911. Museum, Henderson State College.
Minutes of the Board of Trustees of Henderson-Brown College, 1911–1929. Museum, Henderson State College.
Minutes of the Board of Trustees of Henderson State College, 1968–1970. President's Office, Henderson State College.
Minutes of the Board of Trustees of Henderson State Teachers College, 1929–1965. President's Office, Henderson State College.
Minutes of the City Council of Arkadelphia, Arkansas, 1866–1873. On File in City Hall.
Minutes of the First Baptist Church of Arkadelphia, Arkansas, 15 July, 1851–10 December, 1852. On file in the church.
Minutes of the Garland Literary Society, 1905–1915; 1920–1923. Huie Library, Henderson State College.

Minutes of the Henderson-Brown Alumni Association, 1929. Huie Library, Henderson State College.

Minutes of the Henderson-Brown College Club, 1927–1929. Museum, Henderson State College.

Minutes of the Henderson State College Club, 1929–1932. Museum, Henderson State College.

Miscellaneous Record Book 135. Clark County Courthouse, Arkadelphia, Arkansas.

Records Book V. Clark County Courthouse, Arkadelphia, Arkansas.

Records Book 41. Clark County Courthouse, Arkadelphia, Arkansas.

Records Book 51. Clark County Courthouse, Arkadelphia, Arkansas.

Letters and Interviews

Balay, Diane Huie, personal interview, Arkadelphia, February 4, 1971, with the author.

——, personal interview, Arkadelphia, February 18, 1972, with the author.

——, personal interview, Arkadelphia, March 1, 1972, with the author.

Batts, William O., Jr. A letter in my possession, October 12, 1973, to John G. Hall.

Dahlstedt, Waldo A., dean of graduate studies, Henderson State College, personal interview, Arkadelphia, July 28, 1970, with the author.

Duke University, director of alumni. A letter in my possession, February 2, 1972, to John G. Hall.

——, office of the registrar. A letter in my possession, February 2, 1972, to John G. Hall.

Eaves, Royce L., past master, Ancient, Free and Accepted Masons, Lodge 381, personal interview, Arkadelphia, March 25, 1971, with the author.

Ellis, Matt Locke, former president of Henderson State College, personal interview, Conway, Arkansas, April 13, 1974, with the author.

Entler, Fred P. A letter in my possession, July 31, 1973, to John G. Hall.

Fox, Nancy C. A Letter in my possession, October 30, 1973, to John G. Hall.

Galloway, J. J. (Reverend). A letter in Henderson Museum, January 17, 1925, to Mrs. E. H. Johnson.

Galloway, Paul Vernon (Bishop). A letter in my possession, August 23, 1971, to John G. Hall.

Garrett, Frank O. A letter in File Box 3, Farrar Newberry Papers, Division of Social Sciences, Henderson State College, July 10, 1965, to Farrar Newberry.

Glaze, Loretta S. A letter in my possession, February 28, 1972, to John G. Hall.

Greene, Amy Jean, associate professor, Henderson State College, personal interview, September 11, 1970, with the author.

——, associate professor, Henderson State College, personal interview, February 18, 1972, with the author.

Halloran, Ruth. A letter in my possession, July 30, 1973, to John G. Hall.

Harrell, Mrs. D. W. A letter in my possession, October 22, 1973, to John G. Hall.

——, cousin of the late W. W. Brown, personal interview, Camden, Arkansas, October 31, 1973, with the author.

Harrison, Mrs. G. C. A letter in my possession, October, 1973, to Mrs. D. W. Harrell.

Harwood, Dora Sellard, retired Henderson professor, personal interview, Arkadelphia, August 23, 1971, with the author.

Hayes, Albert M. A letter in my possession, August 16, 1973, to John G. Hall.

Hucks, Hubert, Jr. A letter in my possession, September 14, 1973, to John G. Hall.

Huie, Cyrus Richard, personal interview, Arkadelphia, April 19, 1974, with the author.

Kannard, Elizabeth. A letter in my possession, July 23, 1973, to John G. Hall.

Key, Albert Brown. A letter in File Box 3, Farrar Newberry Papers, Division of Social Sciences, Henderson State College, March 22, 1965, to Farrar Newberry.

Key, Annie Lydia. A letter in File Box 3, Farrar Newberry Papers, Division of Social Sciences, Henderson State College, n.d., to Farrar Newberry.

Key, Marcus. A letter in File Box 3, Farrar Newberry Papers, Division of Social Sciences, Henderson State College, April (n.d.), 1965, to Farrar Newberry.

Meier, Roma Garrett, personal interview, Arkadelphia, June 22, 1971, with the author.

——, personal interview, Arkadelphia, August 1, 1971, with the author.

Nelms, Mary Dale Jones. A letter in File Box 3, Farrar Newberry Papers, Division of Social Sciences, Henderson State College, March 28, 1964, to Farrar Newberry.

——. A letter in File Box 3, Farrar Newberry Papers, Division of Social Sciences, Henderson State College, May 4, 1964, to Farrar Newberry.

Nelson, Grace Benton, retired teacher, personal interview, August 26, 1973, with the author.

Ohls, Boulware Martin, retired professor, Henderson State College, personal interview, Arkadelphia, February 18, 1972, with the author.

Powell, William S. A letter in my possession, February 4, 1972, to John G. Hall.

Sasson, Diane. A letter in my possession, February 28, 1972, to John G. Hall.

Sease, Gene E. A letter in my possession, February 11, 1972, to John G. Hall.

Sherrod, Mildred. A letter in my possession, February 23, 1972, to John G. Hall.

———. A letter in my possession, March 6, 1972, to John G. Hall.

———, professor emeritus, Henderson State College, personal interview, Arkadelphia, February 18, 1972, with the author.

Smith, H. Grady, trustee and former bursar, Henderson State College, personal interview, Arkadelphia, July 13, 1971, with the author.

Smith, Lois McNabb, professor emeritus, Henderson State College, personal interview, Arkadelphia, September 16, 1972, with the author.

Thomas, Mrs. R. B., personal interview, Arkadelphia, July 23, 1970, with the author.

Turner, Nila Embree, associate professor emeritus, Henderson State College, personal interview, Arkadelphia, September 9, 1970, with the author.

Turrentine, G. R. A letter in File Box 3, Farrar Newberry Papers, Division of Social Sciences, Henderson State College, May 16, 1966, to Farrar Newberry.

———. A copy in my possession, October 16, 1929, to the Reverend Paul W. Quillian.

Warren, David A. A letter in my possession, August 1, 1973, to John G. Hall.

Washburn, W. C. A letter in my possession, November 14, 1973, to John G. Hall.

Whipple, Mae, professor of music, Henderson State College, personal interview, Arkadelphia, May 4, 1971, with the author.

Whitefield, Clarence E. A letter in my possession, February 4, 1972, to John G. Hall.

Whitten, Dolphus, Jr. A letter in my possession, February 7, 1972, to John G. Hall.

Woodward, C. Vann, Sterling Professor of History, Yale University, personal interview, Atlanta, Georgia, November 8, 1973, with the author.

———. A letter in my possession, April 12, 1971, to Mrs. Louise Saylor.

Workman, James Warthen (Reverend). A letter in my possession, March 2, 1972, to John G. Hall.

Workman, James Warthen (Reverend), former president of Henderson-Brown College, personal interview, Conway, March 19, 1974, and April 20, 1974, with the author.

Published Church, College, Federal, and State Records

Acts and Resolutions of the General Assembly of the State of Arkansas, 1836–1929.

Alumni Bulletin of Henderson-Brown College, IV, No. 6 (May, 1916). Arkadelphia: Henderson-Brown College, 1916.

Alumni Bulletin of Henderson State Teachers College, VI, No. 3 (December, 1964). Arkadelphia: Henderson State Teachers College, 1964.

Alumni Directory: "Who's Who" Among Vanderbilt Men and Women, I. Nashville: Vanderbilt University, 1923.

Bailey, David W., ed. Harvard Alumni Directory. Cambridge: Harvard University, 1929.

Biennial Report of the State Superintendent of Public Instruction, 1899–1900. Little Rock: Arkansas Democrat Co., Printers, 1900.

Bulletin of Henderson-Brown College: Endow the College, Arkadelphia: Henderson-Brown College, 1923.

Bulletin of Henderson-Brown College: Serve and Save Henderson-Brown College. Arkadelphia: Henderson-Brown College, 1924.

Bulletin of Henderson-Brown College: Team Work. Arkadelphia: Henderson-Brown College, 1924.

Bulletin of Henderson-Brown College: To Be Or Not To Be. Arkadelphia: Henderson-Brown College, n.d.

Carter, Clarence Edwin, ed. *The Territorial Papers of the United States.* 22 vols. Washington: Government Printing Office, 1934–1956.

Catalogue of The Arkadelphia Methodist College. Arkadelphia: Arkadelphia Methodist College, 1890–1903.

Catalogue of Henderson College. Arkadelphia: Henderson College, 1904–1910.

Catalogue of Henderson-Brown College. Arkadelphia: Henderson-Brown College, 1911–1929.

Catalogue of Henderson State College. Arkadelphia: Henderson State College, 1967–1970.

Catalogue of Henderson State Teachers College. Arkadelphia: Henderson State Teachers College, 1929–1966.

Catalogue of Hendrix College. Conway, Ark.: Hendrix College, 1891.

Catalogue of Shorter College. Little Rock: Shorter College, 1970.

Henderson State College Handbook, 1970–1971. Arkadelphia: Henderson State College, 1970.

Israel, Fred L., ed. *The State of the Union Messages of the Presidents.* I. New York: R. R. Bowker Co., 1967.

Journal of the House of Representatives of the United States at the Second Session of the Fifteenth Congress in the Forty-Third Year of the Independence of the United States. Washington: E. De Krafft, Printer, 1818.

Lowrie, Walter, and Mathew St. Clair Clarke, eds. *American State Papers, Indian Affairs: Documents, Legislative and Executive of the Congress of the United States, from the First Session of the First to the Third Session of the Thirteenth Congress, Inclusive: Commencing March 3, 1789 and Ending March 3, 1815.* IV. Washington: Gales & Seaton, 1832. J. N. Heiskell Collection, Arkansas Gazette, Little Rock, Arkansas.

Minutes of the Arkansas Annual Conference of the Methodist Episcopal Church, 1836–1914.

Minutes of the Little Rock Annual Conference of the Methodist Episcopal Church, South, 1866–1929.

Minutes of the North Arkansas Annual Conference of the Methodist Episcopal Church, South, 1914–1929.

Minutes of the White River Annual Conference of the Methodist Episcopal Church, South, 1870–1914.

Proceedings of the First Meeting, Association of College and Preparatory Schools of the Southern States, November 6, 1895.

Richardson, James D., ed. *A Compilation of the Messages and Papers of the Presidents, 1789–1817.* I. Washington: Government Printing Office, 1896.

Ross, Arvin A., ed. *Digest of the Ordinances of the City of Arkadelphia, Arkansas.* (n.p.: 1949). Published by the City Council.

Star. Arkadelphia: Henderson State College, 1905–1970.

Transcribed Minutes of the Ouachita Annual Conference of the Methodist Episcopal Church, South, 1859. Rare Books Collection, Bailey Library, Hendrix College, Conway, Ark. In 1866 Ouachita Annual Conference was renamed Little Rock Annual Conference.

U.S., Bureau of the Census. *Compendium of the Eleventh Census of the United States: 1890.* Washington: Government Printing Office, 1892.

U.S., Bureau of the Census. *Compendium of the Sixth Census of the United States: 1840.* Washington: Blair & Rives, 1841.

U.S., Bureau of the Census. *Eighth Census of the United States: 1860,* I, *Statistics of Population.* Washington: Government Printing Co., 1864.

U.S., Bureau of the Census. *Ninth Census of the United States: 1870,* I, *Statistics of Population.* Washington: Government Printing Office, 1872.

U.S. Bureau of the Census. *Seventh Census of the United States: 1850, Slave Inhabitants.* n.p.: n.d. Microfilm copy in the Arkansas History Commission, Old State House, Little Rock, Arkansas.

U.S., Bureau of the Census. *Seventh Census of the United States: 1850,* I, *Statistics of Population.* Washington: Robert Armstrong, Public Printer, 1853.

U.S., Dept. of the Interior, Bureau of Education. *Bulletin* No. 27. Washington: Government Printing Office, 1912.

U.S., Dept. of the Interior, Bureau of Education. *Bulletin* No. 34. Washington: Government Printing Office, 1920.

U.S., Congress. "An Act Making Further Provision for the Sale of Public Lands," *Annals of The Congress of The United States.* (16th Cong., 1st Sess.) II. Washington: Gales & Seaton, 1855.

U.S., Congress, House, Committee on the U.S. De Soto Expedition, *Final Report of the United States De Soto Expedition Commission.* (76th Cong., 1st Sess., House, Doc. 71) Washington: Government Printing Office, 1939.

U.S. *Statutes at Large.* II. Boston: Little & Brown, 1846.

Zook, George F. *Accredited Higher Institutions,* U.S., Dept. of the Interior, Bureau of Education *Bulletin* No. 30. Washington: Government Printing Office, 1922.

Documentary Collections, Journals, and Travel Accounts

Cox, Isaac Joslin. *The Exploration of the Louisiana Frontier, 1803-1806.* VIII. n.p.: 1904. J. N. Heiskell Collection, Arkansas Gazette, Little Rock, Arkansas.

Featherstonhaugh, George W. *Excursion Through The Slave States, From Washington on The Patomac to The Frontier of Mexico; With Sketches of Popular Manners and Geological Notices.* 2 vols. New York: Harper & Brothers, 1844.

Hunter, John D. *Memoirs of A Captivity Among The Indians of North America, From Childhood to the Age of Nineteen: with [sic] Anecdotes Descriptive of Their Manners and Custom: To Which Is Added, Some Account of the Soil, Climate, and Vegetable Productions of the Territory Westward of the Mississippi.* London: Longman, Hurst, Rees, Orme, Brown & Green, 1923. J. N. Heiskell Collection, Arkansas Gazette, Little Rock, Arkansas.

"The Narrative of the Expedition of Hernando De Soto by the Gentleman of Elvas," *Spanish Explorers in the Southern United States, 1528-1543,* eds. Frederick W. Hodge and Theodore H. Lewis. New York: Barnes & Noble, Inc., 1965, 129-272.

Roland, (Mrs.) Dunbar, ed. *Life, Letters, and Papers of William Dunbar, 1749-1810.* Jackson: Press of the Mississippi Historical Society, 1930.

Scott, Robert N., ed. *The War of the Rebellion: A Compilation of the Official Record of the Union and Confederate Armies,* XXXIV, Series I, Part I. Washington: Government Printing Office, 1891.

Switzler, William F., MS Diary, 10 Oct., 1836. Western Historical Manuscripts Collection, University of Missouri Library. Transcribed copy in the Arkansas History Commission, Old State House, Little Rock, Arkansas.

Travels in The Interior Parts of America: Communicating Discoveries Made in Exploring The Missouri, Red River and Washita, By Captains Lewis and Clark, Dr. Sibley and Mr. Dunbar As Laid Before The Senate by The President of The United States in February 1806. London: Richard Phillips, 1807. J. N. Heiskell Collection, Arkansas Gazette, Little Rock, Arkansas.

Wyatt, William N. *Wyatt's Travel Diary 1836: With Comment by Mrs. Addie Evans Wynn and W. A. Evans (Grandchildren of W. N. Wyatt).* Chicago: n.p., 1930.

Newspapers and Periodicals

Arkadelphia *Arkansas Traveler*, 1854.
Arkadelphia (Arkansas) *Siftings Herald*, 1924–1963.
Arkadelphia (Arkansas) *Southern Standard*, 1870–1969.
The Arkadelphian, I, No. 4 (June, 1898).
The Arkansas Technic, 1895–1896.
Brooks, H. W. "Stuttgart Institute and Its New President, Prof. G. C. Jones," Little Rock *Arkansas Methodist*, August 28, 1889, 4.
Camden (Arkansas) News, November 5, 1924.
The Campus, III, November, 1908.
Cannon, G. N. "Objections to the New University Plan," Little Rock *Arkansas Methodist*, April 14, 1927, 4.
Charleston (South Carolina) *News and Courier*, July 28, 1890.
Charleston (South Carolina) *Southern Christian Advocate*, September 30, 1886.
Goodloe, Granville. "Capt. Henderson's Gift," Little Rock *Arkansas Methodist*, August 27, 1902, 2.
———. "The Royal Succession," Arkadelphia *Southern Standard*, February 7, 1901, 2.
Green, James R. "Old Trunk Surrenders Some Interesting Documents Regarding Early History of School City, Clark's County Seat," Little Rock *Arkansas Democrat Magazine*, March 16, 1947, 6–7.
Green, Gleen A. "May Re-Establish Field Day for Diamond Hunters," Little Rock *Arkansas Democrat Magazine*, April 6, 1947, 6–7.
Halliburton, W. H. "Arkadelphia, Rainbow City, Finds Pot of Gold," Little Rock *Arkansas Democrat Magazine*, March 22, 1953, 2–3.
———. "D.A.R. Sponsors Pilgrimage to Residences of Special Note in Arkadelphia," Little Rock *Arkansas Democrat Magazine*, May 3, 1953, 6–7.

Halliburton, W. H. "Dr. Frederick Harwood," Little Rock *Arkansas Gazette*, September 15, 1946, 11B.

———. "Historic Arkansas Homes," Little Rock *Arkansas Gazette Magazine*, June 8, 1941, 8–9.

———. "Historic House in Arkadelphia," Little Rock *Arkansas Democrat Magazine*, September 24, 1967, 3.

———. "The Nation's Rivers Inspire the Nation's Poets," Little Rock *Arkansas Gazette*, November 8, 1964, 4E.

———. "New Bells in Old House," Little Rock *Arkansas Democrat Magazine*, November 17, 1968, 1–3.

———. "Oaklawn Not Site of First Pony Race Course in State," Hot Springs (Arkansas) *Sentinel-Record*, March 2, 1969, 5.

———. "When Salt Was a Sweet Discovery," Little Rock *Arkansas Democrat Magazine*, October 14, 1962, 11.

Jackson (Mississippi) *Clarion-Ledger*, March 25, 1926, 2.

Little Rock *Arkansas Democrat*, 1924–1968.

Little Rock *Arkansas Gazette*, 1820–1970.

Little Rock *Arkansas Methodist*, 1889–1929.

Little Rock *Arkansas True Democrat*, 1854.

Little Rock *Daily Arkansas Gazette*, 1870–1874.

Methodist College Magazine, 1891–1894.

McDaniel, Ann S. "Farrar Newberrys Restore Family Home," Little Rock *Arkansas Gazette*, December 4, 1955, 1E, 4E.

Newberry, Farrar. "Adam Clark: Faithful Recorder," Arkadelphia *Southern Standard*, March 29, 1962, 1.

———. "Arkadelphia in the Gay Nineties," Arkadelphia *Southern Standard*, October 29, 1964, 1.

———. "Arkadelphia Methodists' Early Churches," Arkadelphia *Southern Standard*, April 12, 1962, 1.

———. "The Arkadelphia of 90 Years Ago," Arkadelphia *Southern Standard*, August 24, 1961, 1.

———. "Capt. Henderson—Savior of the College," Arkadelphia *Southern Standard*, May 31, 1962, 1.

———. "Captain Huie, Arkadelphia Enterpriser," Arkadelphia *Southern Standard*, August 3, 1961, 1.

———. "Charles Richardson—Noted Arkadelphia Artist," Arkadelphia *Southern Standard*, July 12, 1962, 1.

———. "City's First Telephone Exchange," Arkadelphia *Southern Standard*, April 25, 1959, 1.

———. "Clark County's Plantation Prince," Little Rock *Arkansas Democrat Magazine*, December 13, 1959, 6–7.

———. "The College Lake," Arkadelphia *Southern Standard*, September 22, 1960, 1.

———. "A Fine Old Home and the Cook Family," Arkadelphia *Southern Standard*, February 4, 1965, 1.

———. "George C. Jones, First President of Old Henderson," Arkadelphia *Southern Standard*, April 16, 1964, 1.

———. "Grand Old Man of Henderson-Brown," Arkadelphia *Southern Standard*, December 10, 1964, 1.

———. "Henderson Won Victory From Disaster," Arkadelphia *Southern Standard*, July 25, 1964, 1.

———. "Historic Spot in Arkadelphia's History Brings Memories to Many," Arkadelphia *Southern Standard*, July 15, 1959, 1.

———. "J. B. Garrett 'Dad' to Hendersonians," Arkadelphia *Southern Standard*, June 10, 1965, 1.

———. "John Hemphill and the Old Salt Works Near Here," Arkadelphia *Southern Standard*, February 6, 1964, 1.

———. "John McLaughlin: Founder of Old Henderson," Arkadelphia *Southern Standard*, December 26, 1963, 1.

———. "John R. Dale—Noted Doctor of Former Days," Arkadelphia *Southern Standard*, July 6, 1961, 1.

———. "The Military Department of Old Henderson," Arkadelphia *Southern Standard*, June 9, 1966, 1.

———. "Old Building Here Holds Historical Interest," Arkadelphia *Siftings Herald*, November 29, 1962, 1.

———. "Old Courthouse Saw Much History," Arkadelphia *Southern Standard*, February 23, 1961, 1.

———. "The Old Market Place," Arkadelphia *Southern Standard*, March 1, 1962.

———. "The Old Mooney Tannery," Arkadelphia *Southern Standard*, January 31, 1963, 1.

———. "The Old Opera House," Arkadelphia *Southern Standard*, April 25, 1958, 1.

———. "Proud Heritage of The Callaways," Arkadelphia *Southern Standard*, August 28, 1959, 1.

———. "R. B. F. Key Christian Benefactor," Arkadelphia *Southern Standard*, April 8, 1965, 1.

———. "A Real 'Forty-Niner' and His Palatial Arkadelphia Home," Arkadelphia *Southern Standard*, October 8, 1964, 1.

———. "The Sloan House," Arkadelphia *Siftings Herald*, January 30, 1963, 1.

———. "Some Arkadelphia Church Bells of Other Days," Arkadelphia *Southern Standard*, October 19, 1961, 1.

Newberry, Farrar. "Some Arkadelphia Hotels of The Long Ago," Arkadelphia *Southern Standard,* October 1, 1959, 1.

———. "Witherspoon Builds Law Offices 105 Years Ago," Arkadelphia *Siftings Herald,* April 16, 1963, 1.

North Central Association Quarterly, IX (July, 1934).

Ohls, Boulware Martin, "Tribute to a Noble Spirit," Little Rock *Arkansas Gazette Magazine,* May 28, 1944, 2, 6.

Oklahoma City *Western Christian Advocate,* March 14, 1906.

Omaha *World-Herald Sunday Magazine,* October 16, 1955.

Oracle, 1908–1971.

The Reddie, 1915–1916.

Ross, Margaret. "Chronicles of Arkansas, the Years of the Civil War," Little Rock *Arkansas Gazette,* 1958–1963.

Sage, J. A. "Is the Little Rock Conference Under Either Legal or Moral Obligation to Maintain Henderson-Brown College as a Senior College," Little Rock *Arkansas Methodist,* April 14, 1927, 5.

St. Louis Post-Dispatch, February 13, 1915.

Vanderbilt Alumnus, February, 1956. Nashville: Vanderbilt University, 1956.

Wilkerson, Sunny. "Why Reddies Are Reddies," *Oracle,* October 4, 1950, 1.

Secondary Sources

Books

Allard, Bessie Newsom, ed. *Who is Who in Arkansas,* I. Little Rock: Pioneer Press, 1959.

Allsopp, Frederick W. *Folklore of Romantic Arkansas.* New York: Grolier Society, 1931.

Anderson, James A. *Centennial History of Arkansas Methodism: A History of the Methodist Episcopal Church, South, in the State of Arkansas, 1815–1935.* Benton, Ark.: L. B. White Printing Co., 1935.

The Arkadelphia Story. n.p.: n.d. A pamphlet published by the Arkadelphia Chamber of Commerce.

Barker, Eugene C., ed. *The Austin Papers,* Part I, *Annual Report of the American Historical Association For the Year 1919,* II. Washington: Government Printing Office, 1924.

Billington, Ray Allen. *Westward Expansion: A History of the American Frontier.* New York: Macmillan Co., 1967.

Biographical and Historical Memoirs of Central Arkansas. Chicago: Goodspeed Publishing Co., 1890.

Biographical and Historical Memoirs of Southern Arkansas. Chicago: Goodspeed Publishing Co., 1890.

Bishop, Morris. *A History of Cornell*. Ithaca: Cornell University Press, 1962.

Blauch, Lloyd E., ed. *Accreditation in Higher Education*. Washington: Government Printing Office, 1959.

Bonds, A. B., ed. *Essays on Southern Life and Culture: A Henderson Symposium*. Arkadelphia: Henderson State Teachers College, 1941.

A Brief History of the First Presbyterian Church, Arkadelphia, Arkansas. n.p.: n.d. Published by the local church.

Cabaniss, Allen. *The University of Mississippi: Its First Hundred Years*. Hattiesburg: University & College Press of Mississippi, 1971.

Capers, Gerald M., Jr. *The Biography of a River Town: Memphis, Its Heroic Age*. Chapel Hill: The University of North Carolina Press, 1939.

Cattell, Jacques, ed. *Dictionary of American Scholars: A Biographical Directory*. Lancaster, Pa.: Science Press, 1951.

Cattell, Jacques, and E. E. Ross, eds. *Leaders in Education: A Biographical Directory*. Lancaster, Pa.: Science Press, 1948.

Coulter, E. Merton. *College Life in the Old South*. New York: Macmillan Co., 1928.

Daly, Lowrie John. *The Medieval University*. New York: Sheed & Ward, Inc., 1961.

Davis, Roy L. *Centennial History of Presbyterianism (U.S.) in Arkansas*. Little Rock: Arkansas Book House, 1954.

Dictionary of American Scholars. New York: R. R. Bowker Co., 1964.

Ezell, John Samuel. *The South Since 1865*. New York: Macmillan Co., 1964.

Finders Keepers: Crater of Diamonds. n.p.: n.d. A pamphlet published by the Murfreesboro, Arkansas Chamber of Commerce.

First Annual Report of the Railroad Commission of the State of Arkansas, 1899-1900. Little Rock: Thompson Lithograph & Printing Co., 1901.

Galloway, J. J., ed. *Dr. Benjamin S. Foster, A Great Teacher*. Little Rock: Epworth League Press, n.d.

Gipson, Lawrence Henry. *The Coming of the Revolution, 1763-1775*, eds. Henry Steel Commager and Richard B. Morris. New York: Harper & Brothers, 1954.

Goodspeed, Weston A., ed. *The Provinces and the States: A History of the Province of Louisiana Under France and Spain, and the Territories and States of the United States Formed Therefrom*. VII. Madison: Western Historical Association, 1904.

Gresswell, Kay, and Anthony Huxley, eds. *Standard Encyclopedia of the World's Rivers and Lakes*. New York: G. P. Putman's Sons, 1965.

Hale, Harrison. *University of Arkansas*. Chicago: R. R. Donnelley & Sons Co., 1948.

Hallum, John. *Biographical and Pictorial History of Arkansas*, I. Albany: Weed, Parson & Co., Printers, 1887.

Haskins, Charles Homer. *The Rise of Universities*. New York: Henry Holt & Co., 1923.

Hempstead, Fay. *Historical Review of Arkansas: Its Commerce, Industry, and Modern Affairs*. I. Chicago: Lewis Publishing Co., 1911.

———. *A Pictorial History of Arkansas*. New York: N. D. Thompson Publishing Co., 1890.

Herndon, Dallas T., ed. *Annals of Arkansas*. I. Little Rock: Historical Record Association, 1947.

———. *Centennial History of Arkansas*. 3 vols. Chicago: S. J. Clark Publishing Co., 1922.

Hollis, Daniel Walker. *University of South Carolina*. 2 vols. Columbia: University of South Carolina Press, 1956.

Houck, Louis. *A History of Missouri From the Earliest Explorations and Settlements Until the Admission of the State Into the Union*. 3 vols. Chicago: R. R. Donnelley & Sons Co., 1908.

Hull, Clifton E. *Shortline Railroads of Arkansas*. Norman: University of Oklahoma Press, 1969.

Hunter, Louis C. *Steamboats on the Western Rivers: An Economic and Technological History*. Cambridge: Harvard University Press, 1949.

Jewell, Horace. *History of Methodism in Arkansas*. Little Rock: Press Printing Co., 1892.

Johnson, Allen, and Dumas Malone, eds. *Dictionary of American Biography*. 20 vols. New York: Charles Scribner's Sons, 1959.

Johnson, Boyd W. *The Arkansas Frontier*. n.p.: 1947.

Johnson, Ludwell H. *Red River Campaign: Politics and Cotton in the Civil War*. Baltimore: Johns Hopkins Press, 1958.

Kerby, Robert L. *Kirby Smith's Confederacy: The Trans-Mississippi South, 1863–1865*. New York: Columbia University Press, 1972.

Kibler, Lillian Adele. *The History of Converse College*. Spartanburg, S.C.: Converse College, 1973.

Lawrence, Alberta, ed. *Who's Who Among North American Authors*. Los Angeles: Golden Syndicate Publishing Co., 1939.

Leflar, Robert A. *The First 100 Years: Centennial History of the University of Arkansas*. Fayetteville: University of Arkansas Foundation, Inc., 1972.

Morrison, Samuel E., and Henry S. Commager. *The Growth of the American Republic*. 2 vols. New York: Oxford University Press, 1962.

Price, Carl F., ed. *Who's Who in American Methodism*. New York: E. B. Treat & Co., 1916.

Rashdall, Hastings. *The Universities of Europe in the Middle Ages*, eds.

Frederick M. Powicke and Alfred P. Emden. 3 vols. London: Oxford University Press, 1936.

Richards, Ira D. *Story of a Rivertown, Little Rock in the Nineteenth Century.* n.p., 1960.

Riggin, J. H. *Lest We Forget or Character Gems Gleaned From South Arkansas.* Pine Bluff, Ark.: Norton-Vail Printing Co., n.d.

Ritchie, William. "Henderson, Today and Yesterday: The Story of the First Fifty Years," *Essays on Southern Life and Culture: A Henderson Symposium,* A. B. Bonds, ed. Arkadelphia: Henderson State Teachers College, 1941, 237–264.

Ross, Margaret. *Arkansas Gazette: The Early Years, 1819–1866.* Little Rock: Arkansas Gazette Foundation, 1969.

Scully, Francis J. *Hot Springs Arkansas and Hot Springs National Park.* Little Rock: Pioneer Press, 1966.

Shinn, Josiah H. *Pioneers and Makers of Arkansas.* Baltimore: Genealogical Publishing Co., 1967.

Taylor, Orville W. *Negro Slavery in Arkansas.* Durham: Duke University Press, 1958.

Thatcher, Herbert K. *Camden and the Ouachita River: A Brief Record of the Founding of Camden.* Camden, Ark.: Ouachita River Valley Association, 1952.

Thomas, David Y., ed. *Arkansas and Its People: A History, 1541–1930.* 4 vols. New York: American Historical Society, Inc., 1930.

Wallace, David Duncan. *History of Wofford College.* Nashville: Vanderbilt University Press, 1951.

Walsh, James Jerome. *The Thirteenth: Greatest of Centuries.* New York: AMS Press, Inc., 1970.

White, Lonnie J. *Politics on the Southwestern Frontier: Arkansas Territory, 1819–1936.* Memphis: Memphis State University Press, 1964.

Who's Who in America. 36 vols. Chicago: A. N. Marquis Co., 1899–1971.

Williams, Charlean M. *The Old Town Speaks.* Houston: Anson Jones Press, 1951.

Williams, Fay. *Arkansans of the Years.* 4 vols. Little Rock: C. C. Allard & Associates, 1953.

Articles

Biedleman, Richard G., ed. "The 1818–1820 Arkansas Journal of Thomas Nuttall," *Arkansas Historical Quarterly,* XV (Autumn, 1956), 249–259.

"The Black Woman," *The Pines,* I (Winter, 1941), 21.

Butler, Laura Scott. "History of Clark County," *Publications of the Arkansas Historical Association,* II. Fayetteville: Arkansas Historical Association, 1908, 552–579.

Buxton, Virginia. "Salt Springs and Salt Works in Arkansas," *Arkansas Historical Quarterly*, XVI (Winter, 1957), 383–397.

Cabaniss, Frances, and James Allen Cabaniss. "Religion in Mississippi Since 1860," *Journal of Mississippi History*, IX (Oct., 1947), 195–218.

Candler, Warren A. (Bishop). "Dr. Cadesman Pope," James A. Anderson, *Centennial History of Arkansas Methodism: A History of the Methodist Episcopal Church, South, in the State of Arkansas, 1815–1935*. Benton, Ark.: L. B. White Publishing Co., 1935, 310–311.

Driggs, Orval T., Jr. "The Issues of the Powell Clayton Regime, 1868–1971," *Arkansas Historical Quarterly*, VIII (Spring, 1949), 1–75.

Galloway, J. J. "The New Educational Plan of the Methodists," *The Dixie Magazine*, III, No. 6 (July, 1927), 31.

Gaughan, J. E. "Historic Camden," *Arkansas Historical Quarterly*, XX (Autumn, 1961), 245–255.

Halliburton, Richard, Jr. "The Adoption of Arkansas' Anti-Evolution Law," *Arkansas Historical Quarterly*, XXIII (Fall, 1964), 271–283.

"Henderson in Song," *The Pines*, I (Winter, 1940), 32.

Hornaday, Clifford L. "An Educational Plan," *The Dixie Magazine*, III, No. 4 (April, 1927), 12.

Huddleston, V. L. "Indians in Clark County," *Arkansas Historical Quarterly*, II (March, 1943), 105–115.

Jones, George C. A letter in *The Arkadelphian*, I, No. 4 (June, 1898), n.p., May 20, 1898, to the Board of Trustees of Arkadelphia Methodist College.

Jones, Robert L. and Pauline H. "Stephen F. Austin in Arkansas," *Arkansas Historical Quarterly*, XXV (Winter, 1966), 336–353.

Lewis, Elsie M. "Economic Conditions in Ante-Bellum Arkansas: 1850–1861," *Arkansas Historical Quarterly*, VI (Autumn, 1947), 256–274.

Littlefield, Daniel F., Jr. "The Salt Industry in Arkansas Territory, 1819–1836," *Arkansas Historical Quarterly*, XXXII (Winter, 1973), 312–336.

Maxted, Mattie C. "Services for the Blind in Arkansas," *Arkansas Historical Quarterly*, VIII (Spring, 1949), 79–94.

"Methodists Plan Unique Educational Plant," *The Dixie Magazine*, III, No. 3 (March, 1927), 7.

Mixon, Ada. "What was Hernando De Soto's Route Through Arkansas?," *Publications of the Arkansas Historical Association*. Vol. IV. Conway: Arkansas Historical Association, 1917, 292–311.

Newberry, Farrar, ed. "A Clark County Plantation Journal For 1857," *Arkansas Historical Quarterly*, XVIII (Winter, 1959), 401–409.

———. "Jacob Barkman," *Arkansas Historical Quarterly*, XIX (Winter, 1960), 314–324.

———. "The Yankee Schoolmarm Who 'Captured' Post-War Arkadelphia," *Arkansas Historical Quarterly*, XVII (Autumn, 1958), 263–271.

Olson, James S. "Harvey C. Couch and the Reconstruction Finance Corporation," *Arkansas Historical Quarterly*, XXXII (Autumn, 1973), 215–225.

Orr, Billy. "Dormitory Life: Boys," *The Pines*, I (Winter, 1940), 24.

Penton, Emily M. "Typical Women's Schools in Arkansas Before the War of 1861–65," *Arkansas Historical Quarterly*, IV (Winter, 1945), 325–339.

Rea, Ralph R., ed. "Diary of Private John P. Wright, U.S.A., 1864–1865," *Arkansas Historical Quarterly*, XVI (Autumn, 1957), 304–318.

Rucks, Pauline. "Dormitory Life: Girls," *The Pines*, I (Winter, 1940), 23.

Scroggs, Jack B. "Arkansas Statehood," *Arkansas Historical Quarterly*, XX (Autumn, 1961), 226–244.

Snavely, Guy E. "A Short History of the Southern Association of Colleges and Secondary Schools," *Southern Association Quarterly*, IX (November, 1945), 423–549.

Stone, Arlington J. "The Dawn of a New Science," *The American Mercury*, August 20, 1928, 446. *The Twenties: Fords, Flappers & Fanatics*, George E. Mowry, ed. Englewood Cliffs, N.J.: Prentice-Hall, Inc., 1963.

Stuart, Martha R. "H S T C Diary: 1891," *The Pines*, I (Spring, 1941), 14.

Thomas, Buford. "The Reddie Blankets," *The Pines*, I (Winter, 1941), 20.

Vinsonhaler, Frank. "Early Doctors in Arkansas," *The Scrapbook of Arkansas Literature: An Anthology for the General Reader*, Octavius Coke, ed. Little Rock: American Caxton Society Press, 1939, 58–60.

Wagnon, William O., Jr. "John Roy Steelman: Native Son to Presidential Advisor," *Arkansas Historical Quarterly*, XXVII (Autumn, 1968), 205–225.

Walz, Robert B. "Arkansas Slaveholdings and Slaveholders in 1850," *Arkansas Historical Quarterly*, XII (Spring, 1953), 38–74.

Williams, J. M. "The Bishop's University Plan," *The Dixie Magazine*, III, No. 4 (April, 1927), 11.

Wright, Fannie B. "H S T C Diary: 1896," *The Pines*, I (Spring, 1941), 14.

Yarbrough, Anna N. "Arkansas' Struggle for Communication," *Arkansas Historical Quarterly*, XVIII (Spring, 1959), 44–49.

Zinn, Edith, "The Story of Laura Lee Henson," *The Pines*, I (Winter, 1940), 19.

Unpublished Works

Alderson, Willis Brewer. "A History of Methodist Higher Education in Arkansas." Ed. D. dissertation, University of Arkansas, 1971.

Hardage, Paul. "A Brief History of Dentistry." Typescript, Museum, Henderson State College, n.d.

Jackman, Eugene T. "The New Mexico Military Institute 1891–1966: A Critical History." Ph.D. dissertation, University of Mississippi, 1967.

Penton, Emily M. "Higher Education for Women in Arkansas Prior to the Civil War." M.A. thesis, University of Chicago, 1930.

Richards, Ira D. "The Urban Frontier, Little Rock in the Nineteenth Century." Ph.D. dissertation, Tulane University, 1964.

Simmons, Guy A. "Hendrix College: A Brief Historical Sketch, 1884–1944." Typescript, Bailey Library, Hendrix College, Conway, Ark., 1944.

Thatcher, Herbert K. "The Ouachita River Basin." Typescript, Ouachita River Valley Association Files, Camden, Arkansas, n.d.

Wilson, William Oscar. "A History of Education in Arkansas." A collection of materials in the Rare Books Collection, Bailey Library, Hendrix College, Conway, Arkansas.

Index